EMPIRES OF THE WEAK

Empires of the Weak

THE REAL STORY OF EUROPEAN EXPANSION AND THE CREATION OF THE NEW WORLD ORDER

J. C. Sharman

PRINCETON UNIVERSITY PRESS

PRINCETON & OXFORD

Copyright © 2019 by Princeton University Press

Published by Princeton University Press
41 William Street, Princeton, New Jersey 08540
6 Oxford Street, Woodstock, Oxfordshire OX20 1TR

press.princeton.edu

LCCN 2018940067
First paperback printing, 2020
Paperback ISBN 978-0-691-21007-0
Cloth ISBN 978-0-691-18279-7

British Library Cataloging-in-Publication Data is available

Editorial: Sarah Caro and Hannah Paul
Production Editorial: Debbie Tegarden
Cover Design: Lorraine Betz Doneker
Cover credit: Color woodblock depicting a Dutch ship of the Dutch East India Company,
c. 1860. World History Archive / Alamy Stock Photo
Production: Jacquie Poirier
Publicity: Tayler Lord
Copyeditor: Jay Boggis

This book has been composed in Miller

Dedicated to my family and Bilyana

CONTENTS

Preface and Acknowledgments · ix

INTRODUCTION   The Military Revolution and
the First International System   1

CHAPTER 1   Iberian Conquistadors and Supplicants   34

CHAPTER 2   Company Sovereigns and
the Empires of the East   65

CHAPTER 3   The Asian Invasion of Europe in Context   99

CONCLUSION   How the Europeans Won in the End
(Before They Later Lost)   131

Notes · 153
Bibliography · 169
Index · 191

ONE OF THE GREAT pleasures of writing this book has been the opportunity to roam around considering historical questions that are fundamental to how we think about politics past, present, and future. The really big changes in international politics have little to do with the European major coalition wars that are often the staple of International Relations textbooks and scholarship. These wars have basically upheld the status quo of a fragmented Europe with a slowly changing cast of great powers (great by parochial European standards, if not always by more cosmopolitan global ones). So when it comes to transformations of international politics, perhaps it would be true to say that nothing interesting has happened in Europe for at least the last 500 years, perhaps even since the fall of the Roman Empire.

For the shifts that have fundamentally altered international politics we have to look elsewhere. Prominent amongst these transformations is first the creation of a global international system and the accompanying multi-civilizational order, second the briefer but vitally important period of European imperial world dominance for around a hundred years or so, and finally the even shorter span that saw decolonization and the return of Asian great powers. I am mainly concerned with the first of these topics, the creation of the first global international system. Dating roughly from the end of the fifteenth century to the end of the eighteenth century, this centers on a process of European expansion that helped to knit together previously separate regional systems.

It's important not to read "European expansion" as synonymous with European conquest or empire. Instead, in Africa and Asia, the process of expansion owed much more to European submission than dominance. Particularly when they encountered Eastern empires far mightier than any European great power of the day, Europeans had little choice but to pay deference. Though they were quick to use violence whenever they thought they could get away with it, more important than military prowess in explaining expansion was the coincidence whereby Europeans' goals were largely maritime—trade routes and port outposts—whereas local great powers were concerned with controlling land and territory, but largely indifferent to the seas. These complementary preferences allowed for a rough-and-ready coexistence. In addition, European ventures in the East and the Atlantic world were crucially reliant on the cultivation of local allies, patrons, and vassals. Finally, in the Americas, various pandemics allowed European adventurers to destroy local empires, though these well-known triumphs were balanced by lesser-known defeats. In the early modern period right through to the present, changes in military and political institutions across civilizations proceeded according to cultural prompts, largely independent of functional concerns about effectiveness and efficiency.

In making and backing these claims, relating to a huge range of times and places, this book either had to be very long or quite short. The reason for writing a short book is the hope of appealing to a somewhat wider audience inside and outside of academia that might not usually be much interested in history, and perhaps a few people who might not ordinarily read social science. But if there are benefits to a short book for both the author and the readers, it's only fair to acknowledge that there are serious costs as well.

The main penalty is the lack of room to really dig into and discuss all the brilliant work relevant to the topic that has informed my thinking. In getting feedback from various generous colleagues and three anonymous reviewers (of whom more below), a recurrent theme was that there are so many other authors, theories, and debates that could and should receive more attention in the text. These commentators are right: there are many authors, theories, and debates that could and should have received more attention (or even a mention). But by and large they haven't. It's very important to stress that this is not a sign of disrespect or disagreement with either the original authors, or those providing comments. Nor is it an effort to overstate the originality of this book by slighting the work I build on. Instead, it reflects a calculation that research, writing, and many other things are based on trade-offs, and that the cost of neglecting vast reams of earlier scholarship is nevertheless justified in having a shorter and more accessible book.

Although this book is less concerned with immersing the reader in existing scholarship, it is in part an attempt to gently nudge (rather than hector) us to think a bit harder about how Eurocentric we still are, and what this costs us. No doubt all right-minded, good-thinking people already agree that Eurocentrism in the abstract is a bad thing. But to see how much the problem is still with us one only has to look at the table of contents or indexes of most books on international politics and history to see the extraordinary predominance of European places, actors, and events, relative to the rest of the world. This book has some of the same bias, but I hope to a lesser degree.

If I have flagrantly disregarded much of the wise advice I received about including a more detailed literature review, it remains true that many of the key elements of my argument here I owe to those who were kind enough to comment on draft text or oral presentations. I was particularly lucky to begin the project at one very stimulating and supportive academic environment, Griffith University, and finish it at a very similar institution, Cambridge University. I thus had two sets of colleagues to exploit.

At the early stages in Brisbane, Sarah Percy and especially Ian Hall gave me crucial steers on what was wrong with my first cut at the project and, even better, how I might go about fixing it. I presented initial versions at Griffith, the Australian National University, and a little later at my current departmental home, Politics and International Studies in Cambridge, and the European International Studies Association. Some of these meetings have featured formal discussants who went well above and beyond their rather thankless mandate in working hard to understand and improve my rough drafts, and so thanks in particular to Daniel Nexon, Sean Fleming, and Alex Weisiger. Similarly selfless was the commitment of the three anonymous reviewers of the draft manuscript; it was a privilege to have my ideas receive such careful and constructive treatment. Andrew Phillips taught me a lot about how to do this kind of research in various discussions over the years, some directly related to this book, others only tangentially. At Cambridge the Department and the History & International Relations group, organized by Maja Spanu and Or Rosenboim, has provided the perfect setting for bringing this research to completion. In Cambridge and in London, Ayşe Zarakol, Duncan Bell, and George Lawson further helped me think through some big historical International Relations questions. I am also very grateful to David Runciman for providing the first link with Princeton University Press. At the Press, Sarah Caro performed an invaluable role in shepherding the manuscript through to acceptance and completion.

Though this research is very different from my other interest in tax havens, money laundering, and corruption, the common thread is that any research takes time, and getting time often requires money. The Australian Research Council has been extremely generous in providing this money through grants FT120100485 and DP170101395. Some similar arguments appearing in this book were first featured in the article "Myths of Military Revolution: European Expansion and Eurocentrism," published in the *European Journal of International Relations*.

In some ways, the book marks a return to an even more ambitious failed project I tried almost forty years ago, "History of the Wold" [*sic*]. With any luck, having completed a primary, secondary school, and university education since that time will make for a somewhat more successful result second time around.

Speaking of the longer term, as ever my biggest thanks go to my family and Bilyana.

EMPIRES OF THE WEAK

The Military Revolution and the First International System

EUROPEAN EXPANSION from the end of the fifteenth century to the end of the eighteenth transformed the world in creating the first genuinely global political and economic systems. It was initiated by near-simultaneous voyages West across the Atlantic to the Americas, and South and East around the coast of Africa, across the Indian Ocean to Asia by explorers like Christopher Columbus and Vasco da Gama. The subsequent growth of the European presence across the oceans is often said to be the result of superior military power: better weapons, and better organizations for using them. Known as the military revolution thesis, it argues that expansion was primarily the result of European militaries and states outcompeting opponents abroad, because Europeans were better adapted to the demands of war, having survived and learned from fierce competition at home. It is based on the assumption that competition produces more efficient organizations that are better adapted to their environment, thanks to a combination of rational learning and Darwinian selection.

In this book I question each element of this account, and suggest an alternative explanation. Europeans did not enjoy any significant military superiority vis-à-vis non-Western opponents in the early modern era, even in Europe. Expansion was as much a story of European deference and subordination as one of dominance. Rather than state armies or navies, the vanguards of expansion were small bands of adventurers or chartered companies, who relied on the cultivation of local allies. Fundamental to the Europeans' success and survival was a maritime strategy that avoided challenging the land-based priorities of local polities, and in the Americas disease that brought about a demographic catastrophe. The greatest conquerors and empire-builders of the early modern era were in fact Asian empires, from the Ottomans in the Near East, to the Mughals in South Asia, and the Ming and Manchu Qing in China. Giving due attention to these great powers helps to correct the Eurocentrism that has so often biased earlier studies, and brings into question conventional cause-and-effect stories about war-making and state-making. A more cosmopolitan perspective reveals the diversity of the relationships between military and political development, in that there were many roads to different outcomes rather than one route to a common destination.

This alternative perspective contrasts with the traditional view of European expansion being a state-directed effort, premised on using the same tactics and technology as in warfare between Europeans. It brings into question the idea of tight cause-and-effect connections between new weapons, tactics, large standing armies, and the rise of the sovereign state. More broadly, the argument put forward here contradicts and supplants the model of military competition producing efficient, well-adapted fighting organizations through some combination of learning and elimination.

The significance of the process by which the first global international system was created is in many ways obvious. Vast, ancient, and previously isolated civilizations came into regular contact with the rest of the world. People, goods, diseases, and ideas circumnavigated the globe for the first time, transforming societies and ecologies in their wake. Yet for the purposes of this book, I concentrate on a few key implications for world politics, but also for the way we study it.

We have had a connected, global international system for around 500 years, a period often seen as synonymous with the era of Western dominance. The assumptions that have underpinned the study of the international system and the theories developed to explain it both start from this premise of Western military and political hegemony. But in fact, for more than half the time there has been a global international system, it was not dominated by the West. On the contrary, European nations were puny in comparison with Asian great powers like the Mughal or Chinese Ming and Qing empires in terms of population, riches, and military might. The fact that this has often not been recognized illustrates how deeply warped our sense of the historical development of international politics is and has huge implications for our understandings of the past, present, and future. Biases of place and time have not only systematically overstated the importance of European powers while understating the importance of those from other regions, they have also fixed a single, deterministic path of military-institutional development as constituting the historical norm.

The history of warfare is crucial as the raw material for generating and testing many social science theories. Military force has been regarded as the ultimate decider in world politics. The military revolution thesis that recurring wars between the great power drove military innovation and state-building in Europe, which subsequently gave these states a competitive advantage they used to dominate non-European polities, is a bedrock of much historically oriented social science. It has informed our understandings of the rise of the sovereign state and the modern state system. Scholars are increasingly interested in the rise and fall of the international orders. The period from 1500 to the end of the eighteenth century gives us an example that is at once intimately connected to our own through myriad historical legacies, while being distinct enough to jolt us into an appreciation of how a pluralistic global order works, absent the domination of any one civilization. How much of what we think we know about the way international politics works is really a parochial, Eurocentric perspective on the way *Western* international politics works? The early modern period uniquely has a potential to answer this question.

From the conventional historical perspective of a "Columbian" or "Vasco da Gama" epoch of military-driven European dominance, the prospect of a global international system not dominated by the West, sparked by concerns about rising powers like Japan, or more recently China and India, looks historically unprecedented—a leap into the unknown. Putting early modern Asian great powers in their proper context would make such a future world seem much less remarkable or strange; perhaps it would be a return to the historical norm after a relatively brief period of imbalance. This is one way that changing our views about the past can fundamentally change our views of the present and the future.

In looking at the way history informs our theories of how international politics works across time, I offer some thoughts on the relationship between the disciplines of history and social science. A key conclusion is that historians and social scientists share more similarities than either often likes to think. I also emphasize what those in the social sciences, especially International Relations and political science, can learn from recent revisionist historians' work about relations between Europeans and other civilizations in Africa, Asia, and the Americas to supplant the military revolution thesis. Any effort to understand a topic as huge as the creation and workings of the early modern global international order requires the insights of different disciplines.

The Shape of the Argument

A recent book observes that "in all the debate, few scholars have actually tested [the] claim that the military revolution underlay European colonialism. To what extent did Europe's military innovations between 1450 and 1700 actually provide Europeans an edge in warfare?"[1] The evidence I present in Chapters 1–3 shows that the military revolution thesis simply does not fit with the evidence from either Spanish conquests in the New World, or Portuguese, Dutch, and English engagements in Asia and Africa.

To begin with, the styles of warfare Europeans used abroad were almost completely different from those that they used at home. With rare exceptions, neither the tactics, nor the armies, nor the organizations fit the templates of the military revolution thesis and great power war in Europe. The volley fire by massed musketeers protected by pikemen that came to dominate warfare in Western and Central Europe was almost never used elsewhere. Instead of the massive armies states deployed in Europe, expansion in the wider world was propelled by tiny expeditionary forces. Furthermore, in most cases these forces were essentially private, being ad hoc bands of adventurers or chartered "company sovereigns." Different circumstances in different locations called for different responses, undermining the idea that there was one, superior, European way of war.

More fundamentally, by and large, there was no general European military superiority over other civilizations in this period. The conquistadors achieved their most famous victories in the Americas thanks to a combination of disease, local allies, and cold steel,[2] while their less well known defeats belie the myth of their invincibility. Europeans maintained their toeholds in Africa under the sufferance of African rulers. On the rare occasions the Portuguese and others challenged African polities to war before 1800, they generally lost. Europeans adopted a general position of deference and subordination to the manifestly more powerful empires of Asia, from Persia, to the Mughals, to China and Japan. Once again, the Portuguese, Dutch, English, and Russians were all on the receiving end of sharp defeats in the exceptional instances they clashed with these empires. Finally, at home in Europe and the Mediterranean, Europeans struggled to hold out against the Ottomans, and experienced consistent disappointment in their military ventures in North Africa.

So far this is all rather negative; if not the military revolution, what, then, does explain the first few centuries of European expansion? It's important to spell out the main elements of my positive thesis. First, a reminder that expansion is not at all the same thing as domination or conquest.[3] In early modern Africa and Asia, the European presence was overwhelmingly maritime, focusing on militarized control of seaborne trade through key ports and sea lanes. In contrast, most powerful local polities were largely indifferent to the seas, being concerned with control of land and people. This coincidence of complementary maritime and terrestrial preferences allowed for a rough co-existence between the "lords of land" and "masters of water." Despite a general European posture of deference to more powerful local rulers, certainly it was not all peace and harmony. Expansion involved a great deal of violence. At a more tactical level, European coercion of weaker African and Asian actors rested on the cultivation of local allies, and military, logistical, political, and cultural adaptations to varying local contexts. Finally, in the Americas, as noted, there was the additional factor of disease and demography that laid low the most powerful empires, and consistently sapped the strength of indigenous resistance thereafter.

Taking a less Eurocentric, more wide-ranging view of the interaction of war, politics, and society from the Western to the Eastern extremity of Asia further undermines key tenets of the conventional wisdom. The Chinese, who invented and developed gunpowder weapons from 900 to 1200, had already reached most of the key milestones of military and administrative modernity centuries before Europeans. The Ottomans and Mughals constructed polities that commanded far more people, money, and military power than any of their sixteenth- and seventeenth-century European counterparts. The Mughals overawed the essentially trivial European presence on the fringes of their domain until the unraveling of their empire at the beginning of the 1700s. The Ottomans steamrollered their opponents, first by destroying the last remnants of the Roman Empire, then conquering Arabia, North Africa, and Southeast Europe.

How does an understanding of these Asian polities change our perspective on developments in Europe? First, it disconfirms the idea of a single path to military effectiveness, of sequences of necessary and sufficient causes, either technological or tactical, by which war makes states. Second, it undermines stereotypes according to which relatively transient successes by small European polities are too often portrayed as epochal triumphs, whereas mighty, long-lived Asian empires are characterized as merely failures waiting to happen.

The discussion so far may seem to be avoiding the obvious retort: the Europeans won in the end. In response, the concluding chapter examines the lessons drawn from the early modern period in light of the subsequent experiences of the nineteenth-century "new imperialism," when European armies carried (almost) all before them. It then contrasts the "new imperialism" with the subsequent European contraction in the twentieth century characterized by decolonization, and Western defeats at the hands of various Communist and Islamist insurgencies. It makes the point that the

Europeans didn't win in the end: their empires fell, and their military capacity shriveled. Even the United States has experienced more defeats than victories against non-Western forces over the last half-century.

I argue that the broad contours of events from the end of the early modern period to the present tend to bear out the primacy of ideas, legitimacy, and culture over explanations based on rational efficiency and selection, and also cast doubt on the idea that technology and battlefield predominance are the mainstays of military effectiveness and geopolitical success. Nineteenth-century empires were often essentially prestige projects that did little to advance the military or economic power of the European nations in question. The struggle over decolonization saw technologically and administratively more advanced societies and militaries consistently lose to less advanced ones. European powers won most of the battles while losing most of the wars, a pattern that recurred in the U.S. counterinsurgency wars of the late twentieth and early twenty-first centuries. This brings into question the importance of technology, and the presumption that military adaptation leads to more homogeneous organizations, rather than more differentiated ones, as part of the now familiar idea of asymmetrical warfare.

I expand on each of these more general points and the relationship between history and the social sciences in the second half of this Introduction. But the priority now is to lay out what the military revolution is, and how it is said to explain European expansion.

What Is the Military Revolution?

Several of the key ideas that provide the foundation for the military revolution thesis, especially the decisive role of gunpowder weapons and military competition in Europe, have been in circulation for centuries. They are found in the writings of Montesquieu, Gibbon, Mill, Burke, Adam Smith, and Schumpeter, among others.[4] Yet in its contemporary form, this argument was first put forward by the military historian Michael Roberts in 1955. Roberts saw the military revolution as sharply dividing the medieval from the modern world, thanks to an interlinked process of rapid military and political change in Europe 1550–1650. (It is worth noting that for

International Relations scholars the Treaty of Westphalia that concluded the Thirty Years War in 1648 conventionally marks the beginning of the modern era.) There are four key elements to Roberts's argument: tactics, strategy, army size, and state development.

Tactical change came about from the 1590s when Dutch reformers adapted classical Roman linear battlefield formations, and began drilling musketeers in volley fire. A few decades later, the Swedish king Gustavus Adolphus combined this innovation with light field artillery and the re-introduction of the cavalry charge. Mastering these new tactics required more training, especially extensive drill, and more officers, in turn necessitating a permanent, salaried, and professional standing army. The coalition warfare of the Thirty Years War in Central Europe saw an expansion in strategic aims, as multiple armies were used to achieve military objectives. The third change was that armies became much bigger, "the result of a revolution in strategy, made possible by the revolution in tactics, and made necessary by the circumstances of the Thirty Years' War."[5] Both the total number of troops rulers maintained under arms expanded, as well as the number committed to individual battles.

Finally, and most importantly, larger, professional, permanent armies required much more money to pay for them. Rulers had to develop a centralized, hierarchical administrative apparatus, and reach deeper into society to extract the necessary resources. Here was the crucial link between changes in warfare and the development of the modern state.[6] In his brilliant essay "War Making and State Making as Organized Crime," Charles Tilly explains the process as follows: "After 1400 the European pursuit of larger, more permanent, and more costly varieties of military organization did, in fact, drive spectacular increases in princely budgets, taxes, and staffs. After 1500 or so, princes who managed to create the costly varieties of military organization were, indeed, able to conquer new chunks of territory."[7] Thus success was said to bring about a self-reinforcing positive feedback loop: greater resources generated greater military power, which then generated yet more resources.[8] Each of these elements was said to require the others in the same set causal sequence, rather than being changes that just happened to coincide with each other. The engine that drove this whole process was said to be military competition: those that failed to keep up were beaten, and perhaps eliminated altogether. This idea of Darwinian military competition spurring military innovation, learning, emulation, and elimination is a recurring theme in both historical and social science scholarship, and is covered in detail at the end of this Introduction.

The Military Revolution and the Rise of the West

Roberts's argument was influential, but was only indirectly related to developments beyond Europe. The next step, taken by Geoffrey Parker, was to link advances in European warfare to the rise of the West more generally. As a result, the military revolution thesis is now more significant for discussions of the rise of the West and developments outside Europe than those inside Europe.[9] Parker began by modifying Roberts's original thesis, emphasizing guns and fortifications rather than tactics as the original source of change. Specifically, in the 1400s new cannons were able to batter down medieval castle walls. Suddenly vulnerable, rulers scrambled for a solution entailing a new style of fortifications with low, thick, artillery-resistant walls, coupled with angled bastions, which caught attackers in intersecting fields of fire. The catch, however, was that these new *trace italienne* (Italian design) fortresses were very expensive to build, and required a large and correspondingly costly army to garrison or attack. Thus by a different route, Parker got to the same point of intersection between war and state-building as Roberts: more money and more troops required the development of a centralized administrative apparatus. Once again, military competition was the engine of change: rulers learned that to remain competitive in war, they had to keep up with these new trends. Those that did not risked being conquered and disappearing from the scene. For both Roberts and Parker, the pressure to centralize and extend the state apparatus was paralleled by the tendency whereby smaller feudal lords and private wielders of violence fell behind the demands of the military revolution, and so were progressively absorbed into the new, "fiscal-military" states.[10]

Undoubtedly the most important innovation of Parker's argument, however, was in the direct link between the changes in the character of European war, and subsequent European expansion in the Americas, Africa, and Asia. The pressures of military competition within Europe were said to have produced organizations with superior military effectiveness relative to those in the rest of the world. Parker summarizes his thesis as follows: "the key to the Westerners' success in creating the first truly global empires between 1500 and 1750 depended upon precisely those improvements in the ability to wage war which have been termed 'the military revolution.'"[11]

A crucial link between the European and global aspects of the military revolution thesis is the accompanying advances in naval warfare. New dedicated warships capitalized on more advanced navigation and design techniques to venture further, while carrying rows of cannon able to sink ships and bombard targets ashore. Like new-style fortifications, these gun-armed ships were very expensive, reinforcing the pressures for more tax revenue and intrusive state intervention in society in order to stay competitive. The feudal and private groups that had carried on medieval naval warfare were unequal to these demands, and hence were sidelined.[12]

The Western advantage in military technology and organization relative to other civilizations was said to pay off quite early: "By 1650 the West had already achieved military mastery in four separate areas: central and northeast America; Siberia; some coastal areas of sub-Saharan Africa; and, in some parts of the Indonesian and Philippine archipelagoes."[13] According to Parker, the combination of new weapons, like muskets and artillery, new tactics, new warships that were able to cross oceans and dominate naval and littoral areas once they arrived, and finally the financial, logistical, and administrative wherewithal of the newly centralized modern sovereign state, enabled Europeans to bring around a third of the world's land area under their control by 1750.[14]

While some historians have queried the timing, duration, and revolutionary character of the changes identified,[15] the thesis has won broad acceptance as an explanation of European expansion, in part because it builds on and complements a much older and established tradition of thought. The idea continues to enjoy wide currency that, from around 1500, Europe began to dominate other civilizations due to superior military technology and techniques developed thanks to especially intense security competition within Europe.[16]

To be sure, there are important variations. Some believe that Europeans' military edge was itself a product of an underlying institutional and economic advantage, which once again reflects the uniquely competitive nature of the European international system.[17] Others point to favorable geography or cultural attributes as preceding or producing European military superiority.[18] Others see the particular type of military competition in Western Europe as especially conducive to stimulating innovation. For example, as one of the few areas of the world not threatened by horse nomads, Western Europeans concentrated on improving early guns that were useful in infantry battles, but not for countering cavalry armies.[19]

Those working in the field of International Relations have tended to take on the same logic.[20] Following Thompson's "military superiority thesis,"[21] MacDonald summarizes the dominant state of thinking in the discipline on why Europe conquered much of the rest of the world by exactly replicating by the military revolution argument:

> European warfare underwent a profound transformation beginning in the sixteenth century. On land, the spread of gunpowder-based weapons, as well as specialized fortifications designed to resist these arms, transformed the nature of combat.... European states were increasingly compelled to raise large standing armies, which were dominated by highly trained and well-drilled infantry.... Although driven by competition between European states, the unintended consequence of this "military revolution" was to widen the gap in military power between Europe and the rest of the world.

Even social scientists who explain the eventual dominance of Europe as being due to economics often still employ the military revolution thesis as a vital part of their account. Thus the economist Douglass North asks:[22]

> What set off the expansion of Western Europe, which led to its ultimate hegemony in the world? A proximate part of the explanation, though certainly not a complete one, is the revolution in military technology that occurred in the late Middle Ages; the cross-bow, the long-bow, the

pike, and gunpowder had implications for the organization and capital costs of warfare. The costs of warfare rose. So, accordingly, rose the costs of survival of political units. Because kings were supposed to live on their own, they were faced with devising ways to increase fiscal revenues.[23]

Those approaching the question from a Marxist perspective also use the logic of military competition to argue the link between deep economic causes and geopolitical outcomes:

> In late medieval and early modern Europe, there was little possibility for a single empire or state to subdue the entire continent.... This lent itself to a more unstable and fluid geopolitical environment in which military competition and war were a near-constant feature of European life over many centuries.... The rapid growth in Europe's military sectors was perhaps a key reason, along with the development of stronger fiscal and organizational capacities, for Europe's later success in overseas conquests.[24]

For most scholars of International Relations, this narrative is no less influential for being tacit, a presumed foundation of why the world is the way it is and how it got that way. As the most consequential sustained use of armed force and conquest ever in world history, with huge consequences for contemporary international politics, examining and explaining the history of European expansion should be a top priority for social scientists. For a discipline whose whole reason for being is world politics, it is surprising how little International Relations research has been conducted on the really big developments: the creation of the first global international system, the relatively brief period of European dominance over the rest of the world in the era of the "new imperialism," and the collapse of these world-spanning empires in the twentieth century. In part this might reflect the legacies of the attitude that the proper concern of International Relations was restricted to relations between "civilized" states.[25]

Having laid out the main features of the military revolution, and how it is said to explain Western global dominance, it is now important to return to three more general topics raised earlier: how we study Europe compared to the rest of the World, the differences and similarities between historians' and social scientists' treatment of the military revolution, and the tendency to reason that learning and competition produce well-adapted, functionally efficient, and effective organizations. To anchor the discussion of this last matter, I use an example from African warfare concerning the use of magic in war that sharply illustrates the distinction between the conventional rational-functionalist logic, and a more cultural approach.

Eurocentrism

The military revolution thesis was initially about developments in Europe, before being extended to explain why Europeans won and everyone else lost. The common puzzle is what was special about Europe. Why, from unpropitious medieval beginnings, did this region later achieve world domination? Earlier scholars had an unabashed conviction that Europeans were inherently superior to other races.[26] Even though this attitude has been discredited, significant biases linger.

To begin with, there is just a lot more history and social science written about Europe, particularly Western Europe, than any other region of the world. Many claims about supposedly unique European achievements have turned out to reflect ignorance about the rest of the world. Any example looks unique if you ignore all the rest. Although this imbalance is far from rectified, new studies of other regions have increasingly debunked claims of European exceptionalism. As one historian puts it: "Any time someone argues that Europe had an advantage in a given area–say property rights, or per capita income, or labor productivity, or cannon manufacture– along comes an Asian historian pointing out that that claim is false. The case for European exceptionalism has unraveled like a ball of string."[27] Despite their ambitions to come up with general theories of politics unbound by particular time and place, International Relations scholars have often been just as bad in their myopic focus on Europe, and their corresponding indifference to the experiences of other parts of the world.[28] One of the main aims of this book is to do something to help rebalance the scales by giving other regions and civilizations equal weight.

More than just a matter of being politically incorrect, Eurocentrism has greatly restricted our ability to explain the past and the present. First, as the quote above illustrates, proving that there is something truly unique about Europe requires careful, detailed studies of other areas as well. For example, was military competition in Europe really so different from that elsewhere? Second, something of a contrast with seeing Europe as *sui generis* is the view of Europe as the universal model, defining the normal and natural pattern for others to follow, even if these others were backward in doing so at a later historical stage. Third, there is a tendency to see events that happened in a certain order in Europe as causing each other, and as necessarily having to happen in that specific sequence. The military revolution thesis provides some good examples here: it is not just that new technology and tactics spread, and then by coincidence shortly afterward armies became permanent and professionalized. Instead, the argument is that new technology (guns) and tactics *caused* the advent of standing professional armies, and that *only* permanent professional armies could use these new techniques. The same type of inevitable, invariant relationship is said to hold between the increase in army size and the development of the modern state. Again, however, it is hard to have confidence in these strong causal claims without comparing them to the way equivalent processes played out elsewhere.

A further subtle but extremely important bias is the way background assumptions set basic questions and starting points. For example, implicit in most of the writings on European intercontinental expansion is the idea that any civilization with the wherewithal to do the same would have, and in some sense should have, gone forth and conquered the rest of the world in the same manner. Aside from the point that this is factually wrong (the Chinese had the necessary naval technology and military capacity in the 1400s without seeking to build an overseas empire), there is the deeper, usually unasked question of why one would make this assumption in the first place. Even more important is the habit of starting at the "end" of the story, European dominance, and then working back through the historical record, which creates a tendency to look for the precursors of supposedly inevitable European success, and the equally inexorable failure of everyone else.[29] The historical starting point of explanations tends to bias their conclusions: "By directing attention to a time period [after 1500] rather than to a region, Western scholars can place the West at the center of any discussion, and subordinate backward Asia to Western history, without explicitly condemning Asian cultures and polities or arguing for a narrowly Eurocentric view of the world."[30] In contrast, if the "end" of the story is any time after decolonization, or the recent resurgence of powers like China, the story is put in a very different light.[31]

Given the importance of deciding when to start and finish the historical coverage, why the heavy focus on the early modern period in this book? Certainly there is some merit to the charge that my starting point at the end of the fifteenth century is itself biased, as it reflects the beginning of the age of European expansion. Yet it would be a major mistake to see Westerners as the only, or even the most important, empire-builders of the early modern era, considering the achievements of various Islamic and Chinese conquerors. Conversely, if the book is about the military rise of the West, why does the story wind down from the end of the eighteenth century, instead of at some point in the twentieth century at the apogee of Western empires, or the beginning of decolonization?

Here historians and social scientists are generally in agreement that explaining European dominance after the onset of the Industrial Revolution is a different kind of problem from that in the previous three centuries.[32] The bounding of Parker's original thesis reflects this periodization. While almost no one questions the idea that the West was dominant in the nineteenth century, there are a growing number of critics who do question this idea as applied to the early modern period, a skepticism that I share. The crux of the argument is whether the West enjoyed military superiority in the period after the beginning of regular interactions with polities in the Americas, Africa, and Asia, but before what many agree to be a "great divergence" at the end of the eighteenth century.[33] Yet in the interest of fairness it is important to consider how my argument fares when assessed from subsequent eras, and thus the last chapter looks at the "new imperialism" of the nineteenth century, and the process of decolonization and insurgency from 1945 to the present. How did Europeans win in the end–before they later lost?

History and Social Science

Historians and social scientists often don't think much of each other's work. As one (anonymous) commentator on an earlier version of my argument put it:

> The author perhaps underestimates or really understates (out of decency) the disdain with which historians regard political science theories, a stance bordering on revulsion and utter disregard. Military historians are slightly less contemptuous of political science than historians as a whole, but that is a very, very low threshold indeed.

Evincing something of the same sentiment, after a rare moment of contact, another eminent military historian is moved to remark, "I apologize for the brief venture into the generally unrewarding woods of International Relations theory" (a little more optimistically he continued with the slightly backhanded point that "Alas ... it should be regarded as inescapable in any book on warfare in any period, past, present, or future").[34] Social scientists often return the favor, with equally unflattering stereotypes of historians.[35]

Despite these differences, historians and social scientists have taken very similar views on the nature and global consequences of the military revolution in European expansion. Those in International Relations and cognate fields have relied heavily, if often only implicitly, on the arguments put forward by Roberts and Parker.[36] Historians for their part have often adopted a very social scientific mode of explanation. Both have often tended to share the same unfortunate Eurocentrism. These commonalities and overlaps show up the falseness of stereotypes that portray those like political scientists, sociologists, and others in the social sciences as engaged in a fundamentally different kind of enterprise from historians. This caricature suggests that historians zoom in to focus on detail and specificity, thereby producing rich descriptions, but that they shy away from the cause-and-effect accounts, and big-picture, universalist theorizing that define social science. When it comes to the military revolution and the rise of the West, nothing could be further from the truth. If anything, historians may be a little too enthusiastic in their simplified, rigid, and universalist causal stories. At least in this area, historians have been surprisingly keen on the idea that organizations in competitive environments are rapid and effective learners, in the ways that economists think of firms in competitive markets. The fact that scholars from a range of different disciplines are looking at the same sort of problems, and trying to explain them via an exchange of ideas across boundaries in the same sort of language, is, however, a notable positive. There is less need to argue about what the questions should be, and more time to look for answers.

So far, however, those specializing in the study of world politics have been surprisingly peripheral to debates about the rise of the West. One might think that the discipline of International Relations, fixated on matters of war and peace, especially the idea of military competition and insecurity, would play a starring role. In fact, with some exceptions, they have been conspicuous by their absence.[37] This is despite the fact that International Relations credits the military revolution, directly or indirectly, with the two most important developments of the last millennium in international politics: the (twin) dominance of the West and of the sovereign state. The mainstream of the discipline tends to unreflectively anchor foundational beliefs in historical accounts that are increasingly coming under challenge. This is a lost opportunity for all concerned.

What, then, do political scientists have to offer historians in explaining the historical developments, if anything? Perhaps strangely, a contribution I aim to make as a social scientist is to urge more skepticism concerning common social science assumptions, concepts, and methods of designing explanations, and to show something of the problems and pitfalls of these assumptions, and ways of reasoning. Specifically, instead of the all-too-easy assumption of efficient, rational learning, and competitive military environments creating better adapted actors, I argue for a perspective where cultural factors are at least as important. What, exactly, are the problems with the conventional model, and how does the cultural alternative work? Below I lay out the problems, suggest how a cultural alternative might be superior, and illustrate the difference with an example about magic in warfare.

What Shapes Organizations?
Questioning Learning and Selection

As well as the big historical argument about what did and didn't drive European expansion, this book is concerned with explaining change in institutions like militaries and states. To this end I first challenge common assumptions about the operation and effects of learning, adaptation, and elimination. These often tacit assumptions underpin the logic of the military revolution, but it is important to realize that they also exercise a vital influence on general beliefs about history and institutions.[38] To bound the discussion, and in the spirit of synthesis, I work mainly from the complementary arguments put forward by two military historians, Jeremy Black and Wayne Lee, and two social scientists, Jon Elster and John Meyer. Working from very different starting points, the historians and social scientists nevertheless level complementary and powerful criticisms of the idea that competitive environments will produce effective and well-adapted organizations, whether it be in war or most other domains.

Learning involves actors identifying successful and unsuccessful strategies and institutions according to judgments of varying organizational performance, working either from a process of trial and error, or by copying successful peers and competitors (survival of the smartest, perhaps). Selection is based on the analogy of "survival of the fittest" in the natural world: unsuccessful or maladapted actors are eliminated from the system, leaving only better adapted actors. As environmental conditions and selection pressures change, so too does the population of successful survivors. Those writing about military history usually draw on both mechanisms. Those that lose battles and wars learn to emulate the features of those who win them, while those who can't or won't learn are eventually conquered. From here it becomes clear why repeated fighting is said to improve military efficiency: warfare gives military organizations the opportunity to evaluate their performance and learn from others, while selecting out those who fail to respond to competitive pressures.

Learning

Black identifies what he refers to as the "paradigm-diffusion" approach as the most common model of change among military historians. This approach holds that particular actors (almost always Westerners) come up with a new technology or technique that is objectively superior, and that this innovation is then copied by others in order to stay competitive in an environment of pervasive insecurity. Thus Black speaks of "a somewhat crude belief that societies adapt in order to optimize their military capability and performance," and identifies historians' reliance on the idea of "some mechanistic, if not automatic, search for efficiency."[39] Lee strikes the same note in speaking of the assumption of a "challenge-and-response" dynamic in military history: "The implicit dynamic ... is one of direct conscious response: historical actors determined the need for a new system or a new technology and therefore developed one."[40]

In contrast to this perspective, Elster has little faith in the ability of actors to reason and learn,[41] especially collective actors. Learning depends on overcoming the effects of uncertainty, which Elster believes are generally overwhelming in the social world.[42] At first glance, it may seem easy for actors to find out what works and what doesn't in improving organizational performance, and then to apply this knowledge successfully. In fact, many demanding conditions must hold for this to work. After all, if determining what causes what in the social world is so easy that rulers and generals can be routinely assumed to get it right, why do social scientists and historians have such a hard time, even with the huge advantage of hindsight?

A parallel might be with Clausewitz's notion of the "fog of war," according to which "war is the realm of uncertainty; three quarters of the factors on which action is based are wrapped in a fog of greater or lesser uncertainty." The idea of the fog of war is much more consistent with the persistence of scholarly uncertainty and disagreement over first-order questions than the view that accurately diagnosing cause and effect is fairly straightforward. Putting lessons in to practice might be frustrated by another of Clausewitz's famous ideas: "friction," said to make even the simplest thing difficult, because "in war more than anywhere else things do not turn out as we expect"[43]

An example of the importance of learning in the military revolution literature is the prominent place Philip Hoffman gives it in his model in *Why Did Europe Conquer the World?* After reasoning that "professional soldiers have every incentive to adopt the most effective tactics, hardware, and organization," he continues: "Rulers fought wars and then used what worked against the enemy. The learning could take place during a war, or afterward, when losers could copy winners and both sides could revise what they did."[44] Yet this process of discerning "what worked" is by no means as easy as it sounds.[45] Victory and loss in war are a result of complex and varying combinations of factors, many of the most important of which, like leadership and morale, are intangible. A study of contemporary military effectiveness stresses indirect and hard to change factors like the international environment, political culture, and social structure.[46] For historians for example, the British defeat of the Qing Chinese forces in the First Opium War 1839–1842 is an unequivocal and paradigmatic demonstration of China's technological and institutional military backwardness compared with Western forces. Yet China's rulers diagnosed this defeat as the result of poor leadership and treachery, rather than indicating any systematic problem or a need for wide-ranging reforms.[47]

Selection

Putting aside the question of learning, what about the impersonal, structural effects of natural selection through war, with conquest the method of elimination? This concept removes the assumption that historical actors were able to diagnose complex causal relations and then re-engineer armies, states, and societies in line with these imperatives. Once again, although the focus here is military competition, the implications of this Darwinian style of reasoning go far wider. Thus social scientists observe: "For those who see history as efficient, the primary postulated mechanism is competition for survival."[48]

Lee speaks of the same logic as being strongly apparent in military history: "Often presented hand in hand with the challenge-and-response dynamic is the idea that successful military innovation produces a new paradigm, quickly copied by nearby competitors in order to survive ... failure to adopt paradigmatic armies or practices leads to societal extinction. War was an existential affair, and those military systems that failed to adapt dropped out."[49] From the perspective of an International Relations scholar explaining the spread of conscript armies, reasoning proceeds along the same lines: "As in any competitive system, successful practices will be imitated. Those who fail to imitate are unlikely to survive."[50] More generally Kenneth Waltz, the doyen of theory in the same field, holds that, thanks to the anarchical nature of the international system, maladapted units "fall by the wayside."[51] Adopting Waltz's logic to nineteenth-century military competition in Latin America, another scholar makes the same point: "Whether firms in the market or states in the system, units in competitive realms are continually pressed to ensure they are internally well organized and equipped to thrive and survive."[52]

The explanation here relies on differential survival rates rather than learning: obsolete or maladapted ideas and organizations give way, leaving more suitable ideas and organizations to diffuse, multiply, and dominate.[53] Firms that don't learn to keep up with the competition will tend to go out of business.[54] If selection is working to weed out inefficient organizations and promote efficient ones, the end result will be very similar to that in which organizations are adept learners. Often these two mechanisms are said to reinforce each other. The threat of elimination provides the incentive to learn. Because inefficient organizations are eliminated, economists assume that firms behave as if they have mastered complex profit-maximization calculations.

Yet, if anything, Elster sees even bigger problems with the idea that organizations' characteristics can be explained as functional adaptations to environmental pressures, in this case the pressures of military competition. Rather like learning, what at first seems to be a commonsense presumption on closer inspection turns out to rely on quite demanding and restrictive conditions. In particular, it is difficult to specify the feedback loop through which the beneficial consequences of an organizational feature cause and maintain that feature.[55] In general, Elster asserts that "Much of applied rational choice theory is a combination of just-so stories and functionalist explanation."[56]

In order for selection mechanisms to create a population of homogenous effective organizations, several conditions have to apply. The "death rate" amongst organizations has to be very high, the differences in effectiveness have to be large and consistent, and the environment has to stay fairly constant. Applying this to warfare between states, for example, the conquest and destruction of states would have to be commonplace, the differences between effective and ineffective states would have to be large and consistently decisive on the battlefield, and the particular features that gave some states this edge over others would have to stay relatively stable. Furthermore, each of these conditions must hold if the selection mechanism is to work; two out of three is not enough to ensure a convergence on the optimal organizational model via Darwinian elimination. It doesn't take too much thought to see how these conditions are difficult to meet in the context of military competition.

First, polities tend to be very durable and are rarely eliminated by conquest.[57] Even powers that are seen by historians as classic cases of military maladaption and ineffectiveness, like the Polish-Lithuanian Commonwealth, or the later Ottoman or Qing Chinese empires, often linger on for decades or centuries. Nor is this surprising longevity limited to great powers. Tiny, essentially defenseless polities routinely survive immense military conflagrations unscathed, like the European microstates of Andorra, Liechtenstein, and San Marino in World Wars I and II.[58] Second, as the chapters to follow make clear, it is rare for a given technology or institutional characteristic to be consistently decisive. Battles and wars are instead decided by varying combinations of often contingent material and intangible factors. Finally, organizational features that might be highly advantageous at one time and place may not confer any such advantage at a different time and place. One of the main conclusions of this book is that the defining features of European armies in Europe were largely absent in the Americas, Asia, and Africa, because they were impractical and ill-suited to local conditions and opponents. Rather than there being one, superior Western way of warfare, the determinants of military effectiveness were, and by all indications still are, highly diverse and variable.

A Cultural Alternative

It is one thing to show why one explanation doesn't work, but quite another to demonstrate a better alternative. Even if all the criticisms above hold true, what is the alternative? In keeping with much recent military history, I stress the importance of culture.[59] But "culture" is one of the most vague and slippery terms used by scholars. I try to make the cultural alternative both clear and persuasive in two steps. The first is to briefly present an argument in favor of a cultural view of military history. Next, I summarize the model put forward by John Meyer designed as a deliberate alternative to the efficiency-through-learning-and-elimination account criticized above. The most succinct statement of the differences between the first view and the second view is as follows. The first view is that organizations are a functional response:

> "Long-term competitive evolution and increasing socio-technical complexity demanded more and more rationalization and standardization."

The second view is that organizations are products of their social and cultural environments, they owe little to efficiency and that the environment legitimizes some forms and stigmatizes others.[60] Finally, I compare these two contrasting models with practices of magic in warfare relating to bulletproofing.

For Black, the proper focal point of discussion in talking about culture is military effectiveness:

> Across the world, the notion of effectiveness was framed and applied in terms of dominant cultural and social patterns. The analysis latent in most military history assumes some mechanistic search for efficiency and a maximization of force driven by a form of Social Darwinism, does violence to the complex process by which interest in new methods interacted with powerful elements of continuity, as well as the manner in which efficiency was culturally constructed, and the

lack of clarity as to what defined effectiveness in force structure, operational method, or tactics.[61]

What does Black mean by a cultural approach? He speaks of the importance of perceptions and expectations in determining preferences and setting goals, interpreting costs and benefits, and creating understandings of victory and defeat.[62] Another prominent military historian, John Lynn, also defines culture as "values, beliefs, assumptions, expectations, preconceptions, and the like."[63] This cultural perspective extends to viewing the development, employment, and understanding of technology from a cultural perspective, rather than technology being some asocial, objective factor that acts to produce military and social change independent of context.[64] For his part, Lee defines culture as "a broadly shared set of ideas about how the world functions and how one can survive and succeed within it."[65] It provides "a repertoire of choices from which to select." He employs the sociological term "institutional isomorphism" in explaining why certain standard ways of doing things can spread and persist for reasons that have nothing to do with their functional effectiveness.

A pioneer of the idea of "institutional isomorphism" is John Meyer,[66] who has argued for a strongly cultural perspective on institutions. This work goes a long way to provide an alternative to mechanisms of learning and selection. It also provides a rich seam of material with which to follow up calls for a more cultural approach to military history. Meyer's starting point is once again suspicion of the presumption that rational organizations face a competitive environment that leads them to become better and better able to do their jobs (i.e., for armies, fighting effectively, and early modern polities, maximizing military effectiveness). According to this logic, organizations are the way they are and do things the way they do for a reason, and that reason is to efficiently and effectively achieve the tasks they were designed for.

Meyer and his colleagues are very much focused on the contemporary period, so there is a need to exercise caution when reading their insights back into previous centuries. Yet if organizations in an era of detailed performance metrics, huge data-processing and analytical capacities, and a whole industry of professional managers and consultants nevertheless can deviate so fundamentally from the rational ideal, there are good reasons to think that their early modern counterparts would have had an even harder time coming anywhere near this idealized mark. This is especially so as early modern actors in all regions tended to explain success and failure by divine providence and supernatural interventions.[67] Rather than distinguishing modern, professional, rational organizations from their backward, primitive equivalents in centuries past, however, Meyer believes that the former are just as likely to be in thrall to myth and ritual as the latter.[68]

For sociologists like Meyer, whether they be government departments, hospitals, universities or firms, organizations are said to be generally indifferent to matters of efficiency and effectiveness, even if they could work out how to achieve these goals, which they probably couldn't. Organizational life is perhaps closer to the theater of the absurd, or satirical send-ups of corporate life like Dilbert cartoons or the television series *The Office*, than it is to the economic theory of the firm or the tenets of management textbooks. Yet organizational life is nonetheless far from meaningless. Instead, the nature and activities of organizations are oriented outward to gain legitimacy, which outweighs all other priorities short of a direct and immediate threat to organizational survival. Organizations are products of their environment, but in a very different sense from the competitive diffusion accounts. They accrue legitimacy by conforming with the expectations of their environment as represented in current cultural models of good practice with regard to both their structure and operations. Thus organizational structure reflects meaning, not function or technical efficiency.

Yet because of the stickiness of internal routines, form and actual functioning often diverge, leading to pervasive window-dressing, ritual, or what is referred to as "de-coupling": the difference between what should happen in theory, and what happens in practice. For example, the ideal contemporary firm (or university) is "client-centric," closely engaged with "stakeholders," has a flat hierarchy with listening bosses and empowered employees, and is deeply concerned with environmental sustainability, gender equality, and corporate social responsibility. But above all, this ideal firm efficiently provides the best goods and services in class at the lowest cost to its appreciative customers. Even when the corporate reality falls far short, this model of how things should be done is very powerful, for reasons that are only loosely connected with matters of profit and loss: "highly professionalized consultants who bring external blessings on an organization are often difficult to justify in terms of improved productivity, yet may be very important in maintaining internal and external legitimacy."[69] In governments likewise, "Administrators and politicians champion programs that are established but not implemented; managers gather information assiduously, but fail to analyze it; experts are hired not for advice but to signal legitimacy."[70] Legitimacy may even be more useful for success and survival than actually getting the job done. Meyer sees actors as performing the roles set for them by the cultural environment, not entities that rationally choose among alternative courses of action.

How does this very abstract contemporary theorizing possibly relate to the historical questions at hand? One brief example might be a discussion of the role and motivations of early modern military entrepreneurs in Europe, like those that did much of the fighting in the Thirty Years War. Even the mention of the term "entrepreneur" might immediately cue the reader to expect cool, dispassionate means-ends calculations about how to maximize profits while keeping costs to a minimum (not to mention preserving life and limb). In fact, however, these individuals often exhibited reckless abandon in both their finances and their personal conduct in battle.

> It was the socio-cultural dimension of military enterprise that encouraged colonels and more senior officers to overreach themselves financially, to make calculations about the maintenance of their regiments that were not economically rational, and to compete for esteem and recognition by high expenditure and heavy levels of personal commitment, both materially and in conspicuous examples of courage and leadership. War remained the primary theatre of social and cultural esteem, and military enterprise harnessed much of the enthusiasm of the actors to play large and impressive roles.[71]

Rather than these "irrational" individuals (and the organizations they led) being eliminated by going broke or being killed in battle, in fact they multiplied under the extreme pressures of seventeenth-century European warfare. Furthermore, "When the role of private enterprise in warfare came under threat and finally disappeared in the late eighteenth century, it was for reasons that owed nothing to an assessment of its actual effectiveness."[72] Instead it was a shift in the climate of opinion, as direct governmental provision and control of military forces became "a marker of sovereignty," and thus states sought to maximize legitimacy by conforming to this expectation.[73] Another leading historian of the era agrees that officers "regarded battle as a theater to display their values of honor and bravery, even chivalry," and that "the look of things mattered even in the most practical concerns."[74] There is still a distinctly dramaturgical aspect to contemporary militaries, for example the tendency to buy hugely expensive prestige equipment that adds little to actual fighting effectiveness.[75]

Can such intangible cultural commitments really survive the bloody and brutal competition of war, with so much at stake? The brief example below is an example of a massive, conspicuous, persistent, and deadly failure of the idea that people and organizations become better adapted to their environment under circumstances of military competition. This is the belief that it is possible to become bulletproof through drinking potions, applying ointments, wearing amulets, or performing certain rituals. I use this jarring instance of maladaptation, so directly at odds with our modern preconceptions of how the world should work, as a concrete example of serious weaknesses in the larger argument that we can safely assume that military organizations get more or less the right answers, given sufficient time and incentives. Even though the practices of bulletproofing discussed here are mainly from the twentieth century, similar beliefs about supernatural intervention on the battlefield have a long history, definitely including in the West.[76] For example, very similar beliefs were held by both locals and Europeans in Southeast Asia in the early modern period:[77] "The Portuguese described an invulnerable opponent in their first Southeast Asian battle, the seizure of a Malay ship off Sumatra. No blood flowed from the man's wounds ... the chronicler reported, until the magic amulet on his arm was removed."[78]

Magic and Military Effectiveness: Bulletproofing

This example is one where choices repeated over decades of war emphatically do not promote military effectiveness, despite the presence of repeated experience, short, unambiguous, feedback loops, low environmental change, strong incentives to learn, the ease of corrective action, and a strong likelihood of elimination. It illustrates how cultural models of best practice can overwhelm even the strongest functional incentives. Though no single example can be decisive, the failure of selection effects to operate even when the highly restrictive assumptions regarding learning and elimination hold in an environment of fierce military competition, strongly counts against the plausibility of this view in general.

According to the conventional perspective, what requirements must be in place for learning to occur in warfare in the way assumed by most historians and social scientists? First, opportunities to learn must be fairly frequent, with regular feedback on organizational performance. Second, the pace of environmental change must be slow enough to allow the accumulation of knowledge. Third, the causal relationships must be relatively straightforward between structures and strategies, on the one hand, and success or failure, on the other. Lastly, acting on lessons learned must be relatively easy, in terms of implementing knowledge acquired through observation. The case below shows that even under extremely favorable conditions for rational learning and Darwinian selection via elimination, culture can dominate.

In 1986 an uprising began in Northern Uganda against the newly installed Museveni government. The Holy Spirit Movement, as it was called, was sparked by Alice Auma, who claimed to be the medium for several spirits. The first, Lakwena, was the spirit of a former Italian military engineer, who through Auma became the leader of the movement. The guerilla army of demobilized soldiers that coalesced was divided into three divisions, each commanded by a separate spirit, who also spoke through Auma when she entered a trance. The battle tactics of the movement were as follows:

> [S]oldiers were forbidden to take cover when attacked.... They had to face the approaching enemy standing erect and with naked torso....

Nor were they allowed to aim at their foe; it was the spirits who were to carry the bullets to the enemy and thus decide who among them deserved death ... [soldiers] were anointed ... with shea butter oil ... and ochre ... to make them bulletproof. .... The Holy Spirit soldiers took up positions and, as ordered by the spirit, began to sing pious songs for 10, 15, or 20 minutes. Then the time-keeper blew a whistle. On this sign, the troops began marching forward in a long line, shouting at the tops of their voices: "James Bond! James Bond! James Bond!"[79]

To say that these battle tactics were suboptimal would be a considerable understatement.

Similar practices have been observed across Africa over the last two centuries: in South Africa in 1819, 1853,[80] and 1991;[81] in the Congo in the 1880s, 1890s, 1960s,[82] and currently;[83] in Tanzania in 1905;[84] in Uganda in 1917,[85] the 1980s, and currently;[86] in Kenya in the 1950s;[87] 1967–1970 in Nigeria;[88] in Angola in the 1970s and 1980s;[89] in Guinea Bissau in the 1960s and 1970s;[90] in the 1970s, 1980s, and 1990s in Mozambique;[91] in Zimbabwe in the 1970s;[92] during the Liberian civil war in the 1990s;[93] and during the same period in Sierra Leone.[94] In his survey of modern African warfare Weigert refers to "the familiar example of guerillas who expected ointments and/or rituals to make them bulletproof."[95]

Tactics relying on magical bulletproofing were used against regular European forces in wars of colonial conquest, and in subsequent anti-colonial insurgencies, as well as in post-colonial Western interventions. This belief was prevalent among groups fighting against post-independence regular government forces, and in interethnic conflict, and against mercenary outfits like Executive Outcomes. Though there were a few instances where cynical elites used such rituals to dupe credulous subordinates, there is strong evidence of genuine belief in the effectiveness of bulletproofing.[96] These unconventional tactics were used instrumentally to attain conventional ends. Thus as Ellis relates: "The abundant evidence that fighters and others who lived through the war believed that power might be obtained from spiritual sources ... does not mean that the act of fighting was some sort of cultic behavior. The main purposes of fighting were to gain wealth and prestige or to take revenge."[97] Wlodarczyk refers to the magic used in warfare as "the ability of an individual to command spiritual power to ends of their own choosing."[98] What is the relevance of bulletproofing to selection effects in military history, and how might it constitute a test of such arguments?

The basic problem of interest is how organizations are shaped by military competition. The force of a test based on this particular example comes from combination of the close fit between the features of the bulletproofing example and the scope conditions and drivers of the selection mechanism (the prerequisites of learning, and elimination), together with the radical difference between the end result predicted (rapid elimination of bulletproofing), and that observed (durability of bulletproofing over centuries in many different locations). The drivers of selection are present to an unusually clear degree, and yet the result equally conspicuously is the opposite of what the explanation says should happen.[99] This example is therefore very relevant to both mechanisms of learning and elimination.

For combatants in societies experiencing long-running civil wars like Uganda, Mozambique, and Liberia, the belief about bulletproofing lends itself to repeated testing. Both at the level of the individual and the group, there were numerous opportunities to judge the effectiveness of bulletproofing in actual combat. Insurgents were disproportionately drawn from former soldiers (like the Holy Spirit Movement),[100] and even those who had not had formal military training often became locked into military violence as a way of life. As such, combatants often had ample first-hand experience to draw upon. There has not been any environmental change that affects the (in)effectiveness of bulletproofing.

There is a very short, simple, unambiguous cause-and-effect relationship in action, that is, being hit by a bullet and being injured or killed by it. This relationship has not changed significantly over time, nor is it likely to, and firearms have been common in African warfare since the 1600s.[101] The cause-and-effect relationship is easily appreciable through personal experience, or through observation of third parties. For combatants there is a very strong incentive to learn the real effect of being shot, all the more so where there is no medical treatment for wounds that are not immediately fatal. Groups are not fighting for otherworldly aims or martyrdom, and thus the incentive is to be pragmatic in adopting effective military tactics and discarding ineffective ones. Corrective action is relatively easy: for the individual, don't trust the bulletproofing procedure, take cover. For the armed groups, which actively inculcated the belief rather than just tolerating it among its members, the solution was to stop the rituals.

For all these reasons, if there is an inefficient belief that should be selected out through conflict-related learning among organizations fighting in an anarchical environment, it is this one. Yet this belief has been widespread and durable. In each case, the conditions favor improving organizational performance by learning and "selecting out" bulletproofing are present in the most obvious and direct fashion one can imagine. Usually organizations receive much less regular feedback, face much more complicated causal relationships, a much less stable environment, a much less direct incentive to learn, and much greater implementation difficulties.

Seemingly unambiguous results were assimilated within the prevailing cultural scripts about cause and effect. Aside from the initial ritual "washing" or charms, remaining bulletproof depends on certain prohibitions being observed. These commonly include not bathing, avoiding eating certain foods, or not having sex. The conditional nature of bulletproofing, only remaining effective as long as these prohibitions were observed, thus gave a frame for interpreting failure at either the individual or group level. African fighters faced the same difficulty as any other soldier, policy-maker, or social scientist: inferring a causal relationship. As one participant put it: "You call them medicine men, but you have your armor in Western armies and sometimes it does not work, which is the same with us. Sometimes we get hurt and sometimes we get killed."[102] Defeat was interpreted as a failure to observe the prohibitions, rather than a disconfirmation of bulletproofing as such.[103] A related explanation, often used to explain the defeat of African forces at the hands of Western colonial armies, was that the latter simply had more powerful magic on their side.[104] In the early 1990s RENAMO in Mozambique came up with a magic "vaccine" to counteract their opponents bulletproofing,[105] while at the same time in Sierra Leone other forces responded to bulletproofing by hacking their enemies to death with machetes.[106]

The predicted workings of the elimination path with respect to bulletproofing should be even more direct and uncontroversial. Individuals who go into combat believing they are immune to bullets are disproportionately likely to be killed or wounded, and groups in which this belief is widespread are disproportionately likely to be defeated. The lack of an elimination effect cannot be attributed to all parties operating with the same beliefs, as there were a variety of armed groups engaged that did not believe in bulletproofing. These ranged from European colonial armies to Communist forces disdainful of "reactionary" and "bourgeois" traditional beliefs, post-independence Western interventions, mercenary forces, and conventionally trained African armies. Sometimes these conventional forces massacred opponents who believed in bulletproofing, but at other times they lost. The balance of losses to wins for magically inspired forces was not sufficient to eradicate or even diminish this practice.

How does the alternative, cultural perspective fare in explaining bulletproofing? The cultural environment creates "the lenses through which actors view the world and the very categories of structure, action and thought."[107] Learning is difficult thanks to pervasive uncertainty, but in any case organizations are largely unreflective, being bound by routine. Organizations put a premium on myths and ceremony.[108] There is a strong sense of actors playing a part, rather than exercising genuine agency.[109] Rational bureaucratic structures may be radically disconnected or decoupled from actual organizational routines.

According to each of these criteria, this cultural explanation produces a reasonably good fit, certainly much better than one based on selection by rational learning and/or elimination. There is a striking homogeneity in the practice of bulletproofing, a practice that is not likely to have arisen by rational action. The cultural environment strongly conditions actors' views, causing them to risk their physical survival as individuals and organizations in line with erroneous beliefs about a cause-and-effect relationship between rituals and bulletproofing. Routine practices persist across decades, even centuries, independent of functional ineffectiveness, and organizations place a pronounced emphasis on myths and ceremonies.

Lest it be thought that this example is some sort of caricature of the dark, irrational African "Other," it is again worth stressing that the underlying theory was developed to be applied to organizations in the United States. There are similar examples of consistent and self-defeating organizational dysfunction in contemporary Western societies, even if the consequences are not as life-threatening. For example, $23 trillion is placed in actively managed investment funds charging high fees for their supposed ability to beat the market in delivering superior returns. This is despite the fact that research consistently shows that the ability to consistently beat the market in this way is illusory.[110] Actively managed funds, like bulletproofing, are highly costly, demonstrably ineffective, and durably popular.

The Road Ahead

Having introduced the military revolution debate, and the models that support or critique the logic underlying this thesis, it is now time to bring forth more detailed evidence to back up the claims made so far. The next chapter surveys the expeditionary warfare of the Spanish conquistadors in the Americas and Portuguese relations with polities in Africa and the Indian Ocean littoral from around 1500. Chapter 2 begins a century later, and focuses on the fortunes of the Dutch and English East India Companies in South, Southeast, and East Asia. Returning to Europe, I argue in Chapter 3 that even on their home ground and in the Mediterranean Europeans did not enjoy any significant military advantage over their Islamic opponents, most notably the Ottoman Empire, until the 1700s. The last section of this chapter examines how a Eurocentric bias of place has distorted understandings of the relationship between technological, military, and political change, while an anachronistic bias of time based on reading back from "inevitable" Western triumph exaggerates European successes, while obscuring the power of Asian empires. Finally, the Conclusion re-evaluates my argument about the early modern era from two later vantage points: first the victory of the Europeans in the age of the "new imperialism" toward the end of the nineteenth century, and then the period from 1945 to the present. I finish the book by briefly returning to the questions about organizational change, effectiveness, and culture.

CHAPTER ONE

Iberian Conquistadors and Supplicants

DID SUPERIOR WEAPONS, tactics, organization, administrative and fiscal support, or some combination of these factors, allow Europeans to dominate the Americas, Africa, and Asia? This chapter and the one following assess the global aspects of the military revolution thesis by studying European expeditionary warfare. The military revolution thesis holds that Europeans sallied forth and won thanks to the application of the same style of warfare they had honed in fierce military competition at home. In contrast, I suggest a new perspective on Europeans' overseas wars from the end of the fifteenth century to the end of the 1700s.

The way Westerners fought in the wider world in the early modern period was almost entirely different from the way they fought wars in Europe with respect to nearly every one of the criteria that define the military revolution thesis. Instead of the tactics of the armies of Holy Roman Emperor Charles V or of the Thirty Years War, Europeans abroad improvised and adapted new methods of fighting in line with local circumstances and conditions. Rather than armies of tens of thousands, the forces of European expansion more commonly numbered only in the hundreds. While cannon-armed sailing ships were superior to anything other powers could put on the open ocean, they did not fundamentally change the balance of power. While Western military technology was far in advance of their American opponents, elsewhere there was a general parity. When there were gaps, these were usually closed quickly.

Remembering that the military revolution thesis is as much about states and taxes as muskets and cannon, the forces that fought, traded, and schemed their way into foreign regions were rarely those of European states, but much more commonly ad hoc bands of adventures and chartered private companies. This was largely out of necessity rather than choice: European rulers were rarely able to transport large armies across the oceans until the nineteenth century. Thus on almost every count, the military revolution thesis that Europeans won by overpowering opponents to the West and East fails to hold. Yet if so, what does explain the first wave of expansion?

Here it is necessary to delve a little deeper into the ambiguous idea of "expansion," which played out very differently in different regions.[1] In the Caribbean, Central and some parts of South America this involved conquistadors destroying major native polities already ravaged by disease and taking over their lands and peoples, though for centuries the degree of actual control exercised by the Iberians was often slight. In Africa and Asia, however, European expansion was very different. The Portuguese, Dutch, and English inserted themselves as relatively minor, marginal players within existing systems of political and commercial relations. Coercion was certainly very important, but European domains in the East were maritime networks that did not challenge the interests of the major powers in the region. In a sentiment that was widely replicated elsewhere, African rulers referred to themselves as "lords of the land," while the European interlopers were the "masters of water."[2] Sometimes this relationship operated on a basis of rough equality, but often Europeans had to implicitly or explicitly subordinate themselves in showing deference to local rulers.

Though it does not get much coverage in this book, disease was a crucial factor in explaining the different patterns of European expansion, as popularized in Jared Diamond's *Guns, Germs, and Steel*. The spectacular destruction wreaked by Europeans in the Americas, particularly the Spanish, owed a great deal to the cataclysmic effects of disease in precipitating the collapse of the largest and most structured polities in the region, and gravely weakening the rest.[3] In contrast, in Africa the advantage was reversed, with locals having a greater tolerance to ambient diseases, while Europeans, and their horses and pack animals, suffered daunting mortality rates. In Asia, disease did not consistently advantage one side over the other to anything like the same degree. It bears noting that those in the early modern period had very little understanding of what diseases were, how they worked, or how they were cured. As with the beliefs of bulletproofing discussed earlier, Europeans responded to sicknesses with superstition: blood-letting, spices, and prayer being the main remedies.[4]

Unless they enjoyed a major epidemiological advantage, Europeans were unable to defeat even middling non-Western powers in the period 1500–1750, and generally maintained their predominantly naval-mercantile empires in the East under the sufferance of the Asian and African rulers of the day.[5] In the rare instances when Westerners sought to challenge this arrangement, they generally lost. This precarious presence is hardly surprising given the tiny, essentially freelance European expeditionary forces involved. As discussed in Chapter 3, in the only instance where large, state-supported Western armies repeatedly faced a major non-Western enemy in this period, the Ottomans were able to win, conquer, and then hold most of their gains in Europe and North Africa. The only evidence of a major shift in the military balance comes right after the end of the period Parker sees as crucial (1500–1750). From this point, the Ottomans began to consistently lose to European opponents, especially Russia, while further East the English East India Company began the long process of uniting South Asia under its rule. Even in the case of Western victories, however, the military revolution thesis is often a poor fit with the way events unfolded.

In the rest of this chapter I evaluate the military revolution thesis in relation to technology, tactics, army size, and the fiscal-administrative supports of warfare. I begin with the Spanish conquistadors and other Europeans in the Americas, before moving on to examine the Portuguese in Africa, the Indian Ocean, and Asia. The following chapter does the same in comparing the tenets of the military revolution thesis in relation to the Dutch and English East India Companies in South, Southeast, and East Asia. Having examined the military revolution thesis and found it a poor guide to the historical experience, the explanation of the essentially modest European early modern successes rests on the importance of local allies, deference to non-Western great powers, and the fit between what Europeans wanted, and what locals were prepared to give. European fortified trading posts ashore posed little danger to Asian and African rulers, and were often incorporated within mutually beneficial networks of exchange. European expansion in this era is thus in no way equivalent to conquest, being in many ways more a matter of European submission than dominance.

What of the more abstract argument of the book about war, learning, and organizational change, and what Black refers to as a paradigm-diffusion model? Here it is important to note the contradiction whereby social scientists and historians find it very hard to tell what caused what in very complex situations like battles and wars, leading to fundamental disagreements about why history turned out as it did. At the same time, there is an assumption that those in the thick of these episodes could accurately diagnose the intricate causal relationships between technology, tactics, logistics, morale, and broader societal factors, on the one hand, and military effectiveness, on the other. Perhaps even more optimistically, the assumption is that, having discerned the causes of effectiveness, these actors were then able to implement efficiency-enhancing reforms. As Europeans rarely enjoyed military superiority over their local foes, there was no process of elimination leading to a convergence on one, superior, Western way of war. In Asia, great power armies that dwarfed their European counterparts had either already anticipated key elements of the military revolution centuries before Europe, or had come up with alternatives.

The Model: Armies of the
Military Revolution in Europe

Before getting down to the analysis of European military actions on other continents, it is useful to consider what an army of the kind described by the classic military revolution thesis would look like. The first battle of Breitenfeld during the Thirty Years War in 1631 saw Protestant Swedes, led by King Gustavus Adolphus, and their Saxon allies defeat an army of the Catholic Holy Roman Emperor. Though he emphasizes sieges as being more typical than battles,

Parker refers to Breitenfeld as a paradigmatic demonstration of the superiority of the new, modern form of warfare.[6] Roberts (who wrote a biography of the Swedish king) also saw the Swedish armies of this time as pioneers of the new style of war.[7] The Protestant forces were made up of 28,000 infantry and 13,000 cavalry, with 51 heavy iron cannons and further light pieces distributed among individual regiments. As the Swedish infantry were deployed in thinner lines than the squares of their imperial opponents, were intensively drilled in volley fire, and had superior field artillery, so they produced a greater rate and weight of fire that proved decisive. The battle was a great tactical and strategic victory, almost 80 percent of the imperial army was killed or captured. Though weapons like swords and pikes were still important, gunpowder weapons had come to dominate.[8] Other historians share the view that Breitenfeld was "the first great test and trial of the new tactics against the old, and therefore the first great land battle of the modern age."[9] The discipline required for the Swedes and others to successfully fire in volleys and perform other maneuvers in battle required training in smaller units with more officers as part of a standing force. Given this and other Swedish victories, "their methods were soon copied by other major armies in Europe."[10] For example, according to Parker, by the very next year after the battle, Imperial forces had learned to adapt and emulate the techniques of their victorious opponents by thinning their lines of infantry and improving their volley fire, as well as deploying more field artillery.

From the beginning of the 1500s to the Treaty of Westphalia that concluded the Thirty Years War in 1648, major European powers typically came to battle with 30,000–60,000, troops and maintained up to 150,000 men under arms in total.[11] Raising, equipping, and provisioning forces of this size required the near-total support of the state, commonly taking 80 percent or more of rulers' revenues, not counting the requirements of servicing debt accrued from previous wars.[12] Hence the link to the broader sociopolitical changes such as state-building: "the costs of war and preparing for war are what lead to societal impacts."[13] For armies of the time, bills were paid (if they were paid) through a combination of official taxation, borrowing, and plunder.[14]

The point here is to provide a rough baseline or benchmark against which to judge the way Europeans fought outside their native region. To be competitive in the new style of warfare in Europe was held to require large gun-armed, standing infantry armies, plentiful cannons, new warships, and new-style artillery fortresses with angled bastions, which together absorbed nearly all the money and manpower that the rulers of the time could muster. Many went through successive bankruptcies under the fiscal strain. The armies themselves, functioning as instruments of states and sometimes under direct royal command, were professional permanent forces extensively drilled in volley fire and combined arms fighting to draw on the complementary strengths of musketeers, pikemen, cavalry, and artillery. It is important to keep in mind that these individual technological, tactical, and fiscal-administrative features are seen as a package deal in constituting the military revolution, not just a check-list of coincidental developments. In considering the way Westerners fought overseas, almost none of these characteristics applied, and hence the tenets of the military revolution are almost completely irrelevant to European expansion in the early modern period.

The Conquistadors

At first glance, the Spanish conquest of huge swathes of the Americas in the early 1500s would seem to be incontrovertible proof of Western military superiority fuelling spectacularly successful empire-building in the face of incredible odds. Tiny forces of conquistadors, far from home in a strange land, repeatedly overcame American armies of tens of thousands, bringing down two empires, and gaining fantastic wealth in the process. The Spanish secured huge new holdings of land, population, and revenue, based on slavery and genocidal violence. Surely if the military revolution thesis works anywhere, it would be here. Aside from being epochally important in their own right, these feats have often shaped perspectives of European expansion in general: "the Columbian experience has escaped geographical boundaries to emerge as the dominant symbol of European expansion in the early modern period."[15] Even a casual familiarity with Western relations with non-Western powers in the Mediterranean, Africa, and Asia shows how wrong this perspective is. But before skipping ahead to other regions, it is important to take a closer look at the Americas. The aim here is not to summarize the historical record, but to evaluate the relevance of military revolution thesis, and to present an alternative view.

The first point of note is the incredibly small number of conquistadors: for Cortes in Mexico only 900 at the climactic Battle of Tenochtitlan in 1521, and for Pizarro only 170 in Peru in 1532. Often presented as proof of Western technological and/or organizational superiority, this fact immediately disqualifies the military revolution thesis, which is fundamentally about mass armies numbering in the tens of thousands, as an adequate explanation of the Spanish conquest. As already noted, the size of the army is the crucial link in connecting the strictly military aspects of the argument with those relevant to the creation of the modern sovereign state. One objection might be that the forces that finally defeated the Aztecs in the battle for their capital Tenochtitlan did number in the tens of thousands (around 70,000), thanks to the Spaniards' local allies. But these allied forces were a world away from the carefully drilled, permanent, professional soldiers of the thesis.

The small size of the Spanish forces was a direct result of the fact that they were essentially private efforts, like Columbus's original voyage of discovery.[16] The Spanish Crown authorized these private expeditions, striking a deal whereby land was claimed in the name of the Crown, and souls for the church, while the right to exploit the new territories for a set period was set down in an arrangement (*encomienda*) with those risking their money and lives in the venture. As was the case with the earlier conquest and colonization of the Canary Islands, "Funds for expeditions were made available through contracts between adventurers and bankers, because expansion was always a question of business, with attendant risks." Kamen[17] continues:

> Not a single Spanish army was expended on "conquest." When Spaniards established their control, they did so through the sporadic efforts of small groups of adventurers whom the crown later attempted to bring under its control.... Thanks to the *encomienda*, the crown was able to mount a military operation in the New World without the necessity, which it would in any case not have been able to fulfill, of sending an army there. [There was an] almost total dependence of the "conquest" period on private enterprise.[18]

The essentially private nature of the enterprise refutes the idea that triumphs in the New World were achieved by state forces financed by public revenues and controlled by the royal bureaucracy. In the main, the early conquistadors were not even soldiers, often being recruited via kinship groups. The majority had none of the military training and instruction in drill that were essential features of new-style armies.[19] There were no officers, and hence no formal chain of command.[20]

Yet if there is a single factor that the proponents of the military superiority thesis might seize on, it is the fact that the conquistadors had guns and their opponents did not.[21] Often authors are careful to stress that when they talk about technology, they mean not just the physical artifacts, but also the organizational skills and perhaps even cultural attributes necessary to employ technology to full effect. However, this caveat notwithstanding, there is a tendency for much of the rest of the discussion to nevertheless default to the physical technology, especially guns.[22] The opposite problem is that if the definition of technology becomes all-encompassing, subsuming organizational, social, and cultural features also, then the word becomes stretched beyond recognition from its commonsense meaning, and such explanations become unfalsifiable.[23] Hence the danger of Hoffman's definition that "technology here encompasses a lot, and intentionally so, because it has to embrace everything that made victory more likely."[24] Explaining victory by superior technology, and then defining superior technology as anything that improves the chances of victory, is circular logic.

What, then, was the role of technology and tactics in the initial Spanish conquests? The difficulty here for the military revolution thesis is that the forces of Cortes and Pizarro in many ways look much more medieval than modern. As noted, the forces were very small and ad hoc, rather than professional soldiers, and as such they had minimal drill and training.[25] Though they had some muskets (harquebuses) and a few small cannons, most of their fighting was conducted hand-to-hand.[26] The most important technological advantage possessed by the Europeans is generally regarded as the conquistadors' steel swords and armor,[27] which had been common across Eurasia for hundreds of years. Thus one historian judges that "Guns were less important than cold steel" in defeating both the

Aztecs and the Incas.[28] Another observes that "Those Spaniards who did have firearms were lucky to get a single shot off before reversing the weapon to use as a club," but that "the one weapon ... whose efficacy is indubitable was the steel sword."[29] A third agrees that "After the initial shock response to their strangeness, firearms lost much of their importance."[30] Guilmartin suggests that the result of these expeditions would have been much the same even if the Spanish had not had any gunpowder weapons at all,[31] remembering that the Spanish also used powerful crossbows. On this basis, if the medieval crusaders had made it to the Americas, they might have been almost as successful as the conquistadors.

Turning from weapons to tactics, given the marginal role of guns, there was no volley fire. Even the pike phalanxes that constituted the main advance of late medieval war were missing. In a 1559 manual on warfare in the Americas, a veteran conquistador explained that "in the Americas the patterns and practices of Europeans warfare were irrelevant ... the treatise proposed that linear formations, hierarchical units, and permanent garrisons be abandoned in favor of small, covert fighting units dedicated to search-and-destroy missions."[32] If artillery was missing, so were artillery forts; and broadside-firing ships, had they been in use at this time (such ships were introduced only after the first Spanish and Portuguese fleets to the Americas and Asia[33]), would have been irrelevant to achieving the Spanish victories against the Aztecs and Incas.

More important than any narrow matter of weapons and particular battles, however, was the support of the conquistadors' American allies.[34] Aside from providing the vast majority of the troops used to defeat the Aztecs, the Tlaxcaltecs and other groups allied to the Spanish were crucial in providing logistical support in the form of porters to carry supplies: "in many ways we might explain European success and failures entirely as an issue of logistics, or, better, how well they succeeded in using indigenous aid to overcome the logistical challenges."[35] For example, building and carrying the small boats used to attack the Aztec capital Tenochtitlan, including digging the canal to deploy them, would have been impossible without the assistance of thousands of Americans. Hassig cautions against the idea of inferring with the benefit of hindsight that the Spanish played a brilliant diplomatic game in manipulating meso-

American politics. He points out that this was impossible, because the Spanish were almost completely ignorant of local politics. It was much more likely that they were in fact manipulated by their allies.[36] Yet the Americans also failed to anticipate the full effects of the epidemics, and the final Spanish betrayal: the pervasive ignorance was mutual. This situation has been described as "Double Mistaken Identity": "each side of the cultural exchange presumes that a given form or concept is functioning in the way familiar within its own tradition and is unaware of or unimpressed by the other side's interpretation."[37] So while the Spanish later believed that the local population had become loyal subjects of the king, the latter considered themselves as being ruled by their own lords.

In dealing with the importance of local allies, Hoffman among others argues that the Europeans only won allies over to their side because of their superior weapons, in that the "decision to ally with him [Cortes] was in fact clear evidence of the power of his technology, not a sign that it was irrelevant. The same holds for the Asian allies of the Portuguese."[38] There are two responses to this point. The first returns to the fact that steel swords and armor were the crucial technology, which, although new to Americans, had been around for centuries in Eurasia. There was nothing modern here. The second point is that even if military superiority may have been a necessary condition for the conquests, it was still less important than disease and local allies.

The Limits of Conquest in the Americas

The famous triumphs of Cortes and Pizarro, as well as the general logic of the military revolution thesis, suggest that the Europeans were invincible in the Americas. Yet after the destruction of the Aztec and Inca empires, the Spanish faced definite military constraints in their further expansion. One of these was simply a shortage of manpower, partly because there were so few Europeans in the New World, but mainly because of the horrifying death rate among their American allies and slaves. But even though they were also wracked by epidemics, some local groups to the north and south were successful in fighting the Spanish to a stand-still until the nineteenth century.[39] When Europeans did finally beat down this opposition, it seems to have been more a matter of demographic weight, as the number of settlers increased, and attrition by disease and war sapped the strength of their opponents, rather than superior military technique as such that was decisive.[40] Thus even in the theater where the Europeans enjoyed a massive non-military advantage (disease), and where the technological gap was greatest, some local polities were able to repeatedly defeat the interlopers from the Old World.

In something of a harbinger of the twentieth-first century notion of "asymmetric warfare," rather than the large, and organizationally specialized societies like the Aztecs and the Incas, it was the loosely organized tribal groups that most effectively resisted the invaders. A possible contributing factor may have been that these societies may have been more resilient to the initial epidemiological shock of the first encounter with Europeans. The idea that more "primitive" groups were more militarily effective runs directly contrary to the logic of the "paradigm-diffusion" model, where the road to success, or at least survival, is to copy technological leaders. Rather than military effectiveness being a product of convergence and homogeneity, either through rational learning or selective elimination of maladapted features, in this case and elsewhere it sprang from divergence and heterogeneity. Though the Portuguese experience in Brazil is excluded here, there was certainly no equivalent of the sweeping early conquests of the Spanish.[41] The experience of the Mapuche (also referred to as the Araucanians), who held the Europeans at bay for more than 300 years in modern-day Chile, is instructive.

The Spanish conquistadors led by Pedro de Valdivia arrived from Peru and founded Santiago in 1541. In 1550 de Valdivia pushed south, and initially matters conformed to the pattern of conquest in Mexico. Thanks to their steel weapons and armor, their discipline, and the use of horses, small numbers of conquistadors defeated much larger Mapuche forces, who lacked metal weapons, and who had been ravaged by smallpox and other European diseases.[42] In short order the Spanish allocated the land among themselves, discovered gold, began setting up mines, and went about enslaving the Mapuche to provide the necessary labor. In 1553, however, the Mapuche rebelled, killing (and eating) de Valdivia (his successor

was also later killed and eaten). Over the next fifty years the conquistadors were consistently defeated, and most of their settlements and forts destroyed. By 1600 they had been thrown back
almost to their starting point in 1550. The Mapuche then crossed
the Andes and drove the Spanish out of what are now four provinces of Argentina (Chubut, Neuquen, La Pampa, and Rio Negro).[43]
Subsequently, endemic warfare saw the Mapuche keep the Europeans at bay until well after the collapse of the Spanish Empire,
only being subdued by a genocidal campaign from the 1860s.

What explains the radically different result of Mapuche resistance here compared to the Aztecs and Incas? Notably even as late
as the nineteenth century the Mapuche generally stuck to using their
own weapons: bows and arrows, slings, clubs, lassos, and long pikes,
though the last were increasingly tipped with steel from splintered
Spanish swords.[44] Tactically, they sought to ambush and encircle
the Spanish, choosing ground that neutralized the effectiveness of
cavalry. The Mapuche mastered the use of horses within a couple
of generations of their first encounter, making them a highly mo-
bile raiding force able to fight Spanish cavalry on equal terms. The
Mapuche were also a decentralized society, banding together in
times of war, but with no capital or political center vulnerable to
attack.[45] On the other side, the Spanish logistical system was consistently abysmal. Garrison troops went so far as to eat the leather
ties that bound together their stockades, and bartered weapons
with their enemies in return for food.[46] The Mapuches' resistance
was cultural as much as military. Christianity or talk of peace with
the Spanish was punished by death, and Mapuche were trained
from boyhood for war. Their resistance continued despite successive epidemics. Interestingly in light of the presumption that repeated defeats are the spur to learning and reform, the Europeans
showed a startling lack of innovation: "In the matter of Indian
strategy and resistance the Spaniards could not see the forest for
the trees. They laid responsibility for their failures on everything
but the Indians."[47] In the mid-eighteenth century a Spanish commentator mourned that:

> In a short time the Spanish conquered the three powerful empires of
> the American hemisphere, those of Peru, Mexico and Bogota, but the

hundred and ninety years that have elapsed since the beginning of this
conquest have not sufficed to end it with the subjugation of the Araucanians [i.e., Mapuche]. Nor has the vast expenditure of fifty million
pesos and more than 25,000 recruits, nor the effusion of blood that has
been spilled done so, even though in the past century the King de-
clared this war to be equal of those of Spain, Flanders, and Italy. Today
the Araucanians posses the fairest portions of Chile ... [and] live in
independence and enjoyment of their coveted liberty.[48]

What of developments far to the north? The Spanish were again
largely halted by native resistance in what is now the southwest of
the United States and Florida.[49] Local forces had begun using guns
as early as the late sixteenth century, but their adoption of the horse
and the mobility this conferred was even more consequential.[50]

In the 1600s the English, French, and Dutch embarked on efforts to carve out their own American empires. They faced nothing
like the Aztec and Incas, though European diseases had a similarly
deadly impact on the native population; to this extent, there was
a very literal process of natural selection shaping American societies. What, if anything, does the military revolution thesis explain
about European expansion north of the Rio Grande? Once again,
there was no question of large armies being deployed from Europe,
and settlement was undertaken largely by private groups under
some form of charter. In the case of the Hudson's Bay Company,
this early arrangement from 1670 swelled over the next two centuries to form a massive domain of 8 million square kilometers. The
Dutch West India Company fought with the Spanish, contested
Portuguese control over the Brazilian Coast, and established the
settlement of New Amsterdam in Manhattan. The absence of native fleets and cities meant that sea power was irrelevant beyond
contests with other Europeans, though riverine transport was certainly important.

Previous stereotypes of American Indian warfare, rather like
those of southeast Asia, emphasized the importance of ritual and
its low lethality, ideas that have now been challenged in both regions.[51] Like the conquistadors further to the south, European
colonists had little scope to practice the standard techniques that
defined the military revolution, such as volley-fire musketry, pike

formations, and shock cavalry charges. The sparsely scattered settlers were rarely professional soldiers drilled in such tactics, and
in any case local conditions were completely unsuitable. In the
heavily forested terrain, the American Indians fought in what the
Europeans referred to as a "skulking way of war,"[52] often relying on
ambushes.[53] Though guns were keenly sought after, they did not
have a revolutionary effect on Indian warfare or society,[54] unlike
the introduction of the horse for the plains Indians and those of
the Southwest.[55] Forts were a crucial element of European success,
but since they did not have to be built to withstand artillery, they
were nothing like the elaborate angled-bastioned designs across
the Atlantic, except where they were built with other European
threats in mind. Europeans were again heavily dependent on local
allies.[56] When it came to the fur trade, which was the primary motivation for the European presence in present-day Canada, Europeans' were dependent on Americans for supply.[57] Rather than any
great tactical or technological superiority, demography may have
been the decisive factor in European dominance of the Atlantic sea-
board, as their numbers swelled, and disease took its toll on local
societies.[58] Unlike in Asia and Africa, Europeans came to out-
number indigenous populations.

Despite the important differences with the conquistadors, European expansion in North America poses equivalent problems
for the military revolution thesis. Technology was rarely decisive,
and the most important technology was the "wrong" kind, steel
weapons and horses, not guns. The tactics of Breitenfeld and other
major battles of the Thirty Years War were nowhere in evidence.
Rather than military forces being instruments of centralizing states,
the relevant groups were private adventures and chartered companies. On a related point, the numbers involved were so small that
the fiscal and administrative effects on their home governments
and societies were trivial.

Africa and the Portuguese

A huge amount of attention has been lavished on the Spanish conquistadors in the New World (if not the resistance that subsequently
blocked their progress). Hassig observes: "I doubt that a more

heavily trodden trail exists than that of Hernan Cortes."[59] In contrast, Portuguese and other Europeans efforts at expansion and conquest in both North and sub-Saharan Africa have been relatively ignored.[60] This selective attention to Western victories but not defeats (what social scientists refer to as "selecting on the dependent variable") is characteristic of a teleological attitude that because the West won "in the end," the victories represent the natural order of historical progress, while the losses were minor, atypical deviations from the fundamental trend. To the extent that there is some awareness of the relations between Europeans and Africans in the early modern era, it is often distorted by the tendency to read nineteenth-century outcomes and Western dominance back into earlier centuries,[61] or to project the idea of dominant conquistadors from the other side of the Atlantic.[62]

Ignoring a couple of centuries of a continent's history because it doesn't fit the traditional story of European triumphalism is to abandon a proper appreciation of the past, and to let the conclusions dictate the evidence considered, rather than the other way around. Examining victories while ignoring defeats means that it may well be impossible to understand the causes of either outcome. Africans' ability to hold off European advances is an important anomaly for those subscribing to conceptions of Western military superiority, premised on the technological backwardness and consequent military vulnerability of sub-Saharan Africa.[63] Many scholars argue that even allowing for Americans' susceptibility to new diseases and the damage this did to their societies, the Spanish conquests are powerful illustrations of Western military superiority. If this is the case, ignoring Africa because the epidemiological playing field was not level is inconsistent. Furthermore, if Europeans were so successful in utilizing native allies and levies to divide and conquer in the Americas, South Asia, and elsewhere, why didn't this work in Africa?

Because African history has been so neglected in this context, here it is given a prominent place. I first look at the Portuguese interactions with Atlantic Africa, especially Angola, then shift to the Swahili Coast of East Africa, before comparing the findings with the main elements of the military revolution thesis. When it comes to North Africa (discussed in Chapter 3), European states invested far more blood and treasure than they did on their more far-flung expeditions, as with the Battle of Alcazarquivir in 1578 when an army of 18,000 Portuguese (far larger than any sent to the east or to the Americas), was completely destroyed in Morocco, a battle that saw the death of the Portuguese king and most of the nobility, ruined the country's finances, and precipitated a successful invasion from Spain.

Rather than the Columbian perspective referred to above of immediate and crushing Western dominance in the four centuries from the 1400s to the mid-1800s, European-African relations were more often than not conducted either on a basis of rough parity, or with the Europeans in the subordinate role. Even the slave trade confirms this picture. European slave traders were either confined to small coastal trading posts, or did business from their ships. The location and nature of the business was dictated by local African supplier polities and middlemen. For example, during these centuries the Portuguese and other Europeans maintained small trading posts on the coast of Guinea operating "more or less at the sufferance of African rulers."[64]

The Portuguese had begun working their way down the Atlantic coast of Guinea from the late 1440s, reaching the southern tip of Africa in the 1480s. These voyages were motivated by the desire to find allies and resources with which to fight the forces of Islam.[65] This geopolitical imperative, particularly the ambition to find and ally with the mythical African Christian king Prester John, remained important through to the establishment of the networks of forts in the Indian Ocean in the sixteenth century. After their initial landings were repelled, from 1456, in an indication of what was to become the norm in dealing with African rulers for centuries to come, the Portuguese changed tack and dispatched emissaries to reach an accommodation with a series of African leaders. Although there were occasional missions to the African interior, Portuguese and more general European interventions were overwhelmingly focused on the coast (and islands). To the extent that European mercantile and political goals in the hinterland were achieved, it was through the cultivation of African groups and polities. Portuguese efforts to colonize Angola from the sixteenth century, discussed below, were the only partial exception to this rule.

Atlantic Africa

Although they didn't find Prester John, the Portuguese did score an early important diplomatic success in central Africa after contact with the kingdom of Kongo led to their king being baptized as João I in 1491, and forming an alliance with Portugal. Over the next sixty years Portuguese forces of up to 600 men assisted the king of Kongo in dealing with various rebellions and local rivals, but their support was useful rather than decisive, and they operated under the command of the Kongolese rulers, rather than as any sort of conquering force. In the early 1570s the Portuguese made a more important intervention in returning King Alvaro to the throne of Kongo. In return, Alvaro pledged allegiance to the Portuguese king, though the practical significance of such pledges was often uncertain.[66]

In 1575 the Portuguese tried their hand for the first time at outright colonization, beginning from Luanda at the mouth of the Kwanza River in present-day Angola. In a manner similar to the way European "conquest" proceeded in most other locales, the Portuguese first sought to exploit local rivalries. They inveigled local subrulers to defect to the Portuguese side and carry out the bulk of the fighting. In return for an oath of vassalage to the Portuguese king, and a promise of further assistance in future, these African allies were able to expand their own domains, which they governed as they pleased. Because the initial Portuguese claims were to areas on the coastal periphery of the major African kingdoms, they aroused little resistance from the two most powerful polities in the area, Kongo and Ndongo. In 1589 the Portuguese tried to up the ante by directly attacking the heartland of the Ndongo kingdom, at which point the Portuguese were routed, and their African vassals/allies deserted them. In the 1600s the Portuguese again sought to take advantage of civil wars and foreign invasions to conquer Ndongo and Kongo, campaigns that either stalemated or ended in decisive Portuguese defeats. In 1641 the Kongolese proved that Europeans had no monopoly on divide-and-rule tactics, inviting the Dutch West India Company to attack the Portuguese in return for lucrative slave-trading concessions. Although the Dutch and Kongolese enjoyed early successes in capturing Luanda, after seven years of indecisive fighting a relief effort from Portuguese Brazil led the

Dutch to abandon their efforts. By the end of the 1600s the Portuguese had given up on conquest, focusing instead on maintaining their costal and riverine outposts, and making money from the slave trade. The next Portuguese expansionary effort did not come until 1857.[67] Warfare in the 1700s was mainly limited to Portuguese punitive missions to enhance its hold on the slave trade.[68]

The Portuguese in East Africa

From Vasco da Gama's first voyage to India, the Swahili Coast of East Africa became a crucial stopping-off point for Portuguese expeditions to Asia. More than this, however, the region was important in its own right for Portuguese imperial aspirations. Although the Portuguese never made as concerted effort as in Angola, in East Africa too efforts to conquer substantial territory away from the coast were defeated by a combination of disease and military resistance, leaving the Portuguese with a series of coastal trading bases. The Swahili Coast (roughly corresponding to the present-day coasts of Mozambique, Tanzania, and Kenya) was dominated by Muslim city-state sultanates that mixed Arabic and Bantu cultures.[69] These traded both with the hinterlands and across the Indian Ocean. Despite their hostility to Muslims in general, the Portuguese once again sought to gain allies by inserting themselves into local rivalries. Because these small, urban, coastal polities were dependent on maritime trade, they were much more vulnerable to Portuguese strategies of bombardment from the sea, blockade and the protection racket that the Portuguese sought to impose in the Indian Ocean as a whole (discussed in the Indian Ocean section) than those in Atlantic Africa.[70]

After forming an alliance with the Sultan of Malindi in 1498, the Portuguese were able to successfully raid and then impose themselves on several other of the sultanates along the coast in the following decades. "In essence, Portugal wanted to force the allegiance of local Swahili rulers and make them pay tribute. They and the merchants in their areas were then to be allowed to continue to trade in items specified by the Portuguese, but not in others in which they [the Portuguese] claimed a monopoly."[71] Later the Portuguese built a *trace italienne* fortress in Mombasa to deter an Ottoman naval threat that emerged later in the 1500s.[72] Once again, Portuguese forces were small, usually in the hundreds, never more than 2000.[73] This compares with the largest Ottoman fleet of just under 10,000 soldiers and sailors with 72 ships in the Arabian Sea and Indian Ocean in 1538, the largest since the Ming Chinese expeditions of the previous century.[74]

Despite their general maritime orientation, the Portuguese sought territorial conquest to capture the source of the gold brought down to the coast, hoping to emulate the spectacular success of the Spanish in the Americas. A 1570–1575 expedition up the Zambezi River in search of gold from the Zimbabwe Plateau was one of the largest the Portuguese mounted in Africa, involving 1700 troops.[75] The Portuguese mission established a presence along the river, but suffered from disease and military reverses. Pearson comments on the Portuguese strategy of inland conquest: "This was a fatal move, for the essence of their strength was their cannon mounted on ships. They had no particular advantage on land, not even when confronted by poorly armed Shona warriors."[76] The expedition was a dismal failure. Thereafter, despite efforts to capitalize on disputed successions in local African polities, the Portuguese presence remained restricted to its coastal enclaves and outposts on the Zambezi until the late 1600s, though informal settlements of Portuguese creoles spread considerably further.[77] In the late 1600s the sultan of Oman pursued a successful maritime strategy of raiding Portuguese settlements and harrying its fleets. This Omani predation culminated in the successful siege of the Portuguese *trace italienne* fortress in Mombasa in 1698 by a 3000-strong force aided by local collaborators.[78]

Africans, the Portuguese, and the Military Revolution

In many ways the Portuguese experience in Angola and the East African Swahili Coast is a natural comparison with the Spanish in Mexico and Peru. Like their Iberian neighbors in the Americas, the Portuguese consistently sought to exploit local rivalries and disorders to cultivate allies who could then be subordinated as vassals. Yet the Portuguese experienced nothing like the same level of success in either their diplomatic or military moves. Why not? One element that looms large is disease: the epidemiological balance was reversed, with no equivalent of the catastrophic population

losses and societal collapse among the Africans; instead Europeans and their animals were at a disadvantage. But as discussed earlier, if scholars can meaningfully study the success of Europeans
in the Americas as a military problem, despite the huge importance of disease, then there is no reason they cannot study the contemporary failures of Europeans in Africa as a military problem
also. This is all the more so because "Although Angola's disease environment was different from that of Europe and its soldiers died
from tropical diseases, Portugal's defeats were usually strictly military."[79] In speaking of the disease factor another historian decries
"an assumption that, had these natural barriers not existed, Western technological superiority would have assured European expansion into the interior, perhaps even as early as the late fifteenth
century.... But, upon closer examination, it would seem that, in
the early modern period at least, Europe's technological edge was
seldom very great, or important."[80] In some sense, European efforts in Africa are actually a better test of the military balance than
the Americas, as European success was overdetermined in the latter. It is important also in disconfirming Parker's notion that the
Europeans easily dominated Africans thanks to superior technology.[81] First, technology was just not that important; and, second,
the technological gap was reduced by trade and transfer of weapons and know-how. Aside from the brute fact of the "wrong" result,
that is, the failure of European efforts at conquest, what is the fit
with the military revolution thesis?

Both the incremental voyages of discovery around Atlantic Africa, and the later rapid development of the *Estado da India* further
east are notable for the prominent role of the Portuguese Crown,
an important contrast with the Spanish adventurer conquistadors,
and the later chartered companies established by the Dutch, English, and others. There were some exceptions: Portuguese missions were often financed with private capital, and sometimes merchants held the temporary right to explore particular areas in the
name of the Crown. The Crown gave temporary grants to private
exploration and settlements, usually headed by the lower layers
of the nobility, but if the initial efforts bore fruit, an official cap-
tain or governor was installed, reporting either to Goa or directly
to Lisbon.[82] As with all their counterparts at the time, the Portuguese Crown thought nothing of employing mercenaries and local

irregulars. Yet these examples do not change the overall picture of the Portuguese kings' singularity in maintaining a much more direct grip (or at least trying to) on their overseas missions and possessions than their early modern peers.[83] "The Portuguese effort in the east differed from that of the Spanish in the Americas in that it was government-directed, underwritten by a sustained commitment of brain power, blood, and treasure."[84] The statist cast of the Portuguese endeavor, prima facie, seems to make it a better candidate for the military revolution thesis, relying as this thesis does on the idea of the decline of private violence as the state centralizes coercive powers.

Aside from being dependent on sea power to get to the African coast in the first place, ocean-going vessels were of little significance in Atlantic littoral, though Portuguese river boats were critical in pushing supplies inland. Closer to shore in the Atlantic, Portuguese attempts at landings were defeated on a number of occasions. The coastal estuaries were too shallow for ocean-going sailing ships, and the Portuguese longboats were overpowered by local forces in their own oared craft.[85] Africans' use of poison arrows was especially effective in driving the intruders back out to the sea.[86] It was a different story on the Swahili Coast, where Portuguese naval cannons were effective in intimidating trading city-states. But even here Portuguese naval superiority was later broken by the Omanis using Western-style ships with Muslim seamen in a century-long contest beginning in the 1640s.[87] Thus with the exception of the small Swahili port city-states in East Africa prior to the arrival of the Omanis, naval superiority did not translate into a decisive strategic advantage for the Portuguese in Africa.

Fortresses and land-based artillery also played little role in Africa, again the Swahili coast being a partial exception. Without the pack animals that were so vulnerable to disease, artillery was extremely difficult to move beyond rivers. The Portuguese base in Luanda was best protected by the logistical difficulties its main rivals had in mounting attacks far from their centers of power. The most imposing Portuguese fortress in Africa, Fort Jesus in Mombasa, was captured by the Omanis with local African support after a two-year siege 1696–1698,[88] allowing them to take Zanzibar and the current coast of Kenya.

Both the Portuguese and Africans used similar tactics on the battlefield, although this similarity seems to have been coincidence rather than emulation or rational learning, the Portuguese having developed close-order fighting to protect against cavalry that was absent in most of sub-Saharan Africa. For both Africans and Portuguese forces in Africa, heavy infantry armed with swords or axes anchored the center, with lightly armed archers positioned on the flanks. Battles started with an exchange of missile fire, at the early stages arrows and crossbow bolts. Initially Headrick judges that "Firearms were even less useful in Angola than in the Americas,"[89] but later in the 1700s, both Europeans and Africans switched to greater use of muskets and skirmishing.[90] Battles were decided by the clash of heavy infantry (horses could not survive local diseases so there was no cavalry). The number of Portuguese was usually in the hundreds, augmented by thousands of African troops, while opponents like Kongo might put anything up to 20,000 in the field. Portuguese steel armor and swords gave their forces an importance far greater than their numbers, but nevertheless they tended to lose as many battles as they won in Atlantic Africa. Portuguese troops enjoyed little success in East Africa, although they were effective in augmenting Ethiopian forces in the mid-sixteenth century.[91] Guns were not decisive early on because of the primacy of hand-to-hand fighting, while later the Africans were able to roughly match the Portuguese in muskets. In sum, when it comes to technology and tactics, there is again very little support for the elements of the military revolution thesis. In each region of Africa, diplomacy and logistics were much more important than any narrow battlefield dynamics in determining outcomes. In the main, whether it was trade, war, or politics, Europeans depended more on Africans than vice versa.

From the Middle East to China

In some ways the Indian Ocean region is the crux of the argument about the military revolution enabling early modern European expansion. Unlike in the Americas and Africa, diseases affected all parties more or less equally. Throughout much of the region technology was also roughly equal. Gunpowder weapons were in use before the Portuguese arrived, not to mention steel and cavalry. Local powers like the Safavid Persians and the Mughals created mighty empires, while even some of the smaller polities of Southeast Asia had populations as large or larger than Portugal or the Netherlands.[92] Parker and others have seen the fact that first the Portuguese in the 1500s, and later the Dutch and English from the 1600s, built empires in the Indian Ocean, despite the lack of any general technological advantage, as clinching proof of the military revolution thesis, and in particular the social and political underpinnings of Western military effectiveness. As one historian puts it, "Moroccans, Ottomans, Gujaratis, Burmese, Malays, Japanese, Chinese, and countless other peoples had guns, germs and steel, too, so what else lies behind the rise of Europe?" Parker draws an important distinction between the Islamic empires and East Asia. He holds that unlike the Muslim powers, the combination of advanced technology and centralized, military-fiscal states made China, Japan, and Korea impervious to the Western threat until the nineteenth century. As this chapter and the next demonstrate, however, the European presence in the Indian Ocean and East Asia are more notable for their similarities than differences: in both cases, European presence depended on deference and subordination to much more powerful Asian empires.

This section examines the Portuguese in Asia, who established a far-flung maritime network all the way from East Africa to Japan with extraordinary speed in the first decades of the sixteenth century, looking first at the balance at sea, and then considering their military fortunes on land.

The Portuguese at Sea

The Portuguese drive to the East around the Cape of Good Hope was motivated in part by the continuing quest to find Christian allies with whom to effect a giant pincer movement against the Muslims in the Holy Land.[93] The Portuguese kings entertained millenarian ambitions of destroying the holy sites of Islam, capturing Jerusalem, and precipitating the second coming of Christ. The second, more mundane goal was to take over the spice trade, useful not just in monetary terms to fund various crusading ventures, but

also to deny this wealth to Muslims (and their Venetian collaborators). The initial Portuguese approach towards the smaller polities
of the west coast of India was very similar to that employed in East
Africa: finding local divisions and rivalries, and offering an alliance
to whichever faction looked more pliable. They quickly captured a
base at Goa in 1510, holding it in the face of a counterattack by
the ruling Muslim sultan only with the assistance of Hindu allies.[94]
It was to remain the headquarters of the *Estado da India* for the
next 450 years, where the viceroy received orders from Lisbon, and
passed them down to the various governors and captains.

Under their leader Afonso de Albuquerque, the Portuguese
pursued a strategy of capturing key maritime choke points through
the length and breadth of the region.[95] Thus after subduing Muscat in the Arabian peninsula in 1507, Albuquerque's forces took
Malacca in 1511, a city at that time larger than any in Europe, and a
crucial entrepôt linking East Asia and the Indian Ocean.[96] In doing
so their small force of 18 ships and 1100 men defeated the sultan's
army of 20,000, including a troop of war elephants. The Westerners' success against these steep odds may well have been facilitated
by the sultan's miscalculation that the invaders would plunder and
then leave.[97] In fact, they stayed and built an imposing fortress on
the site of what had been the largest mosque. An unforeseen con-
sequence was that because the sultanate was a tributary of the Chinese emperor, the Portuguese assault complicated efforts to win
trading rights with the latter. In 1515, at the other end of the Indian
Ocean, the Portuguese seized Hormuz in the Persian Gulf and again
fortified it, though they failed to capture Aden. The next few decades saw slower expansion, as extra nodes were added in the Spice
Islands (Moluccas) and the coasts of India. If the Portuguese do
not measure up to everything said of them, the ability to capture
targets 5000 kilometers apart in the space of a couple of years with
small forces using sixteenth-century technology is an extremely
impressive feat.

An early concerted Muslim effort to expel the Portuguese from
the region was defeated in a crucial naval battle off the city of Diu
in Gujarat in 1509.[98] A Portuguese fleet of 18 ships with 1500 troops
and 400 Cochinese Indian allies faced an unlikely coalition of the
Egyptian Mamluks, unused to war at sea, who had enlisted the aid

of the Ottomans, the Venetians (who were worried that their hold on the spice trade was threatened by the Portuguese), together with the Indian rulers of Gujarat and Calicut (where Vasco da Gama had first made landfall in India). The battle closely fits the script of the military revolution. The Portuguese were out-numbered in both men and ships. The Egyptian-Ottoman galleys had fewer and smaller guns compared with the Portuguese, and the Indian *dhows* none. The Portuguese were able to engage and sink their opponents at a greater distance, as apart from having heavier guns, their ships were built more sturdily to cope with rough Atlantic conditions.[99] Furthermore, the Portuguese ships were much larger and high-sided than those of their opponents, who were thus unable to take advantage of their superior numbers to board. Together with an ability to sail more closely into the wind, heavier guns and sturdier ship construction were a recurring theme in Western naval victories over more numerous Asian opponents at sea.[100] It is important to note, however, that at this time the Portuguese ships were not the broadside-firing warships that became the European standard for centuries after, and their cannons were mounted on the decks and fired stone rather than iron balls.[101]

Perhaps the area of greatest Portuguese naval effort was that of their least success, as they sought to fight their way through the Red Sea to destroy the Muslim holy sites.[102] Here the Mamluks, and from 1517 the Ottomans who had defeated the Mamluks and incorporated their territory, were consistently able to use their galley fleets in defensive victories in 1513, 1517, and 1541, facing the largest Portuguese forces assembled in the Indian Ocean.[103] Despite being synonymous with backwardness in the eyes of some scholars,[104] in shallow waters galleys proved superior to ocean-going sailing ships.[105] Furthermore, together with increasingly capable naval forces from the sultanate of Aceh in North Sumatra, in the mid-1500s Muslims were able to re-open the maritime spice trade to the Red Sea via the Maldives, in defiance of Portuguese efforts to enforce a monopoly.[106] The resulting decline in Crown revenue directly fed through to a military weakening of the *Estado da India* in the late 1500s.[107] The seriousness of this problem can be appreciated by the fact that in 1518 the Portuguese king gained more revenue from the spice trade than from all sources in metropolitan Portugal itself.[108]

From the mid-1600s the Portuguese suffered a grave threat to their Western flank from the sultan of Oman, whose success in capturing Portuguese strongholds on the Swahili Coast has already been described. After expelling the Portuguese from Muscat on the Arabian Peninsula in 1650, the Omanis sacked several Portuguese possessions in Western India including Diu and Bombay, and engaged in extensive commerce raiding using a fleet of up to 50 large cannon-armed ships and 1700 slave sailors.[109]

Another important instance where Western ships were defeated by an Asian fleet were clashes in 1521–1522 between Portuguese and Ming Chinese forces, carefully analyzed by Tonio Andrade.[110] The fighting occurred in Guangzhou harbor as a result of an ill-starred Portuguese effort to force the Chinese to trade. In the first battle five Portuguese ships were able to hold off a much larger Chinese fleet thanks to their superior cannon, but the Westerners were nevertheless forced to beat a retreat after a fireship attack (a sudden thunderstorm that allowed their escape was interpreted by the Portuguese as divine intervention in response to their prayers).[111] The second battle the following year saw a large Chinese fleet with markedly better artillery soundly defeat the Portuguese, who lost two of their ships.[112] Andrade infers: "This suggests that Chinese had learned and adapted,"[113] and sees this as a turning point in spurring China to successfully close the gap with Western cannons. Yet the Chinese cannons in this encounter were more anti-personnel than anti-ship, and it seems that the result may have just reflected a reinforced Chinese fleet, rather than rational learning and innovation in equipment, especially given that only a year had elapsed.

Individual Portuguese ships were easily capable of defeating Asian merchant craft and pirates, an important advantage that enabled them to impose their system of "passes" in the Western Indian Ocean authorizing third-country traders to sail in waters claimed by the Crown.[114] Portuguese maritime domination was greatly assisted by the fact that none of the major powers in the Indian Ocean maintained a navy. Furthermore, these empires were largely indifferent to maritime trade as a product of cultural inclination, and the fact that their fiscal base was very much land-based.[115] The same applied even to archipelagic Japan.[116] A Ceylonese king expressed a common sentiment in his judgment that "whilst the Christians would be Lords of the sea, he would be Lord of the land."[117] There was a similar complementarity of interest between the Mughals and Portuguese: "there developed a reciprocal relationship between two empires, one of the land and one of the sea, based on mutual advantage."[118] Both sides realized that the Mughals were by far the more powerful member of the partnership.[119] In explaining the position of the *Estado da India*, Albuquerque wrote to his king that "if Portugal should suffer a reverse at sea, your Indian possessions have not power to hold out a day longer than Kings of the land choose to suffer it."[120] Thus in general, "Europeans scrambled to find a place on the fringes of Asian orders."[121]

While Portuguese naval prowess was certainly more than a myth, it ran up against significant checks and defeats: the defensive victories of the Ottomans and the Ming in the Red Sea and South China Sea, the ability of the Acehenese to break the Portuguese maritime spice monopoly, and from 1650 the Omanis beating the Portuguese at their own game of naval predation. Asian powers demonstrated considerable powers of naval power projection, with the Omani expeditions to the Swahili Coast, Ottoman missions to India, the earlier Ming Indian Ocean fleets of the 1400s, and the massive Japanese invasions of Korea in the 1590s all being on a much larger scale than any equivalent European efforts. The Ming Indian Ocean fleets mustered around 26,000 sailors and soldiers (around the same size as the Spanish Armada of 1588), while the Japanese invasion force that attacked Korea in 1592 numbered 160,000.[122] Portuguese naval power did not change the *Estado da India's* dependence on land-based Asian empires, and Portuguese maritime supremacy must be put in a context where none of the Asian great powers chose to maintain a navy. Although the Portuguese faced many challenges to individual fortresses, until European competitors arrived from 1600, the *Estado da India* never faced a co-ordinated maritime assault across its network. Thus Chaudhuri's verdict is that Portuguese amphibious victories "were mostly made at the expense of rulers who had had no reason so far to defend their trading ports with strong military forces.... No strong

Asian power at the time, whether in India, the Middle East, or China, considered the Portuguese to be a serious threat to the existing balance of power."[123]

The Portuguese on Land

Though the *Estado da India* was primarily a maritime domain, the ports and forts that were the nodes of this network had to be taken and defended. How closely did the Portuguese correspond to the template of the new-style post-revolutionary European army? The usual point about tiny numbers applies, with Portuguese forces rarely numbering above 1000. As discussed previously, they were maintained by the Crown, rather than being ad hoc companies of adventurers, like the Spanish in the Americas, or employees of a chartered "company sovereign," as with the Dutch and English East India Companies that so effectively eclipsed the Portuguese in the seventeenth century. Contra the teleology of the military revolution, the "modern" state monopolizing armed force was bested by the private wielders of violence.[124]

One of the few instances of the Portuguese trying to conquer territory in Asia was their campaign against the rajah of Kandy in Ceylon.[125] In 1594, 1630, and 1638 this resulted in disaster, as Portuguese forces were ambushed and destroyed, their commanders being killed on each occasion. The Kandy forces eventually combined with the Dutch East India Company to drive the Portuguese from the island.[126] Winius describes the Portuguese as prone to frontal charges and seeking individual deeds of valor, a long way from drilled professionals.[127] Similarly, their weapons were said to be primitive by European standards, as apart from some muskets, they relied on swords, shields, half-pikes, and armor.[128] Kandyan forces did not have guns or armor like the Portuguese, being armed with bows and spears, and thus they tended to avoid frontal attacks.[129] Instead, they used the mountainous and forested terrain to wear down the Portuguese with ambushes and attacks on their supply lines, until the Portuguese were exhausted and heavily outnumbered, at which point they could be overwhelmed. At various points their opponents were also effective in peeling away local Portuguese allies and auxiliaries, who commonly comprised the bulk of the forces deployed. Yet due to their lack of artillery the Kandyans could not capture Portuguese forts, which could not be starved out, thanks to being on the coast,[130] and hence the Kandyan resort to allying with the Dutch, after earlier advances to the Danish East India Company had come to naught.[131]

The Portuguese were much more successful in capturing and defending coastal strong points in an environment of political fragmentation. Here they were favored by their superior ships and ability to provide reinforcements by sea, what is generally regarded as better artillery (even if the gap was small), and better close-order hand-to-hand fighting. This enabled some spectacular victories, as in the capture of Malacca in 1511.[132] Yet somewhat ironically in view of their success in driving the first wave of expansion, Parker holds that the Portuguese generally fought "with all the reckless indiscipline of the street gang,"[133] and that no Europeans in South Asia used the tactics of the military revolution in the field until at least the late 1600s.[134]

Those arguing for the military revolution account of the rise of the West refer to the importance of fortifications in allowing the Portuguese and other Europeans in the East to hold on to their scattered possessions, often in the face of overwhelming odds.[135] Yet this raises the problem that in Europe defending *trace italienne* fortifications was said to require "unprecedented concentrations of men and munitions." For example, it is said that the Dutch were forced to add tens of thousands to their army to garrison these strongholds;[136] hence the ineluctable pressure for larger and larger armies as a crucial component of the military revolution thesis. But neither the Portuguese nor any other Europeans had anything remotely like these numbers for at least the first 250 years of European presence in the region, and in fact Parker himself notes that most of the *Estado da India*'s fortresses were not constructed in the modern, angled-bastion fashion.[137]

If the first few decades of the 1500s may have been too early for the fruits of the military revolution to be evident, the quickening pace of military advancement in the West and the growing gap with other civilizations should have been apparent in the 1600s. Yet at least as far as the *Estado da India* is concerned, there is little if any sign of such a gap opening up. To the contrary, the fortunes of the Portuguese declined as time went on.

As described, the Portuguese were defeated in their efforts to conquer the interior of Ceylon, and lost fortresses in Arabia and East Africa. In 1683 Goa was only rescued from an attack by forces of the Hindu Maratha Confederacy by an imperial Mughal army of 100,000 (who then demanded payment for their services). The Marathas, still a traditional South Asian light cavalry army, then heavily defeated the Portuguese in a war 1737–1740. They successfully besieged a *trace italienne* fortress at Bassein and compelled the abandonment of a second at Chaul, as well as nearly bankrupting the *Estado da India* through a large indemnity payment. Even after substantial reinforcement from Europe, a Portuguese counteroffensive was seen as unrealistic.[138] It might be said that the Portuguese exhibited so little improvement vis-à-vis their Asian and African opponents because metropolitan Portugal was insulated from most of the early modern wars in Europe, and thus was not subject to competitive pressures and lacked the opportunities to learn by doing (unlike Spain). Yet McNeill, Hoffman, and other proponents of the idea that military superiority drove Western expansion proffer the Portuguese as one of their main sources of supporting evidence. If anything, it seems that in many instances the Asians had not only closed the gap with the Portuguese, but had overtaken them in two centuries of their engagement.

Conclusion

The evidence suggests that the military revolution thesis is a poor fit with Western expansion in the Indian Ocean region, for the same sorts of reasons as in the Americas and Africa. The Western forces involved were numerically trivial, reflecting the fact that early modern European states simply did not have the capacity to send substantial forces across the oceans. The combination of small numbers, a reliance on local allies, and the need to fit in with local conditions, meant that the classic tactics of the military revolution again were conspicuous by their absence. The Portuguese and other Europeans did not enjoy any decisive technological advantage in

land warfare. Though they enjoyed an edge in artillery and fortresses, this advantage was slight. (The later French and British
campaigns in India from the 1740s that for the first time saw armies
using the same tactics as used in European great power war, are
explored in the next chapter.) At sea, the role of new ships and nav-
igational techniques was of course crucial in allowing Europeans
to reach and return from Asia, and their warships were decisively
better in the open ocean. Yet even this naval advantage was subject
to severe tactical and strategic constraints and to reversals around
the western and eastern edges of the region, as well as in relation
to the crucial spice trade.

If not by dint of their modern powerful armies and navies,
how, then, did Europeans dominate the Indian Ocean and Asia in
the early modern period? The short answer is that they didn't, any
more than Europeans dominated Africa before the late 1800s.
Though much of the evidence has yet to be discussed—as it will be
in the coming chapter with respect to the Dutch and English company sovereigns—for at least the first 250 years, Europeans in the
Indian Ocean concentrated their coercive efforts primarily on maritime trade, anchored by a network of fortified entrepôts. While
they were successful in using stand-over tactics and protection rack-
ets against smaller polities (though usually even this required local
assistance), Europeans were almost always deferential toward local
great powers. The Portuguese sparred with the Ottomans around
the Red Sea and the Arabian Sea, while other Europeans occasionally clashed with the Mughals and Ming Chinese forces. But in the
main, Europeans were realistic that they stood little chance of mastering foes who could put far superior forces in the field against
them, and so Europeans deferred to the authority of Asian empires.
Aside from military calculations, Europeans also depended on access to Asian markets much more than vice versa. The Mughals,
Japanese, Chinese, and others could bring the Europeans to heel
simply by refusing to trade with them. For their part, the polities of
the region had little desire to contest Westerners' efforts to establish control of key trade routes, resulting in a rough modus vivendi
sometimes referred to as an "age of contained conflict."[139]

CHAPTER TWO

Company Sovereigns and the Empires of the East

THE BEGINNING of the seventeenth century saw the arrival of a new type of European actor in Asia: the chartered company or "company sovereign," epitomized by the Dutch and English East India Companies. The company sovereigns (of which the English and Dutch enterprises were only two of many others) present a puzzle. They were the forerunners of the modern multinational corporation, pioneering crucial institutions of modern capitalism like the legal personality of companies, joint stock ownership, limited liability, and the separation of management and ownership. They were enterprises single-mindedly run for profit. Yet these chartered companies were also endowed with quintessentially sovereign prerogatives and enthusiastically employed them, most notably the right to wage war and engage in diplomacy, but also to found settlements and build fortifications, to administer criminal and civil justice, and to mint coins and exercise religious functions.

Just like the Spanish monarchy that chartered various groups of conquistadors in the New World, the rulers of England and the United Provinces of the Netherlands aspired to foreign conquests and wealth without having the means to fulfill these dreams. Also like the Spanish, the English and the Dutch looked to square this circle by delegating expansion across the seas to authorized private actors. But the institutional form of these actors, the company sovereigns, was very different from the ad hoc groups of conquistadors fighting for gold and *encomiendas*. These companies equaled and perhaps even surpassed the success of the Iberians in driving forward the process of European expansion in the 1600s and 1700s, especially in South and Southeast Asia. Both of these companies came to rule over larger areas and greater populations than the governments of England and the Netherlands. Much more than just extensions of their home states, they became military powers in their own right.

This chapter examines the military performance of the company sovereigns relative to their Asian opponents. The significance of the companies for the military revolution has a broader significance, as this thesis is not just about armies and navies, but is equally about the state. Roberts, Parker, and those who have followed and been influenced by them in history and social science, put forward a theory of state-making as much as war-making, the most famous of whom was the sociologist Charles Tilly.[1] According to their thesis, modern armies require modern states to support them fiscally and administratively.[2] Private agents, therefore, would be priced out of war, especially naval war, due the economies of scale and scope inherent in the military revolution. So the question is not just why a particular region came to dominate the world, but also why a particular political institution, the sovereign state, came to dominate, as opposed to the various other forms that had populated the international system in the past. The dismantling of European empires in the mid-twentieth century in many ways marked the final triumph of the modern state, as the new post-colonial successor states closely mimicked the institutional forms of their European peers.

Just as renewed scrutiny of European expansion leads to hard questions about teleological reasoning in explanations of the rise of the West, so too the prominent role of hybrid private-public actors in European expansion raises equally important doubts about the traditional story of how the progress of modernity entails the monopolization of the means of organized violence by the state. Not only did the company sovereigns compete with states' imperial projects, but often the former bested the latter.[3] Thus in the seventeenth century, the Dutch East Indies Company (the *Vereenigde Oost-indische Compagnie*, or VOC) had the most powerful navy between the east coast of Africa and the Americas. Likewise, the English East India Company (EIC) eventually conquered a vast empire centered on the Indian sub-continent, and came to rule over a fifth of the world's population. Even some of those who do not see military superiority as being the primary driver behind Western expansion nevertheless credit the institution of the sovereign state as being a key cause of this trend.[4] Yet how can the prominence of these companies be reconciled with such an explanation? It is not possible to tell the story of European expansion in the early modern period without taking proper account of the company sovereigns, whose central role has too often been ignored or misinterpreted.[5]

Chartered companies were active in almost every region of the world, including Europe. The English Muscovy Company from 1555 and the Levant Company from 1592 conducted trade and exercised diplomatic functions in Russia and the Ottoman Empire. In North America, English, French, Dutch, and Russian companies formed the vanguards of colonization. The Hudson's Bay Company, explicitly founded on the same principles of the EIC, enjoyed the same far-reaching suite of powers over vast areas of present-day Canada from 1670 until the mid-nineteenth century.[6] From 1621 the Dutch West India Company (part-owned by its Eastern counterpart) was locked in a fierce naval struggle with the Spanish, while it also pursued territorial conquest at the expense of the Portuguese in Brazil and Angola. In West Africa, the English Royal Africa Company was devoted to the slave trade, sometimes leading to conflict with both European rivals and African rulers. In the nineteenth century another wave of chartered companies was formed as part of the "new imperialism" from West Africa to the South Pacific, although in both legal and substantive terms these were much less powerful than their seventeenth-century predecessors.[7] Yet of all these examples, the English and Dutch East India Companies are far and away the most important for the subject at hand. In building corporate empires in the East, the Dutch and especially the English company have been said to epitomize Western military superiority in line with the military revolution thesis. But to the extent that this thesis is premised on the necessity of the state and public authority, the company sovereigns may in fact be an equally powerful disconfirmation of the argument.

This chapter begins by explaining how the Dutch and English company sovereigns were genuine hybrids, in their combination of what are now regarded as essentially private and public functions, and thus cannot be defined as either states, simple merchant companies, or instruments of their home states. After some brief background on the VOC, I assess the extent to which the Company fits the military revolution thesis and come to the conclusion that there is little correspondence. Like the Portuguese before them, VOC troops were too few in number, did not use "modern" tactics, relied heavily on local allies and auxiliaries, and enjoyed only an uncertain technological advantage on land. The Company did enjoy important military successes on land and sea in the islands of Southeast Asia, and against the Portuguese throughout the region, but were most often defeated or deterred by the Ming Chinese, the Mughals, and the Japanese. In the 1700s, the VOC position was severely undermined by local powers in South Asia, while its deepening involvement in Java reflected commercial failure as much as military success.

The EIC was largely excluded from Southeast Asia by its Dutch counterpart, but secured important trading concessions in South Asia and Persia through a combination of diplomacy and the limited use of maritime force. Because the EIC needed the favor of the Mughals much more than the Mughals needed anything from the EIC (or any other Europeans), there was a basic imbalance of power. The 1700s, however, saw massive changes in the South Asian political landscape. The Mughal Empire declined and fragmented, with the global struggle between the French and the British overlaying and interacting with conflicts among the post-Mughal South Asian successor polities. I will then explore to what extent the end result of this time of turbulence, a massive British corporate subcontinental empire, validates the military superiority thesis.

In accord with the thesis, after 1750 the English East India Company did deploy large armies using modern European tactics and technology, but its superior administrative, fiscal, and credit arrangements were even more important in securing its hegemony. So although some elements of this story substantiate the thesis, others are more problematic. The technological and tactical gap between the EIC and its South Asian opponents does not seem to have been decisive. In fiscal-military terms war did not make a state, because the EIC triumphed as a company sovereign. Just as the "modern" statist Portuguese were defeated and displaced by the VOC, so too the more statist French lost out to the EIC. The conclusion briefly reflects on the significance of these findings for the paradigm-diffusion model and theories of organizational learning, change, and military effectiveness. South and Southeast Asian warfare was repeatedly reshaped by the transfer and hybridization of technology and techniques from the West (Ottomans and Europeans) and North (Central Asians and Chinese). But the very frequency of change and variation made cumulative learning difficult or impossible. Those Asian armies that did seek to emulate Western military practice sometimes became less effective as a result rather than more.

What Were the Company Sovereigns?

The company sovereigns were created by a charter issued either by a monarch, or in the case of the United Provinces of the Netherlands, the legislative States-General. These charters gave the company a monopoly on the trade in certain commodities within a specific geographical range, often defined expansively in terms of whole continents or oceans. The logic of the monopoly was that those venturing private capital and bearing the risk had to have the prospect of making a profit. From the rulers' point of view, the easiest and cheapest way of achieving their geopolitical goals outside Europe was by creating monopolies, and then assigning these monopolies to a corporate actor.

Within their territorial and maritime domains, company sovereigns were often granted extensive powers conventionally associated with sovereign states: the right to form colonies, administer civil and criminal justice, mint currency, collect taxes, conclude treaties, and defend and extend their commercial interests with armed force at sea and on land. Despite these powers, company states were also private actors: they were owned by merchants and investors, with profit being their over-riding goal. Beginning with the VOC from 1602 and the EIC in 1657, company sovereigns pioneered two of the fundamental features of the modern corporation: joint stock ownership and limited liability. These two features contrasted with earlier ventures, where merchants and investors had often organized themselves through loose consortia. These pooled capital and resources for individual voyages, and debts and losses could be marked against all of the assets the merchants owned.[8] Company sovereigns were run by a board of directors, the *Heeren* (Gentlemen) XVII for the VOC, and the EIC Court of Directors. These boards ran a variety of more specialized committees, and delegated powers to agents in the East, who, thanks to the distances involved, often exercised great autonomy. Shareholders were also often senior figures in their home polity governments, for example as members of the Dutch States-General or the English aristocracy and Parliament.

Historians emphasize that the company states were more than just contracted extensions of their home states, and there is general agreement that these company states were far from being passive and dependent appendages of their home governments.[9] In this vein, Ward refers to the VOC as "a sovereign entity" and "an empire within a state,"[10] while a member of the seventeenth-century Dutch government spoke of it as "not only a Company of commerce, but also a Company of State."[11] Stern describes the EIC similarly as "a form of government, a corporation, a jurisdiction,"[12] and more generally as "a company state." Wilson classified the EIC as a "state within a state,"[13] Boxer uses the same descriptor for the VOC.[14]

The Dutch East India Company

The Dutch United East Indian Company was founded in 1602, at a time when the Netherlands was fighting for its life in a rebellion against the Spanish Habsburgs, who from 1580 to 1640 also ruled the kingdom of Portugal. From its birth, the company reflected the twin imperatives of profit and geopolitical struggle,[15] in accord with the merged nature of the country's political and economic elite.[16] Dutch merchants had first reached the Indian Ocean in the closing years of the sixteenth century. While these merchants were making money from the trade, they were encouraged by the States-

General to stop competing, which was eroding profits, and to consolidate their efforts in a single enterprise through a merger of the different merchant concerns.[17] The Netherlands itself was a highly decentralized confederation of seven provinces, each with a veto over common decisions. The new company reflected the same confederal culture, being comprised of six regional chambers in Amsterdam, Middleburg, Delft, Rotterdam, Hoorn, and Enkhuizen.[18] Backed by the States-General, the *Heeren* XVII exercised a free hand in running the VOC, routinely ignoring the wishes of the shareholders. The company was granted a twenty-one-year monopoly on all trade in the Indian and Pacific Oceans.

The founding charter stated:

> East of the Cape of Good Hope and in and beyond the Straits of Magellan, representatives of the aforementioned Company shall be authorized to enter into commitments and enter into contracts with princes and rulers in the name of the States General of the United Netherlands or the country's Government in order to build fortifications and strongholds. They may appoint governors, keep armed forces, install Judicial officers and officers for other essential services so to keep the establishments in good order, as well as jointly ensure enforcement of the law and justice, all combined so as to promote trade.[19]

Though it seems that initially the military powers may have been seen as necessary for defense against the Portuguese and pirates, they quickly became the foundation of the VOC's strategy in the East. As one historian puts it, "In the Eastern seas, no European enterprise was more willing to resort to war to gain its objectives than the VOC."[20]

From 1603 the VOC quickly made its presence felt by seizing a rich Portuguese prize ship, the *Santa Catarina*, and establishing its first permanent base in Java. Because correspondence with the Company's officers in Asia took up to two years, the *Heeren* XVII decided to create the position of a governor general in the region to act as their delegate. In practice this officer enjoyed extensive autonomy. As a later governor general in Batavia put it, "the Gentlemen in the fatherland make the decisions there that they consider the best, but we do it here according to our own good judgment."[21]

By 1608 the VOC had 40 ships and 5000 men (roughly half sailors, half soldiers) across Asia. By the end of the century this had swelled to 200 ships and 10,000–15,000 troops under arms.[22] The VOC quickly sought to establish a monopoly on the spice trade, violence being a central part of this strategy.[23] The *Heeren* XVII believed that the welfare of company depended on the VOC being able to "enjoy privately, to the exclusion of all others, the fruits of the trade conferred to her alone."[24] After the Portuguese maritime protection racket (a system copied by the VOC), this move by the Dutch marked a further blow to the largely peaceful, free trade that had been the norm in the region previously.[25] Much of their predation was at the expense of the Portuguese, who lost strongholds including Ambon (1605), Malacca (1641), Ceylon (1656), and Cochin (1663).[26] But it is the military balance between the VOC and their Asian opponents that is most relevant in evaluating the military revolution thesis.

The VOC in Southeast Asia

Rather like the Portuguese refusing authority over the Indian port Diu when first offered in 1508 or Columbo in 1513,[27] the VOC were surprisingly reluctant imperialists, often eschewing territorial acquisitions, even when they were freely offered.[28] As a predominantly maritime organization whose primary concern was the bottom line, the *Heeren* XVII were wary that directly administering large areas and populations might generate more costs than extra revenue. Yet despite their reluctance, the VOC steadily expanded its territorial holdings and vassal domains in its two-hundred-year history.

Given their dependence on seaborne trade for revenue and basic staples, the smaller island sultanates of the Indonesian archipelago were often vulnerable to VOC coercion. In the spice-producing Banda Islands in the 1620s, the company went so far as to exterminate the population to secure its hold over the production of nutmeg, which was thought at the time to ward off plague—another example of the problems of relying on early modern attributions of cause and effect. Those caught stealing, selling, or growing nutmeg elsewhere were executed. The VOC traded Manhattan for Run, the only English-held nutmeg-producing island.[29] The Dutch played on local rivalries, especially with those Southeast Asian polities opposed to the Portuguese and the Spanish. In a few cases in the seventeenth century, the VOC was able to pressure rulers to cede some formal authority and adhere to the Company's highly imbalanced trade demands, as happened in Java toward the end of the century. In most cases, however, the rulers of Southeast Asia negotiated with the company on the basis of equality and to mutual advantage.[30]

From the Company's Javanese headquarters of Batavia, it was progressively drawn into a series of succession struggles and civil wars among its neighbors on the island. Succumbing to something of a "mission creep," the Company's interventions were throwing good money after bad.[31] Punitive campaigns to enforce past financial obligations on Javanese rulers created further debts that were never fully repaid. Because of the Dutch reluctance to exercise direct rule, and their outsider status, they were an attractive military partner for those factions in local political power struggles, who employed company troops as mercenaries.[32] In India the VOC built a system of forts to control the pepper trade, only to find later that the cost of the fortifications often outweighed the profits they made from the pepper.[33]

Opinions are divided as to what extent the intrusion of the Europeans fostered a Westernization of Southeast Asian war. While Tagliacozzo argues that after the Portuguese conquest of Malacca "The military dimension of European arrival also initiated systemic change in Southeast Asian societies, as a failure to incorporate martial technologies quickly and efficiently could prove to be immediately fatal."[34] He holds that Southeast Asian rulers were forced into something of a military revolution of their own, with standing armies and the use of mercenaries coming to replace feudal forces recruited via the nobility, and a greater emphasis on stone fortifications. Another view is that polities in the region were advancing down this track for reasons entirely independent of the Europeans' intrusion.[35]

When it comes to those fighting for the VOC and how they fought, the now-familiar conflicts with the tenets of the military revolution all apply: these were not professional, drilled soldiers;

they did not organize themselves in the standard musket-pike-cavalry-field artillery fashion; the size of the forces involved were trivial by the standards of European warfare (and most others in Eurasia); and lastly, they were in the employ not of a fiscal-military state, but a private corporation with sovereign powers. In that sense there were no wars involving "the Dutch" anywhere in Asia in the early modern period, if this means the United Provinces of the Netherlands.[36] The VOC was heavily dependent on local allies and auxiliaries in Southeast and South Asia who often provided the bulk of the numbers. Even those in the core VOC forces hailed from as far away as Japan. In this sense the VOC became an "Asian Company."[37]

In looking at the technological balance, there is no question that mainland Southeast Asia and perhaps most of the islands too had guns well before the Europeans arrived.[38] For example, the sultan of Malacca was plentifully equipped with cannons by the time of the Portuguese attack in 1511. Sun maintains that "During the late fourteenth and early fifteenth centuries, Chinese gunpowder technology spread to the whole of Southeast Asia via both the overland and maritime routes, long before the arrival of European firearms."[39] He sees the diffusion of gunpowder weapons as beginning in Burma and Vietnam in the 1390s, before advancing to the rest of the region and Northern India through the next century,[40] paralleling the fact that Mamluk and Ottoman guns had reached Western India by 1500.[41] Chinese cannons reached Java by 1421,[42] and the Ottomans sent guns and specialists in their use and production as far as Sumatra in the 1500s to aid their Muslim co-religionists.[43] But were these Asian cannons as good as the European ones? Proponents of Western military superiority hold that they clearly were not,[44] while other historians believe that there was no significant gap,[45] especially given the possibility of hiring Western artillerists and cannon-founders on the open market.[46] The fact that Southeast Asians preferred to buy Western guns does indicate their superiority,[47] but without telling us much about the overall military balance between the two sides.

In the seventeenth century Java had a population of around 3 million (compared to the Netherlands' population of less than 2 million),[48] with the sultanate of Mataram being the most powerful

polity in the interior of the island.[49] The VOC mired itself in a series of succession struggles here from 1677 into the 1740s. Ricklefs
argues that in general no "significant technological differences
appear between the European and Javanese military technology,
mainly because the Javanese quickly adopted those few technological innovations which the VOC introduced from Europe."[50] For example, those in Southeast Asia followed the Company troops in
switching from matchlocks to flintlocks at the end of the seventeenth century.[51] This equivalence was all the closer because the
VOC usually operated with many Asian allies and mercenaries, and
the ebb and flow of these individuals between the different sides in
successive conflicts meant weapons and tactics were readily trans-
ferred. In addition there were many renegade European mercenaries and artillerists willing to work for the highest bidder.[52] In
Java and elsewhere in the archipelago, local conditions necessitated
a different style of warfare from Europe; volley fire was no use in a
jungle, for example.[53]

The out-numbered VOC forces benefited from superior fortifications, though often these were built more to withstand naval
bombardment from rival Europeans rather than land attack.[54] Batavia held out against sieges by 10,000 and 20,000-strong armies deployed by the sultan of Mataram in 1628 and 1629, yet this was
before it was fortified in the modern European style.[55] Like those
the Portuguese stormed at Malacca, many strongholds in Southeast Asia were wood palisades rather than masonry, though the
VOC did occasionally came up against cannon-proof stone walls,
like those of the sultan of Makassar on the island of Sulawesi.

The strategic situation, particularly the ability to move and concentrate forces thanks to control of the seas, while also cutting off
opponents' access to supplies and aid, seems to have been more
important in explaining VOC successes in maritime Southeast Asia
than any narrowly tactical factors.[56] In this vein, Lorge argues:

> Any mistake by a local ruler [in archipelagic Southeast Asia] could be
> mortal; a European failure was merely a temporary setback. The mili-
> tary and political contest was therefore generally one sided because
> the Europeans always retained the strategic initiative. Europeans could
> decide how much effort to gamble on an objective and strike without

warning. Southeast Asian rulers could only react to what were often existential threats.[57]

The VOC possessed a clear advantage over their opponents in naval warfare for similar reasons as the Portuguese, with their larger, more robust, and more heavily armed European designs (the powerful Acehenese navy fought the Portuguese for most of the 1600s, until Aceh fell prey to internal disunity). Relating directly to the bigger themes of this book concerning the cultural framing of goals and strategies, Lorge sees European empire-building in Southeast Asia during this period as deeply irrational on economic grounds. For him both statist and corporate ventures were loss-making enterprises premised on the pursuit of glory.[58]

It is important to remember that outside of the small Spice Islands, Java, and a few other ports, the Dutch had very little control over the archipelago until well into the nineteenth century.[59] Where their naval advantage counted for less, for instance mainland Southeast Asia, the VOC (like other Europeans) had little success in imposing themselves, and experienced some sharp reverses. In 1643 a VOC embassy to the new Cambodian king was massacred in Phnom Penh, and a retaliatory mission of 400 VOC troops was defeated the following year.

In terms of rational learning and military adaptation, the experience of the Southeast Asian polities tends to contradict the logic of what Black refers to as the paradigm-diffusion model, discussed in relation to the EIC and eighteenth century war in South Asia below. The seemingly commonsense idea is that losers will learn to be more effective by copying the military technology tactics and organization of winners. Yet in this region those copying the European system by creating permanent forces of drilled infantry armed and trained along European lines seem to have become less rather than more effective, even according to European observers.[60] Conversely, those forces who stuck to local methods were far more successful in resisting European advances: "It was not the small 'western-style' standing armies that proved effective. Rather, it was the autonomous or semi-autonomous armed bands, whose ideas of warfare were far less influenced by the West and who fought in time-tested, traditional ways suited to local terrain."[61] This conclusion about the benefits of divergence, of an asymmetrical response, rather than mimicking the enemy, also chimes with later experiences of insurgents waging war against Western forces in the twentieth and twenty-first centuries, as discussed in the concluding chapter.

The VOC in East Asia

If the Dutch East India Company had limited success in mainland Southeast Asia, it had even less in China. From the 1620s to the 1660s the VOC made a series of sporadic efforts to offer itself as a tributary, and then forcibly open up Chinese trade, on each occasion leading to Dutch defeats on sea and on land at the hands of Ming forces. The most important of these was the capture of the VOC's *trace italienne* Fortress Zealandia in Taiwan in 1661 by Ming loyalist Coxinga or Zheng Chenggong (in the mid-1640s the Ming had been ejected from power in most of China by the Manchu Qing dynasty).

After being defeated by Portuguese naval forces off Macau, in 1622 the Dutch raided the coast of Fujian, captured ships, and demanded that the Chinese cease trade with Spanish Manila. After two years, however, the company was forced to evacuate its island base just offshore in the Pescadores Islands in the face of a vast Chinese army of "tens of thousands," and retreat to Taiwan.[62] Initial naval clashes had left the Chinese chastened by the size and firepower of the VOC ships, however.[63] Unlike those of the Portuguese in the early 1500s, the company's warships were of the multi-decked broadside firing variety, with dozens of large iron cannons, with which they could successfully take on a much larger number of Chinese war junks and merchant ships. But earlier victories made the VOC complacent, and in 1633 Ming forces made a surprise fireship attack on nine Dutch vessels, reprising their response to the Portuguese a hundred years earlier "[sailors/soldiers] held gourd tubes and boarded small boats, full of firewood, magic smoke, cannon stones, magic sand, [and] poison fire."[64] Four of the Company ships were destroyed or captured, and the VOC gave up on its demands.

Coxinga's campaign against the VOC in Taiwan has come in for close scrutiny as an example of non-Western forces taking a *trace italienne* fortress. A Chinese army of 25,000 besieged the fortress in 1661 after brushing aside sorties by the defenders, who numbered only 2000. Despite their huge numerical advantage, Chinese efforts to storm the fort were repelled with heavy losses. The undoing of the VOC came when a defector pointed out a fatal weakness: a hill that was only lightly defended overlooked the fort. Once this hill was captured, Coxinga's soldiers could fire directly into the interior, and their victory was only a matter of time.

Andrade draws several conclusions from this example.[65] First, that the VOC infantry (and by extension European infantry in general) were inferior to regular Chinese infantry, who were more disciplined, better drilled, and just as well armed. He emphasizes that the Chinese infantry had used volley fire for centuries before Europeans, first with crossbows, later with guns. Second, Chinese muskets and cannons were just as good as Western guns, thanks to the Chinese learning from sixteenth-century Portuguese designs. Third, Western warships were markedly superior, as much for their ability to sail into the wind as for their heavier build and armament. Fourth, Western fortresses were better than their Asian equivalents, because the angled bastions allowed for interlocking fields of fire to make storming the walls a very bloody proposition. While also supported by evidence of Russian clashes with Chinese troops on the Amur River, Andrade nevertheless draws large conclusions on the basis of a few, fairly small clashes. The fact that according to him the Dutch lost in Taiwan because of bad luck (the defector and bad weather preventing the arrival of a relief fleet) indicates the difficulty of drawing general conclusions from individual battles. An interesting side note to the VOC's loss in Taiwan is the Company's diagnosis of the defeat, which was unfairly blamed on the fort's commander. This scapegoating demonstrates the tendency to personalize and dismiss failures, rather than engage in serious introspection and reform, as the tenets of rational learning in the paradigm-diffusion model require.

Strategically, with respect to the Chinese, the VOC faced a situation similar to the one with the Mughals: the Company needed the Chinese much more than the Ming Empire needed the Company. Even allowing for the Ming-Manchu war and the preceding rebellions raging across China in the middle of the seventeenth century, there was far less scope for the sort of divide-and-rule moves that worked so well for Europeans among the small principalities and sultanates of East Africa, coastal India, and the islands of Southeast Asia. Nor was there any close equivalent to the autonomous vassal and suzerain arrangements, as in the Mughal system, which might have given the VOC the opportunity to strike deals with local subordinate polities.

The VOC were highly deferential to the Japanese Shogunate, where the Company was forced "to abandon its usual prerogatives and remake itself in order to meet Tokugawa expectations."[66] An incident in 1610 when the Japanese burned a captured, Portuguese ship containing cargo worth more than the entire capital of the VOC in retribution for the killing of a single Japanese sailor was taken as a cautionary lesson by the company.[67] The Japanese had an equally strict policy of disproportionate retribution if any ship carrying the Shogun's red seal was attacked, a prohibition that was punctiliously observed even by the violence-prone Europeans. In 1707 a Dutch official in Japan reported: "To show our teeth or to use violence is completely impossible, unless we want to leave this land and never come again."[68]

The VOC in Decline

Aside from Southeast and East Asia in the seventeenth and eighteenth centuries, the VOC also fought in South and East Africa (the Cape and Mozambique), Ceylon, the east and west coasts of India, the Middle East, and throughout the reaches of the Indian Ocean. Until the 1660s, many of these campaigns were directed against the Portuguese, while subsequently the VOC faced Asian enemies. If Western Europe was steadily advancing ahead of the rest of the world in military and economic matters, it might be expected that the Company would have gone from strength to strength against indigenous polities. In Java, this was indeed the case, with the Company progressively subordinating native polities and suppressing revolts. Elsewhere, however, the picture was quite different.

On the Malabar Coast of southwest India, the expansion of the kingdom of Travancore threatened the VOC's local vassals and endangered its control of the pepper trade, leading to war in 1739.[69]

After a VOC ultimatum was rejected (the Travancore king threatened to invade Europe in retaliation), the Company landed troops from Ceylon in 1741. After initial victories, their forces were besieged and then starved and bombarded into submission, and the VOC commander subsequently went into service with Travancore. After the defection of its local allies, the VOC, which was struggling to contain a major rebellion in Java at the time and hence could not send reinforcements, abandoned some of its remaining forts in the area and sued for peace. Speaking of the half-century from 1715, a historian observes, "By the end of this period, the VOC would be a minor player caught between two new, large, centralized 'fiscal-military' states: Travancore and Mysore."[70] Thus in the mid-eighteenth century the strategic problem for the VOC was not just that it was failing to keep up with the British and French in the region, but also that it had fallen behind new South Asian rivals.

In Ceylon the VOC broke with its former ally, the raja of Kandy, but struggled in the same way as the Portuguese had (and the British would later) to enforce their claims in the interior. A Kandyan offensive in 1761 almost drove the Dutch from the island, and although they regained the coast, by 1766 the VOC were forced to give up on their efforts to conquer Kandy.[71] At the same time the VOC were expelled from their base on Kharg Island in the Persian Gulf.[72] A more general verdict is that:

> Although we need to acknowledge the general tenets of Europe's "military revolution," the disequilibrium created by such advances [in South Asia], as in Southeast Asia, really had little lasting effect in India until the mid-eighteenth century. There were simply too few Portuguese and Dutch soldiers in the sub-continent to ever force significant changes in trade, and when British armies did appear en masse it was primarily to counter the French.[73]

Ultimately the VOC's very success was its undoing: the more territory that came under its sway, the less commercially successful it became, as largely static revenues were surpassed in the eighteenth century by steadily rising administrative and military costs (in the 1600s military costs took between a fifth and a third of total VOC budget, a very modest share by comparison with European states of the time).[74] The irony of this outcome is that many in the company, including the *Heeren* XVII, were acutely conscious of this very danger, and strongly counselled against it. For example, a pessimistic 1662 report on the outlook for the VOC to the *Heeren* XVII argued that the more it conquered "the less powerful it becomes to govern everything henceforth on its own," and that unless this trend was stopped "the Company will eventually collapse under its heavy burdens and definitively fall apart."[75] Another critic made the similarly prescient argument that "The more the VOC has to govern, the less it can support and augment commerce."[76] A complaint shared by the *Heeren* XVII about the cost of fighting in Ceylon and Malacca stated that "a merchant would do better honorably to increase his talent and send rich cargoes from Asia to the Netherlands, instead of carrying out costly territorial conquests, which are far more suitable for crowned heads and mighty monarchs than for merchants greedy of gain."[77]

Less relevant to the military balance, but crucial to the VOC's overall success and survival, was that its coercive attempts to enforce a trading monopoly created a huge amount of smuggling and piracy, not to mention endemic corruption within the Company itself, all of which sapped the Company's strength.[78] As expenses came to exceed income in the 1700s, the VOC was less willing and able to mount costly new military efforts. By the time the British conquered the Dutch possessions in the East during the Napoleonic Wars, the VOC had already gone broke. In some sense, this failure might be a backhanded endorsement of the military revolution idea that, at least over the longer term, maintaining a modern navy and army required the fiscal resources of a centralized state, rather than a private-public hybrid. Yet against this argument, the paradigmatically modern Dutch state was itself conquered around the same time of the VOC's final demise.

The English East India Company

The English East India Company was formed on the basis of a charter issued by Queen Elizabeth I in 1600. Although founded slightly earlier than the VOC, it took longer to acquire a true joint stock form and the suite of sovereign prerogatives that gave the chartered companies their distinct hybrid, private-public identity.

In its journeys to the East, the EIC was initially overshadowed by its Dutch counterpart, being largely pushed out of the Spice Islands, and instead coming to concentrate its efforts in South Asia. The EIC rose to be the most important company sovereign of all; in the nineteenth century it came to rule a vast empire that took in nearly the whole of South Asia, something like a fifth of the world's population. Those writing about the EIC's history have often divided it into distinct periods before and after the Battle of Plassey in 1757 that saw the Company acquire its first substantial territory of Bengal.[79] In its early period, the EIC established trading posts and forts, and, like the Portuguese and the VOC, stuck to an essentially maritime strategy. The decades following 1757 are crucially important for the main questions of this book. This period saw far more sustained, large-scale fighting between European-led forces and Asians than in the previous two-and-a-half centuries. Toward the end of the eighteenth century, the British government began a gradual process of winding back the Company's sovereign and corporate privileges in tying it more closely to the state.[80] The great Indian uprising of 1857 effectively marked the end of the Company.

I begin the story of the EIC with its relations with the Mughal empire. The Company obtained trading concessions through diplomacy rather than violence, and though maritime violence was always an important part of the EIC's repertoire, its only direct challenge to the Mughals in the 1680s was a failure. In the remainder of this chapter I look at how the EIC began on its path of conquest in South Asia from the 1750s after the collapse of the Mughal Empire, a critical period for evaluating arguments about the military basis of the rise of the West. The assessment looks first at technology and tactics on the battlefield, and then the fiscal and administrative underpinnings of military power and effectiveness.

The EIC to 1750

The EIC was similar to the VOC in being an armed trader intent on enforcing its monopoly to generate excess profits.[81] Thus in the early seventeenth century Sir Thomas Roe, the emissary sent to the Mughal court to seek permission for the EIC to trade, held that local powers "were best treated with the sword in one hand."[82] Like the VOC, the English Company soon clashed with Portuguese ships in the region from 1612, usually winning.[83] The most prominent early military success of the EIC was the capture of the Portuguese fortress at Hormuz at the mouth of the Persian Gulf, a victory won in coalition with Persian forces in 1622. The Safavid emperor Shah Abbas had offered trading access, customs concessions, and a subsidy to offset the cost of the expedition, in return for naval assistance in recapturing the stronghold held by the *Estado da India* for over a century, and defended by modern *trace italienne* fortification.[84] The small English force of five ships successfully drove off the Portuguese ships, bombarded the fortress, and helped transport the Safavid forces that pressed the final assault. Yet while a military success, the commercial consequences for the EIC were much more mixed, and showed the as yet uncertain legal status of the Company. As England was at peace with Portugal at the time, the Lord High Admiral in England threatened to sue the Company for piracy, only being mollified by a £10,000 personal cash payment.[85] In response to his question "Did I deliver you from the complaint of the Spaniard [Portugal and Spain were joined in a personal union at the time] and do you return me nothing?" King James also received a £10,000 payment from the EIC.[86] The EIC subsequently felt that they received rather less from the Persians than was their due.

It is important not to overstate the militancy of the EIC in its early days. As a matter of law and practice, it was far less bellicose than the VOC in the Spice Islands.[87] Where the English tangled with their Dutch counterparts, the EIC usually came off second-best. In Europe, King James I and the Netherlands States-General were on good terms, and sought to broker a compromise between the two chartered companies according to which the trade in spices would be shared. However, the VOC officials in the East were fiercely determined to enforce their monopoly, executing ten EIC employees on the island of Amboyna in 1623. The EIC was more successful in reaching a lasting accommodation with the *Estado da India* from 1635.

After a series of expeditions to South Asia, the Company came to see the need for a permanent base in the region. The EIC's first toe-hold was in the port of Surat in 1619, as with subsequent outposts secured by diplomacy at the Mughal court rather than force. The conventional story of Company-Mughal relations in the 1600s sees a rough balance, whereby local Mughal officials exploited the EIC, who responded when these depredations became too great by harassing Mughal shipping traveling to the Red Sea, leading to a return to the uneasy status quo.[88] Working from Persian Mughal sources, however, Hasan argues that historians have overstated the degree of conflict and obscured the degree to which the relationship was generally harmonious.[89] Rather than being exploited by local imperial officials in Gujarat and later Bengal, in fact the EIC colluded with these local agents to evade the emperor's customs duties.[90] The EIC's entry into the empire was greatly eased by the permeable nature of the Mughal polity, which routinely shared and delegated sovereign prerogatives. In part this reflects the manner in which the empire was constructed, relying more on co-opting and subordinating rivals than destroying them.[91] In particular, merchants and ports enjoyed substantial powers of self-government,[92] and thus the EIC's autonomy was easily accommodated within existing precedents. The Company pledged their servitude to the emperor, and he graciously extended certain privileges to them, including the right to trade.

The Company's first fortified outpost, built in 1639 at Madras, beyond the reach of the Mughals, was the product of local intrigue rather than any military preponderance. The main obstacle to the fort was not the local ruler, whose enthusiasm extended to a commitment to pay half the expense of construction, but the directors in London, who were wary of excessive costs. The directors' suspicions proved to be well-founded when the ruler reneged on his end of the bargain and refused to pay, but by that stage it was too late, and the fort was built.[93]

The only significant seventeenth-century collision between the EIC and the Mughals occurred in 1686. At this time, Emperor Aurangzeb was pressing for more revenue to fund his campaigns against the rebellious Marathas, and so his officials cracked down on EIC evasion of customs duties. At the same time, under the influence of the Bombay governor, Sir John Child, the Company decided to adopt a more aggressive posture toward the Mughals: "The merchants had decided to become warriors."[94] The Company made a serious miscalculation, however, in thinking that the Mughals had been weakened to the point that English could win land victories. An initial amphibious assault in Bengal failed with heavy losses. Irked by EIC raiding of ships taking the faithful to the Hajj pilgrimage, the emperor ordered that the Company be expelled.[95] The tables were turned, as an Abyssinian fleet commander commissioned by the Mughals blockaded Bombay, forcing the surrender of the Company garrison in 1690, at which time all of its possessions bar Madras had fallen. The EIC sued for peace. It issued a "most humble and repentant" supplication to the emperor, and agreed to pay a huge indemnity, as well as the higher taxes that had sparked the war, in return for the restoration of its privileges.[96] This experience demonstrated not only that the Company was inferior on land, but even that its maritime redoubts were vulnerable.[97] "Private" pirating by Englishmen unaffiliated with the Company proved to be a continuing irritant in the following two decades, leading to occasional skirmishes. But by this time Aurangzeb was fully committed to his long-running campaign against the Marathas, and was unwilling to divert troops to capture Bombay and Madras.[98]

The Importance of South Asia in the 1700s

The 1700s were a time of turbulence and huge change in South Asia. Above all, it witnessed the decline of the Mughal empire and the rise of the East India Company. Several scholars draw parallels between the intense military competition in India in the eighteenth century, and the conditions that are claimed to have fostered the military revolution in Europe one or two centuries earlier.[99] The period after the death of the Mughal emperor Aurangzeb in 1707 saw frenzied court intrigue, a series of bitterly contested imperial successions, and the peeling away of powerful regional rulers, who continued to pay lip service to Mughal suzerainty, but increasingly governed as they saw fit.[100] The Hindu Maratha Confederacy that had plagued the Mughals with their hit-and-run attacks from the late 1600s went from strength to strength. In 1739 the empire suffered a crushing defeat at the hands of Persian ruler Nadir Shah, as a huge Mughal army was routed and Delhi sacked; even the emperor's gem-encrusted peacock throne (which had cost twice as much as the Taj Mahal) was carted away. It is worth underlining that the Mughals were not defeated by Europeans, and that though internal dynamics were the determining factor in their fall, their most dangerous military foes were Persians and Afghans, not the Portuguese, Dutch, or British.[101] Though nearly all players on the South Asian scene, including the EIC, continued to acknowledge the supreme authority of Mughals until well into the nineteenth century,[102] the pretense grew increasingly threadbare.

The decline of the Mughals saw both an intensification of conflict between Mughal successor polities, and between Europeans, in particular the British and French. By the end of the Napoleonic Wars, the British had conclusively eclipsed all of its European rivals in Asia. As well as besting the French in the middle of the eighteenth century, and briefly occupying Manila, EIC forces also helped conquer Java. The Dutch were given back their possessions in the East only as part of a British strategy to maintain a viable Netherlands as a European buffer state. The VOC had gone broke in 1799. In large part as a result of its success, however, after its conquest of Bengal, the Company was incrementally subordinated to the British state. From the late 1700s onwards the EIC began to lose its hybrid company sovereign character, as mercantile concerns were increasingly replaced by the imperatives of rule. In keeping with the aim of assessing whether the military revolution explains European expansion and empire-building, the focus here is on the balance between Europeans and South Asian powers, rather than the frequent wars both groups fought among themselves. It is only fair to acknowledge that there is a cost to this pragmatic decision: perpetuating the Eurocentric bias decried by Black and others whereby non-Europeans only feature where they engage with Europeans. As such, it bears repeating that Europeans were entirely absent from two of the most decisive victories won in South Asia in the 1700s: the defeat of the Mughals by the Persian Nadir Shah in 1739, and the defeat of the Maratha Confederacy by an Indo-Afghan army in 1761.[103]

To begin, it is worth briefly re-emphasizing that there was considerable variance in how the Europeans fared at the hands of South Asian opponents. While the EIC rose to dominance and the French first introduced important innovations like volley fire, the

Dutch VOC and the Portuguese suffered important defeats at the hands of South Asian opponents in the 1700s. The Dutch were marginalized on the Malabar Coast (present day Kerala),[104] while the Portuguese were confined to Goa after defeats at the hands of the Marathas.[105] The only Europeans who gained dominance in the 1700s were the British, while the other European powers were defeated by the EIC or local South Asian powers.

Historians put particular stress on European (really British) expansion in South Asia: first, because in terms of population and economic size, these territories were by far the most important conquests made by Western powers before the Industrial Revolution.[106] Bengal alone had a larger population than Britain in 1750. Also, for the first time, the period from the mid-eighteenth century saw reasonably large armies led and trained by Europeans (although most of the troops were nevertheless local) engaged in sustained fighting against a variety of relatively equally matched Asian forces. This experience provides better evidence than seeking to extrapolate about general trends from isolated skirmishes. In addition, Parker identifies certain key tactical advances, especially drilled infantry using volley fire, as being used in South Asia for the first time outside Europe in the 1740s.[107]

The Conquering Company: A Military Revolution from 1750?

The step-change that would occur in EIC military capacity in the eighteenth century was nowhere in evidence in the first few decades. In the 1720s the Company was still wary of the Mughal's diminished power.[108] As late as 1740 there were only 2000 Company troops across South Asia.[109] What changed the EIC was not the collapse of the Mughal imperium directly, but rather a new European challenge from the French East India Company.[110] While loosely modeled on its English and Dutch predecessors, the French venture was much more closely tied to the Crown in both its finances and strategic direction.[111] Indeed, these two sources of dependence became mutually reinforcing: because the Company relied on state subscriptions and bailouts it was amenable to political direction, and because it was pressed into service as an arm of the

French state, its commercial viability remained weak.[112] Yet this tension did not stop the French from introducing the innovation of training local troops in the contemporary European style of war, that is, infantry using flintlocks and bayonets, drilled in volley fire, complemented by field artillery, officered by Europeans.[113] It is important to emphasize in speaking of the nationality of armies that all sides made up the bulk of their manpower with South Asian recruits, and even the forces in the service of Indian rulers were sometimes led by European mercenaries. The importation of European military techniques did not mean the importation of European armies.

The British and French fought many of their wars by proxy, sponsoring local allied powers and hiring irregular forces.[114] The splintering of the Mughal empire created a plenitude of succession struggles in which the Europeans could interfere to advance their own ends (local powers were just as willing to play the Europeans off against each other). In the south of India between 1746 and 1763, the British and French backed rival claimants from their respective bases in Madras and Pondicherry in a struggle that overlapped with and merged into the War of Austrian Succession and the Seven Years' War in Europe. What is conventionally regarded as the most consequential battle of the era, Plassey in 1757, saw a severely outnumbered EIC force under Robert Clive fight and (more importantly) bribe its way to victory over the ruler of Bengal, who was supported by the French. Widely if misleadingly regarded as the break point between the Company's merchant and governing phases (the EIC was a hybrid body before and after),[115] the resulting conquest of Bengal, cemented after a further victory at Buxar in 1764, granted control over the population and tax revenues of one of South Asia's richest and most populous regions. This is often regarded as having started a self-reinforcing cycle of success reminiscent of Tilly's aphorism that states make war and war make states.[116] With a massive increase in revenues, the Company could pay for larger and more capable armies, which increased the territory and population under its control, which generated more revenue, and so on.

The Company's main opponent in the Southwest was the expansionist sultanate of Mysore. A series of four wars saw Mysore at first compete with EIC on even terms in 1767–1769 and again in 1780–1784, before being decisively defeated by an EIC-led coalition of rival Indian powers (1790–1792), and eliminated in 1799.[117] The Hindu Maratha Confederacy was defeated in three wars 1775–1782, 1803–1805, and 1817–1818.[118] Although the EIC and then the British Raj fought important campaigns in South Asia throughout the nineteenth century, especially responding to the near-death experience of the Indian "Mutiny" of 1857, these were to enlarge and preserve British hegemony. There is a strong temptation to see this eventual victory as inevitable, and to read back from the end result in explaining the key military trends of the eighteenth century.[119] Yet it is important to note that the wars against Mysore and the Marathas were evenly matched for most of their course before decisively tilting toward the British,[120] rather than being some sort of triumphal procession from start to finish.

Explaining the EIC's Victory: Technology and Tactics

How to untangle the causes of British victory? At first glance, the military revolution seems to provide a powerful explanation of the process that was complete by the mid-nineteenth century: Western, or at least British, domination of the vast area of South Asia, including something like 200 million inhabitants.[121] According to one view, the introduction of new European tactics based on drill and superior guns transformed the Western presence in South Asia from marginal, maritime bit players, into peer competitors, before culminating in British hegemony.[122] Drilled, flintlock-armed infantry in disciplined formations proved superior to cavalry and individual deeds of valor.

Yet there are immediate problems with the argument that technological and tactical advantages were determinative:

> The proposition that the Europeans possessed superior military knowledge lives uneasily with the fact that there was convergence in knowledge even as there was a divergence in battlefield outcomes. The practice of hiring European mercenaries by the Indian regimes was so extensive that a distinction cannot be maintained between European and Indian spheres of knowledge in the second half of the eighteenth century.[123]

Relating to technology transfer between Europeans and Asians more generally, Chase cautions against an "unconscious double-standard": "When experts travel from Italy to England, it is taken as a sign of openness to new ideas; when they travel from Italy to Turkey, suddenly it is a crippling dependency on foreign technology."[124] Roy and others are keen to stress that transfer and adaptation was a two-way street, with the Europeans also copying from South Asians.[125] Aside from technology like rockets, Europeans improved their forces by adopting local cavalry tactics; indeed, the most important lessons probably concerned local arrangements for supplying and financing armies, too often overlooked given military historians' fixation on particular battles.[126]

Historians debate the extent to which Europeans actually enjoyed an advantage in guns. Some sixteenth-century Portuguese sources claim that local artillery was as good as or better than their own.[127] Roy argues that there was a gap in the early 1700s, but that this was closed by 1770, meaning that the EIC won most of its victories after its technological advantage had been canceled out.[128] Even Chase, who puts superior guns at the center of his explanation of the rise of the West, notes of South Asia that "On land, European muskets and pistols were also superior to local weapons under many circumstances, but not nearly enough so to offset European numerical inferiority until the Industrial Revolution."[129] Even if European-led forces did enjoy an advantage of superior weapons, this is unlikely to be the primary cause of their overall military success, given the importance of other factors like logistics, diplomacy, finance, and their control of the seas.[130]

What about the size of the armies on the battlefield, another crucial component of the military revolution thesis,[131] and a factor that was conspicuously lacking in the history of Western expansion in the period 1500–1700? Although in some instances smaller forces led and trained by Europeans could beat South Asian opponents many times their number, the armies commanded by the French and English Companies steadily expanded from the 1740s. By 1790 the EIC had over 70,000 troops.[132] From the 1750s Company forces began to be supplemented with regular military and naval units under the command of the British and French Crowns, but these did not challenge the primacy of the Companies. In the

British case "Ministers, who hardly knew anything about India, showed little inclination to try to impose their views on how the war should be fought.... They generally left it to the [EIC] directors' secret committee to draft the outlines of instructions to be given to admirals or senior army officers departing for India."[133] If the armies the Europeans put in the field in the late 1700s were much larger than anything they had mustered since first arriving in the East, they were not especially large by seventeenth- or sixteenth-century or even medieval South Asian standards.[134] More important is not the question of army size in isolation, but the way this serves as a link to the monetary and administrative underpinnings of the military revolution thesis.[135]

Explaining the EIC's Victory: Military-Fiscalism

Moving away from the focus on the battlefield, both Roberts and Parker believed that building and sustaining modern armies could only be achieved by rulers with the administrative wherewithal to extract the necessary money and manpower. European polities supposedly either had to conform to this sovereign state model or face extinction. These administrative and fiscal matters highlight the second half of the military revolution thesis: that the increased demands of modern warfare necessitated a centralized state. How does this component of the military revolution thesis fare in eighteenth-century South Asia?

Rather than numbers or technology, a more important difference seems to have been the different ways in which Europeans and South Asians built up their armies, with the latter often being shaped by Mughal precedents. The Mughals had raised huge cavalry armies in a manner that reflected the segmented, shared authority structure of their empire.[136] Aside from the emperor's relatively small core of personal troops, he retained an ennobled multiethnic retinue, each noble allocated the tax from a particular area of land in return for providing a specified number of cavalry in proportion to the size of the award.[137] The awards were revocable, non-transferrable claims on a particular source of revenue, not heritable fiefs as in European feudalism. Importantly, these huge cavalry forces, totaling something between 100,000 and 200,000, owed allegiance to the particular noble, not the emperor or the empire.[138] They absorbed around 80 percent of all imperial land revenue.[139] Nobles also served as the regional governors.[140] In addition, the *zamindars*, who ruled and collected taxes on small estates, maintained their own troops.[141] These latter constituted the bulk of a vast military labor market numbering up to 4 million from which the Mughals supplemented their nobles' cavalry. There were no formal officers or ranks, and such was the Mughals' wealth that their campaigns were financed directly from the treasury, rather than on credit as in Europe.[142] The Mughals incorporated guns into their existing mode of cavalry-based warfare, further undermining the idea at the center of the military revolution that a given military technology necessarily required a given tactical or institutional approach.[143] Gommans, Hasan, and de la Garza argue that the Mughals' spectacular success in building their composite empire by incorporating military entrepreneurs and local power holders also sowed the seeds of its unraveling,[144] and a segmented, composite model of political power crucially formed the post-Mughal polities and their armies.

These successor polities tended to build armies by assembling coalitions of warlords, drawing on the local military labor market, and supplementing these forces with European mercenaries.[145] Although this enabled the creation of large armies capable of fighting European-led forces on equal terms, this fiscal-military arrangement was also brittle.[146] For one thing, allies, warlords, and mercenaries could be bought off either to sit out battles, or to change sides, again following the Mughal precedent, a tactic that the EIC used to great effect on several crucial occasions including Plassey in 1757.[147] Even apart from direct inducements, forces comprised of different elements owing loyalty to their particular warlord were more difficult to command, and could disintegrate into their component parts if the tide of battle turned against them.[148] "The *sirdars* [warlords] were not bureaucrats whom the central government could transfer at will. They were military entrepreneurs who held hereditary land tenures with the right to maintain armed followers."[149] Another problem was that enlarging territories and armies by ceding revenue rights left central rulers with less and less money, making it difficult to continue to supply troops and pay mercenaries consistently.[150] While these potential weaknesses were manageable in the short term, the tendency to fight repeated campaigns and sequences of wars over decades made these problems acute. It also made it more difficult for these polities to recover from particular reverses, such as a loss in battle or the death of a leader.

In some ways, seeking to Westernize such forces created at least as many problems as it solved. The relationship between warlords and European mercenary officers in the service of the same local ruler was often strained, with the former refusing to subordinate themselves to a regular chain of command. Echoing the point made earlier in relation to Southeast Asia, Black argues that attempts by South Asian powers to reform their armies along European lines sometimes actually reduced military effectiveness rather than increasing it.[151]

Not surprisingly, paying and supplying these new huge armies over long campaigns and successive wars also created immense financial stresses for the Companies. While the French Company could rely on the Crown, the EIC was in the main forced to rely on its own resources, though after a time it too was also supported by British Crown regiments, and especially the Royal Navy (for which the EIC had to foot the bill[152]).

A crucial advantage held by the EIC, like the Mughals in their heyday, was its superior ability to buy military success, whether directly, by bribing opponents, or indirectly, through ensuring the mercenaries were paid consistently and that its armies were well supplied.[153] The Company became the preferred employer of many mercenaries precisely because of its dependability in paying wages.[154] Although the Company was by no means averse to hiring warlords, and was also heavily dependent on irregular cavalry, it built up an increasingly large stock of locally recruited standing troops who signed long-term contracts.[155] These were organized in line with European regimental templates, with around 2000 soldiers being officered by 50 Europeans. Aside from regular pay, soldiers were also promised a pension on retirement. These forces created a dependable core of the Company's army that most other South Asian polities lacked.

In part the Company's superior financial capacity came from revising the land tax regime in its territories to reduce the share taken by intermediaries,[156] while the Company's cumulating military successes brought it more plunder and tribute.[157] Yet by itself this revenue was insufficient, and so the Company increasingly borrowed to sustain its war, with 90 percent of this credit originating from local lenders.[158] As a result, the English tended to drain the pool of credit potentially available to its rivals and enemies. Even so, the EIC definitely felt the strain, coming close to bankruptcy in 1803 during a war against the Maratha Confederacy. The Company's debt-to-revenue ratio rose from 120 percent in 1793 to over 300 percent in 1809.[159]

Assessing the Military Revolution Thesis in South Asia from 1750

All things considered, then, how does the military revolution thesis stack up in explaining the EIC's rise to dominance in South Asia in the second half of the eighteenth century? The idea that superior Western gunpowder technology (e.g., flintlocks) and tactics (e.g., volley fire) were themselves decisive, or even major factors in explaining European dominance, seems unlikely.[160] Aside from the fact that European powers like the VOC and the Portuguese were militarily marginalized by South Asian polities in the 1700s, thanks to the transfer of weapons and knowledge between all sides, the gap was slight at best. The weight of evidence favors the idea that it was the EIC's superior institutional and financial capacity that allowed it to eventually triumph over a succession of South Asian and European rivals.

Given that the military revolution thesis is only partly an account of what happens on the battlefield, however, the underlying determinants of fiscal and administrative capacity might seem to be a better fit with South Asia in the years 1750–1800. Parker and others stress that over the longer term, military success is predicated on state-building in order to create and sustain modern, effective armies and navies. According to this Darwinian logic, polities either adapted this form to keep up with the competition, or fell by the wayside. If the EIC's victory was more a matter of build-

ing and funding the durable military, fiscal, and administrative bu-
reaucracies that could put effective armies in the field year in and
year out more consistently than their South Asian rivals, isn't this
an endorsement of the military revolution thesis?

Saying that some aspects of the military revolution thesis have
purchase in South Asia may be setting the bar too low, given the
range of elements that comprise the intellectual whole. The idea
that military success is explained by some combination of superior
weapons and/or tactics and/or discipline and/or strategy and/or
the fiscal-administrative institutional characteristics of the polity
is hardly a demanding test. It is very difficult to think of any imag-
inable result where one or more of these factors was not at play.
The thesis is not a menu of possible causes from which individual
terms are selected, mixed, and matched on an ad hoc basis, but
rather a set and sequence of interrelated parts. Very little of the
sequence and logic progression summarized earlier in this book
fits with South Asian history of this period.

Even the state-building military-fiscal component, which has
more purchase than the technology-and-tactics aspect, faces the
obvious problem that it was a private company, or at least a private-
public hybrid, that eclipsed the states, both European (the Portuguese and French) and Asian. Neither the idea that the EIC was
simply an extension of British state, or a state in its own right,
holds water.[161] The Company was simultaneously a privately owned
joint-stock company, a vassal of the Mughal emperor, the suzerain
of various South Asian tributaries, and a direct ruler of increasingly vast populations in its own right. Aside from its legal status,
as a matter of practicality the large majority of troops and treasure
committed to conquering South Asia in the eighteenth century
were raised and controlled by the Company itself, not the Crown
or Parliament. Although the British government vetoed or directed
the EIC with respect to relations with France and other European
powers, and contributed troops and ships to beat back these European competitors, it was much less likely to involve itself in matters involving Asian powers. Although the EIC later lost much of
its commercial character in the nineteenth century as it was subordinated to the British state, this followed rather than preceded the
establishment of its hegemony on the subcontinent.

Conclusions

In summing up, a comparison of European relations with the Mughals and the Chinese shows some interesting similarities and differences. First and most obvious, the European land forces were trivial compared to those of the Asian empires. There was little if any sustained fighting between Europeans and Asian empires before the nineteenth century, mainly because Europeans had a realistic appreciation that they would lose. There was thus no sign of a military revolution–induced advantage in this respect. Second, this European military inferiority meant that accommodation of, and usually formal subordination to, Asian great powers was the typical modus vivendi, especially given the Europeans' need for access to trade. Third, as in Africa, none of the Asian great powers had an interest in controlling sea routes or maritime trade in the way that Europeans obsessed about, making compromises and accommodations between the two groups much easier to strike. Echoing the same conclusion as many others is the view that "If we are seeking 'difference' between the European and Indian cultures in the early modern period, its most obvious point lies at the shoreline ... the Europeans sought to 'arm the sea' in ways wholly novel to India where sea-borne trade had long been 'free' and largely detached from political power."[162] Fourth, when the Europeans did fight on land, they were crucially dependent on local allies, including the EIC's campaigns in the late eighteenth century.

For proponents of the military revolution thesis to identify South Asia in the mid-1700s as the turning point for Western expansion, where the advantages of the military revolution belatedly came into play, is in essence a backhanded endorsement of both the critique and positive thesis at the heart of this book. The inescapable implication is that European expansion before this point, in the Americas, South Asia, Southeast Asia, and Africa, must have been due to other factors, at least when it comes to expansion on land. Though the date range in the subtitle of Parker's book is 1500–1800, the key statement of his argument shortens this period to 1500–1750.[163] A puzzling feature of Parker's work is that his wide-ranging, subtle historical investigations often undermine his own relatively simple thesis about the military revolution and the rise of the West. This point again raises the danger of reading later industrial-era trends and causes back into the very different early modern period.

The final matter is the plausibility of the paradigm-diffusion model of organizational learning. There certainly was a great deal of military transfer in South Asia in the early modern period. The Mughal military system was itself a hybrid of Mongol, Turkic, and Persian models. South Asians enthusiastically adopted gunpowder weapons in the 1500s, though the Ottomans were at least as important here as Europeans in introducing this technology. In the 1700s, rulers like Tipu Sultan of Mysore sought to closely emulate European armies, and Western mercenaries were in strong demand. But as set out in the introduction, there are specific conditions that must hold for the logic of the paradigm-diffusion model to work: learning about causal relations must be relatively easy (through simple relationships and plentiful information), it must be possible to learn about the environment faster than the environment itself is changing, and it must be possible to implement lessons learned through reform. Reflecting on the material presented in the previous chapter, it is hard to be confident that any of these conditions hold.

The point about the difficulty of organizational learning in war is illuminated by a sixteenth-century example.[164] In 1519 the Hindu Vijayanagara Empire, which ruled South India, went to war against the sultanate of Bijapur. Bijapur had hundreds of cannons, while the Vijayanagara army had few or none, instead relying on its cavalry, archers, and war elephants. In the resulting battle and siege, the "modern" Bijapuris were decisively defeated by "backward" Vijayanagara. Both sides interpreted the result as an endorsement of their existing force structure, with the vanquished redoubling their efforts to acquire more guns. Despite their contrasting responses to the utility of guns, the end result for Bijapur and Vijayanagara proved to be the same, with both polities later being swallowed up by the Mughal Empire.

By all accounts, South Asia in the 1700s was changing rapidly, as the slow splintering of the Mughal Empire was an effect and cause of socioeconomic changes. For the first time Europeans became major players in the politics of the region, while there were also new threats from the Northwest with the Persian and Afghan invasions of the 1730s and 1760s. The various polities were seeking to hybridize old and new military ideas, techniques, and technology from domestic and foreign sources. At such a time of turmoil and uncertainty, with so much change and so little stability, the chances for learning faster than the environment was changing were poor.

CHAPTER THREE

The Asian Invasion
of Europe in Context

JUST AS EUROPEANS were beginning to expand into Asia, Asians were expanding into Europe. Indeed, in the 1500s and 1600s there was probably more European territory and population under Asian rule than vice versa. This situation lasted until the 1750s, when British forces began to conquer substantial populations in South Asia. Even here it was a company with sovereign powers, the British East India Company, professing allegiance to an Asian (Mughal) empire that was the agent of conquest, not a modern European sovereign state. The Asians in Europe in the early modern era were the Ottomans, a Turkic group originating from Central Asia that conquered an empire in Europe, Africa, and the Middle East roughly on the same scale of that of the Romans, centered from 1453 in the last Roman capital, Constantinople. Throughout the 1500s and until the late 1600s the Ottomans were feared as an existential threat to Europe as a whole.[1]

Why is the Ottoman Empire important to the central claims of this book? The first part of this chapter explains why as their primary non-Western opponent for several centuries, and the only one to engage in sustained, high-intensity warfare with the European great powers, the Ottomans are the most appropriate case for testing claims of a shifting military balance between Western and

Eastern powers. The next section then gives a brief overview of the Ottoman military system. The most important points are the Ottomans' ability to productively combine and adapt different styles of warfare, and even more significantly their anticipation of key innovations that are said to define the military revolution. The Ottomans had a permanent, standing infantry army equipped with guns, directly commanded by the sultan, well-supplied by a complex bureaucratic logistical system, and paid for with central tax revenues well before the European great powers started to do the same.

I then look at the wars between the Ottomans and their various Western opponents in Central Europe and the Balkans, which has been the traditional focus of Western historians, but I also consider the contest in North Africa between local, Ottoman, and European forces, which has received far less attention. The repeated European disappointments and defeats at the hands of Islamic foes in North Africa right through to the nineteenth century conclusively scotches any notion that Western overseas expansion swept all before it. These reverses are even more significant given that the Spanish and Portuguese committed far more resources in their failed expeditions across the Mediterranean than they ever did to those across the Atlantic or to the East. The Ottomans were dominant in Europe right through what is said to be the key century of the military revolution, 1550–1650. The fact that their eclipse came only in the second half of the eighteenth century, and then at the hands of the Russians, is an awkward fit with the tenets of the conventional story. It is a strangely underappreciated fact that the Ottoman Empire enjoyed far more extensive and longer-lasting military and geopolitical success than supposed paragons of modernity like the Dutch or Swedes.

This last point leads me to explore some important general themes. Putting the Ottomans and the historical evidence considered in the previous two chapters in context, much of the myth of Western dominance from 1500 rests on pervasive biases of place and time. The first—a Eurocentric interpretation of a sequence of technological, military, and political changes seen as leading by necessary cause-and-effect to the military revolution as the only possible outcome—does not stand up when compared to evidence from other regions. The most important innovations, like gun-armed professional standing armies supported by an extensive administrative apparatus, were pioneered in Asia. Furthermore, the fact that the same gunpowder technology was successfully accommodated within very different institutional settings undermines the idea of deterministic causal sequences, within or beyond Europe. The bias of time leads to a view of the nineteenth-century period of Western dominance as the defining essence of the modern era, with the history of the preceding centuries read as the precursor to the inevitable Western triumph. Non-Western powers are portrayed as mere failures waiting to happen.

An Overview of the Ottoman Empire

Beginning in the late thirteenth century in northwest Anatolia, the Ottomans launched their conquests in the Balkans, and took Constantinople in 1453. Sultans thereafter claimed the mantle of the Roman emperor. In the next fifty years the Ottomans came to dominate the Balkans, and extended their hegemony over the Black Sea littoral, in part through securing the vassalage of the Crimean Tatars.[2] Their most spectacular conquests, traditionally downplayed by military historians, were to the south and east.[3] In 1514 at the decisive battle of Chaldiran, the Ottomans defeated a Safavid Persian army, with subsequent campaigns leading to the conquest of eastern Anatolia and northern Mesopotamia. Led by Sultan Selim I, in 1517 the Ottomans destroyed the empire of the Mamluk slave soldiers, winning possession of Egypt and Syria, and doubling the size of their own empire to 1.5 million square kilometers.[4] Later conquests saw the Sublime Porte take control over Baghdad, Yemen, North Africa, the Western Caucasus, and the Eastern Mediterranean, win access to the Persian Gulf and the Red Sea, claim the holy cities of Mecca and Medina, and with them the title of caliph. The Ottomans developed a powerful navy, and extended their influence even further by sending expeditionary forces and artillerists to aid allies as far afield as Gujarat, Ethiopia, Uzbekistan, and Sumatra.[5]

The focus of historians' attention, however, has generally been the Ottomans' drive into Central Europe following the conquest of much of Hungary in 1526–1541. This initiated the long contest with the Habsburgs and a varying cast of Christian allies, including

Venice, the Polish-Lithuanian Commonwealth, and Romanov Russia. After reaching their greatest territorial extent in 1683,[6] Ottoman expansion into Europe then began to be rolled back from the end of the century.[7] Though they scored significant victories against the Russians and Habsburgs up until the end of the 1730s, thereafter the Russians convincingly won a long series of wars against the Ottomans.

The Ottomans as a Test
of the Military Revolution Thesis

Why are the Ottomans the best test of the military revolution thesis? At first glance, the basic chronology of the struggle between Christian European powers and the Ottomans seems to support its argument. Before the military revolution, the Ottomans consistently defeated their Western opponents as they advanced to the gates of Vienna, but once Western forces began to modernize, they were better able to stem the sultans' advances. Then, after the lessons of the Thirty Years War had been absorbed by the forces of the Holy Roman Emperor and his allies, they managed to inflict the first major defeat on the Ottomans at the end of the 1600s, defeats that became chronic in the eighteenth and nineteenth centuries. Parker brackets the Ottomans with the Mughals and Safavids as possessing modern military technology, but nevertheless failing to keep up with their European competitors, because the Islamic empires were supposedly unable to adapt their existing military systems and political institutions.[8] The related gunpowder empire thesis, advanced first by Hodgson and later McNeill,[9] similarly condemns the Ottomans to failure, supposedly because their initial adoption of cannons gave rise to political centralization that then blocked the path of further reform.

Challenging the tacit assumption that the early modern era was one of inexorable Western progress, the situation in North Africa was in fact one of Western frustration and failure throughout this period. The Western set-backs and defeats, the non-conquests, are just as important and instructive as the Western victories, and an excessive focus on the latter at the expense of the former has produced a distorted overall picture. Thus Black notes the tendency to string together Western victories from Cortes and da Gama to Plassey in 1757 to the nineteenth century to produce a false story of four centuries of unbroken Western dominance.[10]

As some historians have noted, in many ways the wars between the Ottomans and the Christian powers of Europe from the fifteenth to the twentieth century are the most obvious testing ground for arguments about the changing military balance between the West and the rest of the world, and yet this centuries-long struggle has attracted less attention in this context than one might expect.[11] The Ottoman case solves many of the problems of trying to apply the military revolution thesis to the expeditionary campaigns flagged in the previous chapters. Whether applied to the conquistadors in the Americas, or the Portuguese, Dutch, or English in the East, the recurring problem for the military revolution thesis is that these tiny expeditionary forces looked almost nothing like the armies that fought great power wars in Europe at the time. European expeditions engaged in what were essentially skirmishes, rather than sustained campaigns that tested the institutional or socioeconomic mettle of either side (with exceptions like the Aztecs and Incas) until after the 1750s.

Because the collection of private adventurers and company sovereigns active in the Americas, Africa, and Asia did not deploy or represent "real" European military forces, or at least forces that resembled the armies and navies which fought major power wars in Europe, it is hard to assess whether Western great powers benefited from a military revolution that gave them a pronounced advantage over their non-Western peers. The simple fact is that no European great power fought a large-scale war against an Asian great power apart from the Ottomans until after the Industrial Revolution. For this reason, and the fact that most of these Western overseas forces were only very loosely connected to states at all, it has been difficult to test the key proposition that high-intensity warfare forced political, social, and economic change on combatants, specifically the formation of centralized sovereign states, thanks to the fiscal and administrative demands of such military competition. Yet on each count, the Ottomans are the great exception, as they engaged in regular large-scale wars with Europeans in Central Europe, the Balkans, the Mediterranean, and North Africa for

500 years, and thus provide the best case for testing central propositions of the military revolution thesis.

If this confrontation between the Ottomans and the Christian powers of Europe is such a compelling test of the military revolution thesis, linking developments within the European theater and the military balance with other civilizations, why hasn't it received more attention? One reason is that Parker, Roberts, and others have suggested that the early modern revolution in warfare was centered on the Western half of the continent (the Netherlands, France, the Italian and German states, Sweden, and Spain), while Europeans in the East only adopted the crucial innovations belatedly and imperfectly.[12] In speaking of the Polish-Lithuanian Commonwealth (the elimination of which is scholars' favorite cautionary tale of what happens to those who fail to keep up with military trends),[13] Parker holds that their continuing commitment to predominantly cavalry armies made sense given that they were facing relatively backward Ottoman and Tatar opponents.[14] There are also traces of some of the same logic with reference to the Habsburg armies fighting the Ottomans,[15] though elsewhere Parker does include these forces as products of the military revolution.[16] Elsewhere he suggests the Ottomans only "imperfectly practiced" the military revolution.[17]

Yet in looking at both sieges and operations in the field, it is difficult to sustain the point that war on this front was somehow backward or isolated from military changes in Western Europe. Agoston has convincingly argued that from the late 1500s Habsburg imperial forces in Hungary responded to Ottoman victories by adopting the measures that constituted the core of the military revolution:[18] "On the battlefield against the Ottomans, the Habsburgs employed troops that were at the cutting edge of European military technology and tactics as early as the late sixteenth century."[19] Imperial forces were shaped by the experiences of the Spanish-Dutch wars in Flanders, the well-spring of innovation for military modernization, according to Roberts, Parker, and others. Habsburg forces then changed further thanks to the effects of the Thirty Years War (remembering that for Parker the period 1500–1650 saw the key advances),[20] once again putting them at the forefront of the military revolution according to its proponents. These changes included a higher proportion of musketeers, a further increase in the proportion of officers to rank and file in order to execute more complex tactical maneuvers, more drill, the centralization of command, and the formation of military training academies and libraries. As such, from the 1590s at the latest, the Ottomans fought the most advanced forces Europe had to offer in and around Hungary. Though Agoston sees a process of centralization in the Habsburg domains, even after the Peace of Westphalia in 1648, the financial and military support of the distinctly confederal Holy Roman Empire remained important. It is very hard to see this entity fitting the template of the centralized sovereign state. Yet for all their complexity, the Habsburg domains were notably more unified than the seven provinces of the Netherlands (described by one prominent historian as more of an alliance than a federation),[21] each with its own separate navy, regiments, and veto on common decisions. It is surprising that historians and other scholars have not reflected more on the fact that what is presented as being early modern Europe's most advanced state, the Netherlands, and what is stereotyped as its least successful, the Polish-Lithuanian Commonwealth, had pronounced similarities in their strongly decentralized character with multiple veto-points on political decision making.[22]

With these facts in mind, it is hard to disagree with the point that for the military revolution thesis to be accurate "Logically, then, the Habsburgs should not only have contained the Turks, but rolled them back" from the mid-1500s.[23] Yet this did not happen until at least a century and a half later. Parker claims that the key military innovations of the military revolution occurred in the 1500s,[24] while Rogers puts the break point even earlier, with the rise of infantry and artillery in the 1400s, which he further sees as critical to Western dominance overseas.[25] Regardless of the exact date, the earlier the revolution, the more relevant the Ottomans become, and the bigger challenge their strong performance is for the thesis of Western military superiority. Furthermore, the Ottomans successfully fought off the Spanish, the paragons of military modernity for most of the 1500s, in North Africa, which thus comprises a second source of evidence for Ottoman military effectiveness vis-à-vis European forces. The Moroccans and Portuguese also engaged in major battles in this theater. In sum, it is the Balkan and North African frontiers that constitute the best testing ground for arguments about a purported Western military superiority in the early modern period.[26]

Although the naval component of the struggle was also critical in the contest between Muslim and Christian powers, this is a less useful domain for testing the propositions of the military revolution thesis. Mediterranean naval warfare was focused on the oared galley for most of the early modern period, rather than on the cannon-armed ocean-going sailing ship. Whether this is regarded as evidence of a general backwardness, or merely adapting to local conditions that differed from the Atlantic, Indian, and Pacific Oceans is an open question.[27] Hess argues:

> The short range–200 to 500 yards–and unpredictable behavior of cannons, the lack of rigging flexible enough for the light winds of the Mediterranean, and the deep draft of Atlantic vessels all limited their effectiveness against the Mediterranean war galley. The oared vessel's maneuverability in calm weather and shallow water, and its ability to beach, often neutralized the greater fire power and cruising capacity of the Atlantic sailing ship in Mediterranean regions.[28]

In any case, the Ottomans managed to maintain their Mediterranean island and littoral possessions intact largely until the 1800s, while harassing their Christian opponents through the Barbary privateers, so it is difficult to see a major strategic cost of sticking with galleys in this period.[29]

The Military System of the Ottoman Empire

At the heart of the Ottoman military success was their flexibility in combining very different styles of warfare, from the horse archers of the steppe, to professional standing infantry formations armed with firearms, to formidable siege engineers and artillerists, to powerful galley forces. From the 1300s until the end of the 1500s, the bulk of the Ottoman army was comprised of cavalry recruited via a system reminiscent of the Mughals. Individuals were granted the right to revenue from a specific non-heritable piece of land (a *timar*), and in return they were required to serve as fully equipped cavalrymen together with a specified number of retainers. These forces, which numbered around 50,000–80,000 in the 1500s,[30] were referred to as the *sipahis* or *timariot* cavalry.

From the late 1300s the sultan also maintained a corps of salaried standing troops of household cavalry, artillerists, but especially the Janissaries ("new soldiers"). These latter forces, numbering around 20,000–30,000 in the period c.1400–1650,[31] were military slaves, taken from the sultans' Christian subjects as boys, and then trained as infantry, from the early 1500s particularly in the use of muskets. It is notable that in creating a large standing army so early the Ottomans were significantly ahead of their European counterparts.[32] The Habsburgs, for example, only formed their first equivalent standing forces in the mid-1600s.[33] More recent works claim that the Janissaries were using volley fire (something of a totem of modernity) decades before their European opponents.[34]

The Ottomans also took on ad hoc irregular cavalry raiding forces,[35] and were supported by tens of thousands of additional light cavalry archers from their Tatar vassals.[36] In the 1500s, the ratio of cavalry to infantry in Ottoman armies was around 3:1, their mobility being a key part of these forces' successes, while in the 1600s and subsequently the proportion of foot soldiers steadily increased,[37] reaching about 1:1 in the forces fighting the Habsburgs in the 1690s.[38]

It is generally agreed by historians that the Ottomans' gunpowder technology was the equal of the Europeans at least until the late 1600s, and was a crucial determinant of their successes against the Persians and Mamluks.[39] The gunpowder empire thesis suggests that their early success with large siege guns constituted a low equilibrium competence trap (being stuck with a "good enough" solution that removed the incentive for further reform), however, in that the Ottomans then failed to adopt lighter field artillery.[40] More recent accounts, based on Ottoman archives only open since the 1980s, suggest that this is something of a myth, and that in fact the sultan's troops had a full range of medium and light artillery produced at foundries in Constantinople and elsewhere in the empire.[41] Chase's encyclopedic study of guns concludes: "As far as firearms were concerned, the Ottomans were a clear success story."[42] Murphey has argued that the religious toleration of the Ottomans relative to many Christian monarchs (e.g., the sultans' acceptance of Jews expelled from Iberia) meant that they were more open to technology transfer from abroad.[43]

Until the 1700s, the Sublime Porte was more capable in logistics, finance, and recruitment than its main European adversaries. The Ottomans were able to consistently put larger forces in the field than their European rivals, and they were also better able to sustain their combat power.[44] The sultans could draw on a population of 20–40 million,[45] around the same number as France,[46] or all of the Habsburg lands under Charles V[47] (although it bears noting that until the retreat of the nineteenth century, the population of the Ottoman Empire was more than half Christian).[48] Their logistical success was all the more notable given the need for the Ottomans to fight very different wars against the Safavids in the deserts of Mesopotamia, and the Habsburgs in Central Europe. The empire was self-sufficient in guns and ships thanks to foundries and shipyards working at the direction of the sultan.[49] Their navy—once again directly built, armed, recruited, and commanded by the ruler—was similarly ahead of its time compared with Europeans' reliance on private solutions (with the exception of the Venetians),[50] though the Ottomans also employed privateers operating from North Africa.[51] Finally, the Ottomans were able to muster and sustain large armies and navies year after year while being less prone to the ruinous bankruptcies that were the norm among many European powers at the time.[52]

Ottoman Warfare in Europe

The Ottomans crossed into Europe as early as the 1300s and reduced most of the Balkans to subservience in the following two centuries, but their challenge to the heartland of Europe came in the sixteenth and seventeenth centuries. After subduing various rebellions in the Balkans, the Ottomans attacked the kingdom of Hungary's southern defensive perimeter, taking the crucial fortress city of Belgrade in 1521. In 1526 Suleiman the Magnificent led an army of up to 100,000 further into Christian territory, meeting the Hungarian and allied forces at Mohács. The Hungarians were crushed, and their king killed in a battle that exhibited the technological, tactical, and logistical edge of the Ottomans over their Western counterparts. The core of professional, drilled Janissary musketeers proved vital, as did the Ottoman's superior artillery.[53] Guilmartin argues that their victory at Mohács which led to the Ottomans' occupying most of Hungary and positioning themselves within striking distance of Vienna (around 220 kilometers away) was far more strategically significant than the Spanish and Portuguese conquests outside Europe to this point.[54] It allowed the Ottomans to besiege Vienna in 1529, though they failed to breach the walls before the end of the campaigning season.

Politically, the death of the king of Hungary at Mohács had produced two claimants to the throne: John Szapolyai, and the Habsburg Ferdinand of Austria. The Ottomans supported Szapolyai, and were drawn back into the fighting in Hungary to defend his claim and that of his son against that of the Habsburgs. Hungary became divided three ways, between Royal Hungary, ruled by the Habsburgs but formally outside the Holy Roman Empire; Transylvania, ruled by a Christian prince owing suzerainty to the Ottomans; and lastly Ottoman Hungary, at first ruled by Szapolyai. In 1541 the Ottomans extended their control by capturing Buda, while taking further Hungarian territory in 1551. A period of peace followed later in the sixteenth century as the Ottomans and Habsburgs devoted their efforts to fighting in Persia and Northern Europe, respectively.

As in the Dutch-Spanish struggle, sieges rather than battles dominated warfare in Hungary. Exhibiting an unparalleled prowess in siege warfare, the Ottomans had taken a multitude of strongholds constituting the defensive line from the Adriatic to Northern Hungary up to 1540.[55] Drawing on the resources of the surviving Hungarian nobles, their ancestral lands, and funds granted from the Holy Roman Empire, the Habsburgs embarked on a massive program of creating a new defensive line almost 1000 kilometers long anchored by state of the art *trace italienne* fortifications. These efforts were largely in vain, however, as the Ottomans were able to capture many of these new-style artillery fortresses. In their turn, the Ottomans proved to be dogged in defense, although the Christian powers' disunity may have been the sultans' biggest asset.

Outside of campaigning seasons, the Ottomans kept a garrison of around 25,000 in Hungary,[56] and skirmishing and low-level warfare was nearly constant, even during truces. Fighting resumed in earnest in the Long Turkish War of 1593–1606, which saw initial Ottoman military and diplomatic defeats associated with the defection of their Christian vassals reversed later in the war. While the Christian powers improved their performance on the battlefield, the Ottomans nevertheless managed to fight them to a standstill and hold on to their earlier gains.[57] At the same time, it became clear that the Ottomans were operating at the edge of their logistical range in Western Hungary: the need to transport and supply large armies from the core of Ottoman domains meant they could only campaign for a relatively short period.[58] For most of the first half of the seventeenth century the Habsburgs were consumed in the great struggle of the Thirty Years War.

The last Ottoman attempt to take Vienna occurred in 1683. Early success in undermining the walls proved in vain when the cavalry army of the Polish-Lithuanian Commonwealth (the sort that had supposedly been rendered obsolete by the advances of the military revolution) routed the besiegers. The ensuing sixteen-year war posed major problems for the Ottomans, who for the first time had to simultaneously confront a unified coalition of their Christian foes, formed as the Holy League: the Habsburgs in Hungary and the Balkans, the Poles in the Ukraine, the Russians around the Black Sea, and the Venetians in Greece. The Ottomans lost, and in the Treaty of Karlowitz in 1699 they ceded their Hungarian territories, as well as making many concessions elsewhere (some of which were regained in the early eighteenth century). Although, as ever, it is difficult for scholars (let alone participants at the time) to tease apart the different factors at play, it seems that it was the challenge of facing all of its major Christian enemies at once that led to the first substantial defeat for the Ottomans.[59]

This impression is strengthened by the fact that the Ottomans were able to defeat the Russians, Venetians, and Habsburgs individually in separate wars in first half of the eighteenth century, while the Poles succumbed to internal dissension and military decline. Thus in the last major war between the Ottomans and the Habsburgs 1737–1739, it was the sultan's troops, not those of the Holy Roman Emperor, that came away victorious, following on from Ottoman victories over the Russian army of Peter the Great in 1711 and the Venetians in 1715. Although the Habsburg and Ottoman armies clashed in 1787–1791, this was mainly a sideshow to the concurrent Russo-Turkish War. The Russians won important military and diplomatic victories at this time, but the Habsburgs were forced to return early gains, leaving the status quo intact. Shortly afterwards the Holy Roman Empire was conclusively defeated by Napoleon and dissolved.

The Eclipse of the Ottomans from the Mid-Eighteenth Century

What explains the military eclipse of the Ottomans in the eighteenth century? In some ways, rolling back the Ottoman challenge to Europe mirrors the contemporaneous East India Company conquests, first in Bengal and then more broadly in South Asia, in providing early signs of a more general change in the military balance between East and West.[60] The evidence presented earlier demonstrates that claims of a general European military superiority from 1500 to 1750 are wrong. But beyond this period, and especially during the nineteenth century, Western military superiority became increasingly real and consequential. It is the mistaken tendency to read the experiences of this era back into the early modern period that has done so much to distort our understanding of European military effectiveness relative to their non-European foes.[61]

In the period of the Ottomans' dominance over their European opponents from 1453 to 1683 rather than being defined by frequent pitched battles, warfare was more often a matter of sieges and near-constant border raids, both forms at which the Ottomans excelled.[62] Given that Parker sees attacking and defending fortifications in an age of cannons as the first driver of subsequent military, institutional, and political changes, Ottoman mastery of sieges is highly significant for the broader military revolution thesis. The war of 1683–1699, however, saw an unusual number of battles, fifteen, with the Ottomans losing all but two.[63] This coincided with major structural changes in the Ottoman military and polity beginning in the second half of the 1600s, which accelerated and deepened in the following century. The *timar* system of non-hereditary land grants in return for providing an allotted number of horsemen fell away, in part as a result of the greater need for infantry, in part because the agricultural revenue was no longer sufficient to meet the associated military obligations.[64] This increased the pressure to field more Janissaries, yet these had to be paid for directly by the imperial treasury, creating considerable fiscal stress.[65] From their origins as a slave army recruited as boys from the Empire's Christian population, the Janissaries increasingly become a hereditary cast that took side jobs to supplement their income.[66] The sultans began to bulk out their infantry with temporary forces, often recruited by local notables in the provinces.

In turn, this led to the growing fiscal and military strength of these local notables, which gave the empire an increasingly decentralized cast.[67] From a system in which the imperial treasury had taken almost 60 percent of tax revenues in the 1500s, by the end of the 1600s these local figures came to control 75 percent of tax revenues,[68] and they later increased their share to more than 80 percent.[69] Aksan makes the significant comparison that in the period 1768–1770 the English East India Company spent three to four times as much on its military than the sultan did.[70] One downside of the new arrangements favoring local recruitment of temporary forces was that during lulls in fighting former soldiers turned to banditry, or joined rebellions against the sultan, further accentuating the empire's revenue problems.[71] In the first half of the 1700s the traditional Ottoman strengths of mobilizing very large forces, excellent logistics, and support from their irregular Tatar allies were nevertheless generally sufficient to ensure that these more ad hoc forces remained competitive vis-à-vis European armies.[72] Yet after a generation of peace, the Ottomans experienced repeated defeats and disasters in a series of wars with Russia from 1768. The Sublime Porte suffered a further substantial decline in tax revenues, the military logistical system broke down, and, in part as a result, the tactical deficiencies of the new forces became unsustainable.[73]

The conventional picture of the Ottoman military decline, both at the time and afterward, is that some combination of religious, cultural, and domestic political factors locked the sultans into an increasingly outmoded style of warfare, when European armies were rapidly modernizing.[74] Yet rather than stasis and stagnation, the empire was experiencing rapid and fundamental changes during the period 1650–1800. Although these changes as described above were primarily institutional and fiscal, they directly fed into a changing military. By and large, technology was not the problem, since both the Ottomans and their Russian opponents found it easy to acquire arms and expertise from Western Europe.[75] The Ottoman military in the 1700s was very different from that of the 1600s, but some of the most important changes tended to undermine rather than improve effectiveness.[76] For example, the Janissaries seem to have given up drill around 1700.[77] As noted earlier, the Ottomans had in fact adopted most of the key features of the early modern revolution well before their European opponents, so there was nothing necessarily incompatible with the way the empire was set up and the requirements of modern warfare. Hence after the defeats of the late eighteenth century, it was not clear whether the correct course was to accelerate change by closely mimicking Western European models (assuming this was possible within broader political and societal constraints), or to try to restore traditional Ottoman strengths which had fallen into decay. As one scholar pithily states the problem: "it may be clear that one has lost; it is often far from clear why one has lost, or what an individual defeat might say about one's longer term military potential."[78]

Ironically the European agent of destruction for the Ottomans was the one that had the most tenuous claim on a Western identity. For it was Romanov Russia, not the Habsburgs, who won four wars against the Sublime Porte in the period 1768–1829, in addition to their role in the winning Holy League coalition of 1686–1699. Given its social foundation of serfdom, and the fact that it was probably just as dependent as the Ottomans on technology transfer from further West,[79] Russia is an unlikely exemplar of the military revolution thesis, since it was some distance from historians' and social scientists' paragons of modernity like the Dutch, Swedes, English, and French. Indeed, the "backward" Russians defeated not only the Ottomans, but ended the great power status of the paradigmatically modern Swedes much earlier after the conclusion of the Great Northern War in 1721.[80] Parker, Chase, Hoffman, and others tend to argue that Russia too often fought the "wrong" opponents: that is, horse nomads, to fully benefit from the benefits of military competition.[81] In a similar vein, even at the time

Frederick the Great of Prussia condescendingly dismissed Russia's victories over the Ottomans 1768–1774 as an instance of "one-eyed men who have given blind men a thorough beating."[82] Yet as Frost notes of its success, "Petrine Russia was an early demonstration of the fact, all too clear in the twentieth century, that modern military technology enables a small, militarized social elite to secure and maintain great power status on the basis of a backward and under-developed rural economy."[83]

North Africa

The limits and reversals the Portuguese and Habsburgs experienced in North Africa are a salutary corrective to the notion of European invincibility in early modern overseas campaigns against non-Western foes. These campaigns illustrate how ephemeral the European technological lead in gunpowder technology was, and, more importantly, show once again how broader contextual factors often outweighed narrow battlefield concerns. Perhaps because this theater does not conform to the standard tropes of Western triumphalism, it has received comparatively little attention.[84] This relative obscurity, however, cannot be attributed to the fact that the battles in this region were a sideshow. Both the Ottomans and the Portuguese mounted their largest-ever fleet-borne expeditions in the early modern period to North Africa, involving forces that were far larger than anything committed in the Indian Ocean or the Americas. For a little more than a century, until 1580, the Iberians entertained recurrent dreams of extending the reconquest of the peninsula (only completed in 1492 with the capture of Granada) over to the other side of the Mediterranean. The Portuguese king even adopted the title "King of Portugal and the Two Algarves, on this Side and the Other Side of the Sea in Africa" in anticipation of victory.[85] Yet the Portuguese experienced their greatest and most consequential defeat in Morocco. The Ottomans and their allies bested the Europeans, who later expended vastly disproportionate sums in maintaining insignificant outposts along the North African coast.

The prelude to these later efforts was the Portuguese seizure of the city-state of Ceuta just near the Straits of Gibraltar in 1415. Historians note that there were economic motivations for the conquest: Ceuta was an important node in the trans-Saharan gold trade, and the surrounding territories were rich in both cereal crops and textile production. Yet they also hold that the crusading ethos was probably even more important. The Portuguese somewhat improbably justified their claim to this land as rightful successors to the North African kingdom of the Visigoths.[86] While the mission (led in person by the king and his three sons) was a success, for several decades there was little follow-up beyond defending Ceuta. From 1458 to the second decade of the sixteenth century, the Portuguese captured and fortified a string of other ports and outposts, particularly along the Atlantic coast of Morocco. In important respects, their success conforms to the patterns of the military revolution, in that the Portuguese initially enjoyed a near-complete superiority in ships and artillery, enabling them to capture and hold coastal enclaves like Tangiers, even when severely outnumbered.[87] Habsburg forces enjoyed similar success further east along the Mediterranean coast in capturing ports like Melilla (in 1497, still held by Spain today) and Algiers (1510), again due in part to a clear edge in military technology.[88]

Yet perhaps at least as important in explaining these early victories was the disunity among the local polities along the Maghreb, wracked by tribal in-fighting and chronic succession struggles. Even before the tide began to turn, however, the Europeans came to appreciate the strategic limits of their conquests in terms that are reminiscent of similar limits elsewhere in Africa and in Asia. The Portuguese and Spanish often dominated within range of their ships' guns, but beyond raiding from coastal strongholds, their armies' effectiveness dropped off sharply inland. Though they were able to cultivate some local Muslim notables as allies and vassals, the religious hostility between Christians and Muslims, especially those Muslims recently expelled from Spain, greatly complicated efforts to win the acquiescence of local populations to European rule. Financially, early conquests paid dividends, as Saharan trade was diverted to ports dominated by the Portuguese and Habsburgs.[89] Yet as other European interlopers, particularly those from Northern Europe, thrust themselves into this trade, and as local merchants found alternative routes, the expense of maintaining fortifications and garrisons in North Africa came to substantially exceed any plausible return. The Portuguese ended up paying fifty times more to maintain their settlements in the Maghreb than these outposts generated in revenue.[90] The Portuguese and Spanish eventually realized that they couldn't win in North Africa, and they couldn't break even either.[91] Their decision to pour resources into this region, and then hang on to residual outposts for decades or even centuries, evidenced the primacy of prestige and ideology over rational cost-benefit calculations.

The two key military developments that halted and then reversed the European tide were first the strengthening and unification of Moroccan forces, and then the arrival of the Ottomans spreading west from their conquest of Egypt. Thanks to a combination of Muslim refugees from Spain, European gun-runners and defectors, Ottomans artillerists, and local inventiveness, the Moroccans closed the gap in artillery with their Portuguese opponents (it is important to note that a majority of the gunners fighting for the Portuguese were also foreigners—French, German, and Italian).[92] The Portuguese lost some important strongholds (e.g., Marmora in 1515 and Agadir in 1539), and then faced the considerable expense of having to rebuild their remaining fortresses to the modern artillery-resistant designs in order to hold out against the cannons of their Islamic enemies. Of course this requirement further increased the net loss the Crown made from its North African possessions. As a result, in the period 1542–1545 the Portuguese withdrew from all but three of their settlements. But much worse was to come.

In 1578, the young king Sebastian led a Portuguese army of nearly 20,000 that had cost around half the kingdom's annual revenue to utter defeat in Morocco, where the king himself and a large proportion of the country's nobility were killed on the battlefield.[93] The Moroccans matched the Portuguese in guns in the battle, and won thanks to superior leadership, discipline, and cavalry.[94] One historian refers to this episode "as undoubtedly the greatest military disaster the Portuguese ever suffered in the course of their overseas expansion."[95] The kingdom was left without an heir, and the resulting period of uncertainty and weakness saw a lightning Spanish invasion, as a result of which the Spanish king also became king of

Portugal. Portugal's extra-European efforts thus had crucial, even fatal, implications for the independence of the kingdom itself.

The Ottoman-Habsburg struggle in North Africa developed from 1518. Spanish forces had taken Tripoli in 1510. At this time, Habsburg strongholds and shipping on both sides of the Mediterranean were threatened by the Turkish Barbarossa brothers, private military entrepreneurs who had assembled formidable amphibious forces that had been hired out to various patrons. In 1517 Oruc Barbarossa sought help from the Ottomans, who had just conquered Egypt from the Mamluks, in return for his allegiance. The sultan agreed, and his name was read at Friday prayers and his likeness added to coinage to symbolize his suzerainty over these new realms. Algiers and Tunis were created as two new provinces of the empire (Tripoli later came to form the core of a third), with Oruc's brother Hayreddin Barbarossa becoming governor of Algiers, and later grand admiral of the entire Ottoman fleet. The sultan shipped in substantial supplies and Janissary troops to secure his hold over the new territories and help fight off the Christians.

The Holy Roman Emperor Charles V was devoting more and more effort to capturing the coast of present-day Algeria and Tunisia, at one stage enlisting the help of the conquistador Hernan Cortes. From the 1540s to the 1570s Habsburg forces of up to 30,000 were employed to take and hold key ports, larger than the army earmarked to conquer England in the Spanish Armada of 1588. For their part, in 1574 the Ottomans assembled a gargantuan force of 100,000 to recapture Tunis, their most expensive expedition of the entire century, and a larger fleet than they had deployed at Lepanto just three years earlier.[96] The modernization of the Habsburg fortifications according to *trace italienne* designs complicated the Ottomans' task, but still these ports proved vulnerable.

After this climactic battle for Tunis, won by the Ottomans, both empires began to direct their attention elsewhere. The Spanish Habsburgs were increasingly focused on their Protestant enemies, while the sultan decided to strike east against the Persian Safavids. While the Spanish successfully held on to a few outposts, Ottoman influence largely prevailed. Muslim privateers and corsairs continued raiding shipping and coastal towns, using cannon-armed sailing ships to strike as far away as England, Ireland, and even Iceland.[97] Meanwhile, throughout this period much of the Ottoman fighting had been against local Arab and Berber opponents. The superior discipline and firepower of the sultan's troops had usually proved decisive.[98] As such, the Europeans had no monopoly on either conquest by sea, nor the particular battlefield innovations of the sixteenth century associated with gunpowder weapons. The Sublime Porte maintained its suzerainty (though generally not direct control) over North Africa until the nineteenth and twentieth centuries.

In considering the limits of Western expansion in this region, it is important to note that the Portuguese devoted far more soldiers, ships, and money than they did to any of their other extra-European ventures. Even during the first crucial decade of the *Estado da India* and Albuquerque's conquests of Goa, Hormuz, and Malacca, Morocco remained the priority for the Portuguese with "repeated, massive, and expensive deployments."[99] While Portuguese campaign forces in the East almost never exceeded 2000 troops, the original attack on Ceuta in 1415 involved forces of 20,000, that against Asilah in 1478 30,000 men, and the final, fatal expedition of 1578 another force of almost 20,000.[100] As Cook puts it, "with all Asia to win and few resources to waste, Lisbon still poured men and money into Morocco."[101] The Habsburgs had sent similarly sized forces to battle with the Ottomans in Algeria, Tunisia, and Libya. Thus the failure of the Portuguese and the Habsburgs to achieve their strategic aims in North Africa cannot be put down to a lack of commitment. Both the Christian powers and the Ottomans were fighting at roughly equivalent distances from their centers of power, although the Moroccans were on their home ground. While European naval strength was crucial in the early victories against the smaller North African polities, it was not sufficient to conclusively defeat the Ottoman navy (even after Lepanto), or stop them from deploying and supplying large expeditionary forces to the Western Mediterranean, or even to suppress the Barbary corsairs.[102] In terms of the broader lessons of the book on how military organizations learn (or don't learn) in war, it is worth noting how the Spanish explained their failures against the Ottomans in North Africa: "the Spanish acknowledged the martial abilities of the Turks—especially their discipline; but the reasons for Christian failure were attributed not to the strength of the enemy but to bad leadership or the positions of the planets."[103]

Conclusions on the Ottoman-Western Military Balance

What can we say about the Ottomans in light of the military revolution thesis and the East-West balance? The first is the importance of periodization and the danger of anachronism. From 1400 to 1650 the Ottomans were the most successful conquerors in Europe and the Mediterranean, and for a century after this point they were largely able to hold onto their vast conquests and best any individual Western great power. Although there was undoubtedly a decline in Ottoman power during the second half of the eighteenth century, there is a tendency to inaccurately read "the sick man of Europe" portrayal of the Ottomans back into the seventeenth or even the sixteenth centuries. In this way, the superpower of its day is falsely presented as merely a failure waiting to happen. As discussed later, it is also vital to point out that even once they had definitely passed their zenith, the Ottomans did not fall anywhere near as far or as fast as states that are said to epitomize European modernity, such as the Netherlands, Portugal, or Spain. Each of these European powers was conquered long before the Ottoman Empire fell at the end of the First World War.

What of the military revolution thesis more specifically? For the period that Roberts and Parker identify as the heyday of the revolutionary changes, the Ottomans were superior to their European opponents, including those like the Spanish and the Holy Roman Empire that are said to be at the forefront of the new techniques. If the military revolution is dated earlier, in the late medieval period as Rogers and Guilmartin argue,[104] then the Ottoman defeats of Western forces are still more significant, and their early advances in technology, tactics, and logistics still more noteworthy. Thus as Black puts it, "so far as there was a military revolution either in the Roberts period [i.e., 1550–1650] or earlier, it had not hitherto led to a decisive shift in the military balance or movement in the frontier between Christendom and Islam, a point that was further underlined by the peripheral nature of the Christian military impact on North Africa."[105]

In some sense Parker himself is one of the most acute critics of his own thesis in noting:

> The Turks conquered Crete from the Venetians in the 1660s, and soundly defeated Russia in 1711 and Austria 1737–39.... Spanish attacks on Algiers failed in 1775, 1783 and 1784; even Napoleon failed to take Acre in 1799.... [U]ntil the late eighteenth century, thanks to their ability to mobilize and maintain enormous armies, the major Islamic states–like the empires of Asia–proved able to keep the West at bay. Although the Europeans managed to inflict great defeats on Muslim forces during the seventeenth century, such as the rout of the Turks outside Vienna in 1683, it must be remembered that it was the Turks at the gates of Vienna and not the Europeans at the gates of Istanbul.[106]

He revises his position to say that the Ottomans were only outclassed by the West with the advent of the Industrial Revolution. Parker nevertheless holds that the early modern military revolution was still significant, not in offensive terms, but because it enabled the West to check the on-rushing Ottoman tide in the 1500s.[107] But, as has been noted before, Western defensive victories, as with those of the Safavids in the East, may well reflect the fact that the Ottomans were operating at the extremes of their logistical range more than technological or tactical innovations on the part of the Europeans. If so, this would confirm Black's frequently made point about historians' tendency to exaggerate the importance of technology and the battlefield at the expense of underlying factors.[108] It also raises the more general question of how both contemporary participants and scholars looking back centuries later can judge military effectiveness. And it is directly relevant to determining how or whether military organizations adapt to improve their effectiveness and competitiveness. Murphey observes that Ottoman military performance, like most others' of the time, was determined by five factors: "technological constraints; cost constraints; physical barriers and environmental constraints; motivational limits; limits of state power and coercion."[109] It is difficult to see how much room these constraints leave for deliberate organizational reform.

In sum, there are several reasons why considering the Ottomans and their long confrontation with European powers is vital in evaluating the military revolution thesis. First, notwithstanding excellent recent revisionist work, there is still a huge imbalance in military history toward the Western experience, as is discussed in the section to follow. Second, the general historical literature, and even more so social science scholarship, is still premised on the conventional picture of Western dominance thanks to the military revolution, and the equally conventional picture of the Ottoman Empire as the sick man of Europe. Recent work like that by Hoffman shows the staying power of such models.[110] In exactly reproducing the military revolution thesis in explaining the rise of the West,[111] Gennaioli and Voth conclude of the Ming and Ottoman Empires that "As our theory would predict, neither evolved a highly centralized structure of government or high levels of uniform tax collection."[112] Other scholars are equally dismissive of the Ottomans, but for exactly the opposite reason: they were too centralized, lacking the separation of powers and checks on the executive that supposedly explained the success of the Dutch and the English.[113] The "fiscal-military" state thesis, eagerly taken up by social scientists, suggests that it is precisely the need for the monarch to bargain and negotiate with autonomous domestic actors that is decisive in fostering advancement.[114] Finally, by putting the Ottomans in comparative perspective, the aim is not just to change the perception of this historical instance, but also to modify the general argument about the rise of the West, the rise of the state, and the dynamics of change in and through war.

Conclusions on the Early Modern Revolution

The previous chapters put early modern European expansion in the Americas, along the coast of Africa, and in the Indian Ocean littoral of Asia at center stage in assessing whether and to what extent the conduct of these expeditionary campaigns fit the template of the military revolution thesis. By and large, they don't. Directly contrary to the military revolution thesis, before 1750 Europeans were not militarily dominant relative to other civilizations anywhere, including in Europe. The partial exception of Spanish success in the Americas owes more to disease and local allies than to military technique as such. The military revolution cannot explain Western expansion in the early modern period because there was no effort, let alone ability, to transport the sort of armies that fought major wars in Europe to other continents. The agents of Western expansion were primarily chartered companies or freelance adventurers, rather than state officials or officers.

European expansion in Africa and Asia is instead explained by Europeans' willingness to compete among themselves for bits of the Earth's surface that were not of interest to existing great powers, namely the oceans, and then their ability to ingratiate themselves and reach accommodations with local polities in Africa and Asia to secure small coastal trading outposts. Deference toward, and partnerships with, foreign rulers were generally more important than campaigns of conquest. These approaches owed as much to cultural inclinations as technology, tactics, or fiscal-military institutions. Major non-Western powers chose not to compete for the oceans. Aside from the important baseline fact of traveling transcontinental distances, Western maritime advantages did not change the military balance vis-à-vis any major non-Western power. In sum, there simply was no Western military dominance for at least 250 years after the emergence of the first truly global international system.

In the period 1500–1750, European conquests were much less significant and extensive than those of the Ottomans, the Mughals, and the Manchus, both in terms of the economic and demographic resources captured, and the extent of the military resistance overcome. The Chinese and Ottomans have a stronger claim to pioneering key military innovations like professional, permanent, drilled, gun-armed forces supported by a complex, centralized administrative, fiscal and logistical apparatus than does any Western power. Yet fixating on any single model as providing the litmus test of modernity, and then equating it with effectiveness, is a dangerous move. In terms of war and organizational change, the relationship between convergence and homogeneity, on the one hand, and effectiveness on the other, varies more than the paradigm-diffusion model can accommodate.

If the evidence for the military revolution as the motor of a purported Western global hegemony in the early modern era is so weak, why has this thesis continued to be so influential? In two sections below I argue that the answer hinges in large part on biases of place and time in the way that the historical record is arranged and interpreted. As a result, it is not just our understanding of the wider world that has been distorted by these biases (though it certainly has), but also our understanding of Europe itself. A bias of place (Eurocentrism) has meant that a certain sequence of military and political developments in Europe has been falsely interpreted as constituting a tight, necessary, and universal causal story. The bias of time (anachronism) has isolated one atypical and fairly transitory period of Western dominance as the natural order of things, and then sorted and sifted the rest of the historical record in support of this contention.

The bias of time is reflected in the highly misleading tendency to read the outcomes of the nineteenth century and the dynamics of the Industrial Revolution back into a very different pre-industrial era. To regard the Western victories of the late nineteenth century as the natural order of things, as the defining *leitmotif* of European relations with other civilizations, according to which all other experience should be evaluated, while ignoring the earlier period of European inferiority, as well as the later collapse of European empires after World War Two and the contemporary rise of non-Western powers, is simply not defensible. If there is a contemporary "end point," it is the atrophy of European military power, the geopolitical rise of Asian great powers, and Western defeats in wars against Southeast Asian and Islamic insurgents from the 1950s to the present day, as covered in the concluding chapter.

Turning to the bias of place, how does the picture change if we take the Europeans out of the frame, and ask whether military and societal changes outside the West fit the sequence specified by proponents of the military revolution? The evidence shows that neither new tactics nor gunpowder technology had a transformative effect in other regions. Considering a broader range of evidence from the world at large is a good thing in and of itself, but zooming out in this fashion also brings into question what we think we know about Europe. Did guns, new-style fortifications, and new tactics really cause or require armies to get bigger, or was this just a coincidence? Did these larger armies really cause or require centralized, sovereign states, or is that just the way things happened to turn out in Europe for contingent, idiosyncratic reasons?

Bias of Place: Eurocentrism

What is the evidence of a Eurocentric bias among scholars? Andrade estimates that there are "two or three orders of magnitude" more military history work on Europe than any other region.[115] Rather than just being a quantitative problem, Jeremy Black describes how this bias shapes the terms in which history is conceived and written:

> [The] tendency [is] firstly to focus largely, if not exclusively, on Western developments, and secondly to consider those elsewhere in terms of Western paradigms and the interaction of non-Western powers with the West, these latter two factors being closely entwined.... Thus, for example, the focus in discussion of military revolutions is the West, the definitions are Western, and in so far as non-Western powers feature it is to record the success of their Western counterparts.[116]

Authors like Parker and McNeill do pay attention to developments outside Europe. Both recognize that many of the advances during the military revolution did in fact have counterparts that had occurred centuries earlier in China. Parker in particular conducted extensive primary research in Japan, India, Sri Lanka, and East and South Africa.[117] Nevertheless, the focus is still squarely on Europe. It is notable that in a key edited volume on early modern military history, eight of twelve chapters relate to Europe.[118] The most important collection on the military revolution debate includes only one chapter looking beyond West-Central Europe.[119]

This tendency is at least as pronounced in International Relations. Levy is forthright in introducing his work on the great powers since 1495: "The concern of this study is with the modern Great Power system, which originated in Europe about five centuries ago.... The Eurocentric bias of this study is deliberate. The system centered on Europe is of greatest historical interest to most Western scholars, and most theories of international behavior and war

Table 3.1. Eurocentrism in International Relations: Number of articles written on the events during the period 376–1919 published in 12 leading IR journals from 1980 to 2007 by geographic region of focus.

Geographic focus	Number of articles
Europe and Canada	205
East Asia	66
United States	35
Middle East and North Africa	21
South Asia	6
Southeast Asia	6
Sub-Saharan Africa	5

Source: Information from the Teaching, Research, and International Policy (TRIP) project at the College of William & Mary. Republished from J. C. Sharman, "Myths of Military Revolution: European Expansion and Eurocentrism," *European Journal of International Relations* 24 (3) (2018).

have been derived from it."[120] Scholarship since has so far failed to correct this situation, as evidenced by the geographic focus of articles published in leading journals in the field in the table above. Writing about "the international system" or "great powers" in general, while only using examples and evidence from Europe, remains reasonably commonplace, and is considered unremarkable. Although authors may compare France, the Netherlands, the Habsburg Empire, Sweden, England, and other European powers, to the extent that systemic competition and diffusion are vital components of the explanation, they are still only looking at one regional case.[121]

Basing the military revolution thesis so disproportionately on evidence from one region, and positing necessary and sufficient causal relationships, leaves many of the core tenets open to challenge in considering a broader range of evidence. In part as a result of this bias, explanations tend to be deterministic and imply that there is only one route to a particular outcome.[122] Rather than allowing that the same outcome was a product of independent contingent precursors, the argument tends to be that a definite, specific set of events necessarily followed from each other in a set sequence, and that they were jointly necessary and sufficient to produce a given result. Looking at other regions undermines almost all of these purportedly necessary and sufficient relationships. By underlining the importance of contingency and causal complexity, I hope to put some aspects of European history in a new light also.

Stereotypes might suggest that historians eschew the sort of simple cause-and-effect accounts common in the social sciences in favor of richly detailed narratives. In fact, the original military revolution thesis was articulated in terms of necessary causes. Thus Roberts states, "The transformation in the scale of warfare led inevitably to an increase in the authority of the state.... Only the state, now, could supply the administrative, technical and financial resources required for large-scale hostilities."[123] The initial tactical changes "were indeed the efficient causes of changes which were really revolutionary."[124] Individual components of the military revolution argument are said to be necessarily related to each other; one part of the causal sequence requires that the others be present too. For example, the new-style fortifications necessarily required large armies to defend them, gunpowder required infantry-heavy armies, the cost of advanced navies necessitated public not private ownership, and so on.[125]

Not only have historians found that the military revolution argument does not hold outside Europe, but their findings also suggest that this account may not even hold in Europe. For example, the development of gunpowder weapons, new linear tactics, or new-style artillery fortresses may not have had any causal impact on the growth of army size or the rise of the state. The fact that several Western European polities developed the features that later came to define the modern sovereign state after their armies had increased in size may simply have been a coincidence.[126]

In *The Asian Military Revolution*, Lorge argues: "Early modern warfare was invented in China during the twelfth and thirteenth centuries,"[127] and thus that military developments in early modern Europe represented a belated Sinification of Western warfare.[128] China first developed large, professionally trained standing infantry armies that made extensive use of gunpowder weapons and volley fire, artillery-proof fortifications, and a highly developed bureaucratic administrative apparatus almost a thousand years ago. Neither new artillery nor new styles of fortification had much impact in changing existing political institutions. Medieval armies in China had long been larger than any in Western Europe prior to the eighteenth century. Given Chinese innovations like professional armies, gunpowder, and guns, Western culture was clearly not a prerequisite for major military-technical advancement.[129] In detailing distinctive paths taken in China, Japan, South, and Southeast Asia, Lorge is specifically critical of the notion of necessary conditions, most importantly that the spread of gunpowder weapons requires any single institutional response.[130]

If guns cemented the dominance of infantry over cavalry in Europe, they did the same in Japan, but in South Asia, where guns fitted into the existing tradition of horse archers, there was nothing that matched the template of the military revolution.[131] Horse archers were more revolutionary than cannons and muskets.[132] Artillery made relatively little difference to the conduct of sieges, and in some ways favored defenders more than attackers.[133] Certainly gunpowder weapons did not remake polities. There was thus nothing natural or inevitable about the sequences that happened to occur in Europe. Specific investigations of the "gunpowder empire" thesis, that dominant empires outside the West blocked military-technological progress,[134] are contradicted by closer analysis of Mughal and Chinese practices.[135]

Turning from history to International Relations, with reference to East Asia, scholars like Johnston, Kang, Suzuki, Hobson, Hui, Ringmar, and others similarly argue that European history can be a very misleading basis for forming general explanations.[136] International Relations work derived from explicitly Eurocentric datasets, such as the Correlates of War and Great Power Wars 1495–1815, has been shown to be profoundly misleading in the conclusions it suggests about international systems.[137] Victoria Tin-bor Hui's scholarship comparing Chinese and European history is particularly relevant as an example of the new insights to be gained from a comparative regional approach, particularly as she aims to answer many of the same basic questions as historians like Roberts and Parker concerning the role of war in the rise of the state.

Hui compares the diverging paths of the ancient Chinese and early modern European systems.[138] Ancient China is held to be similar to Europe around 1500, both being characterized by "disintegration of feudal hierarchy, prevalence of war, conditions of international anarchy, emergence of sovereign territorial states, configuration of the balance of power, development of the centralized bureaucracy, birth of state-society bargains, expansion of international trade."[139] For Hui, war may make states, but sometimes it makes empires. For despite these similar initial conditions in ancient China and early modern Europe, the end points were radically different. The warring states period in China was succeeded by imperial unification, whereas Europe retained its fragmented, anarchical system. Hui's conclusion is the same as historians like Lorge: what have been put forward as universal and necessary relationships are instead idiosyncratic and contingent.

Scholars of Europe have posited mechanisms of the balance of power and diseconomies of scale to explain the pluralistic European international system, but have then assumed that these mechanisms apply universally. Looking at the Chinese experience, however, Hui discerns two other mechanisms that tend to produce the opposite result: bandwagoning and positive returns to scale. In China these promoted the conquest of separate states to form one empire. The Chinese comparative perspective puts fundamental trends in Europe in quite a different light. The victors from the warring states period in China introduced conscription to enlarge their armies and thereby out-competed their rivals. Rather than the "logic of balancing," the "logic of domination" explains the development of the system. What the military revolution thesis sees as a muscular process of state-building in early modern Europe is portrayed by Hui as a series of short-term improvised expedients that she terms "self-weakening." Important examples are the extensive reliance on debt, rather than the states' own resources, and the use of mercenaries rather than conscript armies,[140] in short the tendency to throw money at problems (often someone else's money at that), rather than build institutions. In this way the basic orienting question changes from one of explaining European success to that of explaining the failure of European unification.[141]

In sum, comparing the historical experiences of different regions conclusively undermines any idea of European exceptionalism in pioneering the path to military modernity in the early modern period. Taking a broader view also demonstrates that the effects of particular technologies and tactics were strongly shaped by cultural and political contexts. Because these contexts varied widely, there was no master logic dictating that developments had to occur in a set sequence.

Bias of Time: Anachronism and Teleology

The biases of place are closely related to those of time. There is a pronounced tendency to write about the past in terms of the present by looking for the precursors of Western success and Eastern failure. Lorge notes historians' tendency to work backward from a time of Western dominance and Asian weakness and then to mine the preceding centuries for evidence of the "prerequisites" of "inevitable" Western success and Asian failure.[142] He cautions that "By emphasizing the rising power of European nation-states after 1500, particularly the economic, technological, and political developments that led in a neat Hegelian progression to our perceived Western-dominated world, the actual histories of these non-Western polities are relegated to the realm of antiquarian interest."[143] Echoing a theme emphasized by Black about the danger of running together Western victories over the centuries as one common trend,[144] Thornton similarly decries the same tendency to read the nineteenth-century conquest of Africa back into the very different circumstances of European-African relations in the preceding centuries.[145]

All the early modern great powers rose and fell at some point, but some cases are discussed mainly in terms of their rise, others predominantly in terms of their fall. The Dutch or Swedes were conclusively relegated to minor power status in the early eighteenth century, while the Portuguese were defeated and occupied by Spain in 1580–1640, yet they are most often written about in terms of their rise and successes. The Ottoman, Mughal, Ming, and Qing Empires conquered and controlled far greater territory, population, wealth, and military power than any of these European counterparts. With the possible exception of the Mughals, they were also far more enduring as great powers. Seemingly on any objective metric the non-Western empires were more successful. Yet the Ottomans, Mughals, and Chinese are most often written of as being in decline, and in terms of crucial missteps and lost opportunities that condemned them to backwardness and defeat. While the temptation is to look back from the subsequent success of Western Europe to find the earlier precursors of later victories, with the Asian cases it is the reverse: to look back from the collapse of these empires to find the origins of decay, failure, and defeat in all the previous developments across the preceding centuries.[146]

The fixation with the "end" of the story forms the rationale for the concluding chapter. If the end of the story shapes the way we see what goes before, how well do the claims I have put forward so far stand up to a change of perspective? To what extent does my argument depend on a particular cutoff date around the time of the French Revolution? In particular, some might object that the West does win, dominating and dethroning the Asian great powers, and expanding Europe's control from around 35 percent to 85 percent of the Earth's surface by the time of the First World War. Might it be a case of the military revolution being right after all, just a couple hundred years late? To address these sorts of questions, I next assess how the story changes from different end points. The first is the zenith of Western power at the dawn of the twentieth century. The second is the collapse of European empires and the success of insurgencies waged against European and U.S. forces from the 1950s to the present.

How the Europeans Won in the End (Before They Later Lost)

DECIDING WHERE TO FINISH a story without a natural ending can make a lot of difference about the lessons drawn. To conclude an account about the limits of European expansion immediately before the greatest period of Western dominance, roughly from the end of the Napoleonic Wars to World War One, and especially the second half of this time span, may well seem like stacking the deck, leaving out the part of the historical record that doesn't fit my argument. For as the nineteenth century went on, Europeans brushed aside the obstacles that had previously constrained their dreams of empire. The English East India Company completed its conquest of South Asia, with the Europeans later colonizing Southeast Asia as well. The settlers in the Americas crushed the last indigenous resistance. By this time the European great powers had cowed the Ottoman and Chinese Qing Empires, as well as the Japanese. Finally, Africa (along with the South Pacific) was apportioned among the various colonial powers. It is only a slight overstatement to say that by the early twentieth century, every part of the Earth's surface was subject either to formal Western rule or informal Western hegemony. Doesn't this unprecedented and near-total global victory discredit the verdict of the previous chapters, which critique the idea of European military superiority, and emphasize the power of non-Western polities? In short, how can my argument account for the fact that the Europeans won in the end?

In looking at developments after the early modern period, I address this very reasonable objection about periodization, and explore how preceding events look different when viewed from different ending points. The coverage of the book so far reaches until around the end of the eighteenth century. The idea of Europeans' total victory is to conclude the story from the vantage point of the beginning of the twentieth century. Yet of course the Europeans didn't win in the end. From the perspective of the early twenty-first century, we know that the spectacularly rapid empire-building of the nineteenth century was followed by an even more rapid process of imperial collapse in the few decades after 1945. This vast process of empire-building and decolonization produced the contemporary international system of sovereign states,[1] yet International Relations scholars have given these twin transformations much less attention than they warrant.[2]

This short concluding chapter cannot and does not try to be a whirlwind tour of all the military relations between the West and every other region of the world in the two centuries from the end of the Napoleonic Wars to the present. The purpose of the very selective survey of developments in the nineteenth, twentieth, and twenty-first centuries is not to engage in sustained historical or analytical arguments about the causes and consequences of the new imperialism or decolonization. Instead, it is to see how my argument about the early modern period stands up in light of later events.

In the preceding chapters, I argued that advantages in military technology were seldom decisive, and that even where Europeans held such an advantage (e.g., cannon-armed sailing ships), this did not alter the strategic balance. Does this claim really still hold up when one side is armed with modern rifles and machine guns, and the other with spears, swords, and muskets? Doesn't military-technological superiority explain how often quite modest European forces humbled Asian empires and conquered vast swathes of territory in the 1800s? If so, doesn't this invalidate the claims made throughout the previous chapters that differences in weaponry are almost never decisive?

The advances of the Industrial Revolution marked a basic change in the relations between Europe and other civilizations, which is in part why the dynamics of the preceding early modern period were so distinct.[3] Nevertheless, drawing on recent histories, I argue that in the nineteenth-century wars of imperial conquest, European logistics and organization, their ability to mobilize local allies and resources, and the disunity of their opponents were at least as important as superior weapons for victory. Somewhat like the Ottomans before them, the Qing Chinese Empire suffered from a process of internal institutional decay that led to an absolute decline in military capacity. More recently, experiences from 1945 to the present demonstrate that a similar, and perhaps even greater, technological superiority enjoyed by contemporary Western forces over their opponents has counted for surprisingly little. The wars of decolonization, and more recent insurgencies, demonstrate how even when Western forces have a huge technological advantage and win most of the battles, they have nevertheless often lost the wars.

Thus if conclusions from the early modern period are put in a different light looking at them from the perspective of the nineteenth century, then so too the experiences of the nineteenth century are put in a different light from the perspective of the twenty-first century. In this way, the period c.1850–1914, from whence many scholars draw their understandings of European expansion, is very unrepresentative, and a poor guide to understanding either the broad sweep of international politics over the last 500 years, or the determinants of victory in inter-civilizational war.

The process of empire-building and collapse also mandates further scrutiny of claims about the pre-eminence of cultural factors. I have argued that the Europeans' preference for maritime, networked overseas domains was crucial for their ability to co-exist with more powerful Asian and African polities that had a firmly terrestrial orientation in the early modern period. If the triumph of the West in the nineteenth century was underpinned by the science and technology of the Industrial Revolution, and the associated rise of the modern bureaucratic state, where is the influence of ideas and culture?

Once again, the Industrial Revolution was certainly a vital part of explaining how Europeans were able to build their new empires. But the prior, perhaps counterintuitive, question is why Europeans wanted to build huge empires. Given the at-best uncertain returns in military and economic terms, in many cases later imperial expansionism seems to have reflected concerns about prestige and status in an international context where great power standing required colonies. In the decades after World War Two, however, the possession of colonies went from being valorized to being deeply stigmatized as part of a fundamental change in the mores of international society. Europeans generally maintained their industrial and administrative superiority over the forces of decolonization arrayed against them, but somehow this didn't seem to be decisive anymore, and European empires collapsed. Thus both the rise and the fall of European empires were crucially driven and shaped by changes in ideas and cultural contexts, rather than just, or even mostly, material factors and rational means-ends calculations.

If seeing how the story told so far changes when the historical end point from which it is assessed is moved, the other main goal of this chapter is to conclude the earlier discussion of models of war and institutional change. I draw together the reasons why the functionalist model, premised on rational learning and Darwinian survival pressures, is implausible. Against the expectation of convergence on a superior Western style of warfare, it is striking how often non-Western opponents have improved their performance by adopting a very different style of war. Success has often been a product of tactical and institutional differentiation, rather than rational emulation and/or homogenizing elimination pressures in a competitive environment. These more general points about organizational learning and change fit closely with perspectives centered on the importance of culturally constructed perceptions and expectations in determining preferences and setting goals, interpreting costs and benefits, creating understandings of what counts as victory and defeat, and shaping the appropriate form and functions of military institutions. Not only does this view provide an alternative model to explain war and institutional change in the abstract, it also has particular relevance to the transformative geopolitics of the "new imperialism" in the nineteenth century, and the equally fundamental process of European contraction and collapse that followed.

Winning in the End: Motives and Means in the New Imperialism

Perhaps the starkest example of the changed military balance between Europeans and non-Europeans is the "Scramble for Africa" in the last quarter of the nineteenth century. From a position of controlling less than 10 percent of Africa in 1876,[4] European empires came to span 95 percent of the continent by World War I.[5] Not since the time of Cortes and Pizarro 350 years earlier had Europeans achieved such out-sized military results. The image of repeating rifles and machine guns against African spears and bows is one of the enduring tropes of a technology-based account of Western triumphs. How can these lopsided victories be explained in the context of an argument that has consistently played down Western strengths in general, and the decisiveness of technology in particular? I first take a step back to ask why these battles and wars were fought, and what motivated the new imperialism

As discussed in Chapter 1, from the period of the first sustained interaction between Europeans and Africans in the late 1400s until well into the 1800s, Europeans played a marginal role in African politics. European trading and slaving posts along the Atlantic and Indian Ocean coasts were generally dependent on the goodwill of local rulers. The process of military innovation in the intervening centuries had not produced any substantial shift in balance of power. In the early 1880s, however, new land grabs by the French and German governments, and a quixotic bid by the Belgian king for a vast personal fiefdom, set up a dynamic that culminated in the Berlin conference of 1884–1885 and the subsequent division of Africa among the European powers over the next couple of decades.[6] This huge change, the conquest of a continent, raises the questions of first why Europeans embarked on the "Scramble for Africa," and then how they were able to succeed. The first was often a matter of following cultural prompts on the markers of great power prestige, while the "how" of European conquest was at least as much a matter of politics and logistics as battlefield technology.

The Motives of the New Imperialism

Taking the "why" question first, one of the most relevant books on the subject observes:

> Historians have by now abandoned the search for the philosopher's stone that will reveal the identity of the universal motivation that underlay European imperialism. If little else about that contentious subject has been agreed, it has at least been accepted that the motives for participation in the imperial venture were multiple and complex and varied considerably among nations.[7]

There is certainly nothing like enough room to survey this huge historical literature here.[8]

Perhaps the baseline presumption from an International Relations point of view (to the surprisingly limited extent that the discipline takes an interest in the process of colonization) might be that European states sought new conquests overseas to augment national wealth and power.[9] In the nineteenth and early twentieth centuries, empire-building was often justified as a strategy to increase national security and wealth. Such a rationale chimes with baseline social science presumptions on what motivates behavior in international politics. Thus: "Empire forms a means of internal balancing. By subjugating and annexing other territories, states gain access to useful commodities and manpower. At the same time, this strategy denies the adversary access to those same resources."[10] According to this logic, even otherwise defensively minded European states might be sucked into the scramble so as to avoid a deterioration in their security relative to potential future opponents, especially given the sharpening intra-European rivalries of the day.

Despite the caveat above about the varying and mixed motives in play, the extent to which status or prestige concerns were important in driving the new imperialism is notable. At the time, socialization worked to promote imperial ambitions, and disparage the idea of being a "mere" sovereign state.[11] Great powers with overseas empires were set on retaining them; the others aspired to acquire them. States new to the international system like Germany, but also Italy and Japan, sought to emulate the transcontinental empires of existing great powers.[12] In a clear echo of the selection mechanism discussed later, Bosworth notes of Italian Eritrea: "The simplest and most persuasive argument in defence of the colony was a variety of social Darwinism. In going to Eritrea Italy had joined the great struggle of the internationally fittest, a failure to compete in which would mean 'national death.'"[13] The leading newspaper of the day noted that Italy must acquire an empire in Africa or "cease to have any pretence to assume the role of a Great Power and ... have to content itself with being a big Switzerland."[14] Thus it was to counter an insecurity of standing, not military insecurity, that "The main goal of Italian foreign policy and military planners in the late nineteenth century ... became the acknowledgment of the new nation's status as a great power. In the late nineteenth century such a position seemed to demand possession of an empire."[15] Economically, the Italian empire was a story of unremitting losses and "heroic over-investment."[16] Militarily, it ranged from a distraction to a disaster, the defeat at the hands of the Ethiopians at Adowa in 1896 marking the nadir of Italian fortunes.

Japan's late nineteenth-century imperialism was driven by a similar logic to that of Italy:

> imperialism and a strong military to support this was also regarded as an integral part of a "civilized" state's identity.... Being a powerful imperialist power would not only militarily protect Japan, it would also help Japan to be recognized as a full member of the "civilized" society of states and be accorded its protection. After all, the great "civilized" powers were at the same time the most militarily powerful and possessed vast colonies to further their mission of "civilizing" the "uncivilized" states.[17]

Though an imperial power of long standing, various French colonial expeditions from the 1830s (Algeria), and those in sub-Saharan Africa fifty years later seem to have owed at least as much to the pursuit of grandeur, and wiping out the stain of the humiliating defeat at the hands of Prussia in 1871, as the pursuit of material advantage.[18]

Even the late expansion of Dutch colonialism in Southeast Asia re-flected a similar dynamic from the 1890s, with prestige concerns again said to outweigh economic factors or concerns regarding Eu-ropean rivals.[19] Along these lines, Lorge dismisses Europeans' empire-building as a product of "their willingness to spend blood and trea-sure in what were, on balance, unprofitable ventures all in the interest of glory."[20] He explains the "failure" of Chinese and other Asian pol-ities to build maritime empires as a result of their reluctance to subsidize such loss-making vanity projects.[21]

Whether colonial empires did in fact enhance military or eco-nomic capacity is fairly dubious, especially considering the cost of establishing, garrisoning, and administering these new posses-sions. The fact that the new wave of chartered companies formed to reap the benefits of these new overseas opportunities (while sparing the metropole the costs of imperial governance) almost always lost money, and often went broke, or only survived at the expense of the taxpayer, indicates the scanty commercial benefits of the new colonies.[22] One calculation suggests that "The British Empire ... generated no profits, at least in the years 1880–1912. In fact it required a subsidy."[23] Even where colonies did bring profits, typically to small sections of the elite, it is unclear whether these same or greater profits could have been gained through arm's-length trade or investment, minus conquest and formal subordi-nation.[24] Though the imperial powers did recruit troops in the colonies, the main duties of these forces was to garrison and ex-tend imperial borders, rather than improving the defense of the metropole itself.[25] Perhaps more importantly, if scholars are still arguing about the economic and security benefits of empire (if any), it is highly unlikely that contemporary leaders were able to make accurate calculations. This once again underlines the point about the implausibility of the assumption that leaders can in fact tot up costs and benefits, or assess the causal impacts of different trends and decisions.

The point here is not that European powers engaged in a delib-erately irrational foreign policy that they knew would leave them poorer and more vulnerable. Rather, the spirit of the age suggested that empires were the normatively appropriate institutional form for great powers, and suggested that possessing colonies was the route to national greatness. Empires were seen as both a means to national success and security, as well as being an end in themselves. Empire constituted the legitimate great power form in the context of the time.

The Means of the New Imperialism

Putting to one side the question of motives in the new imperialism of the nineteenth century, how do the means by which Europeans conquered their new empires fit with the drivers of military success in the early modern era discussed in the preceding chapters? There I argued that Europeans generally did not enjoy significant military technological advantages over non-Western opponents in Asia, Africa, or Europe itself, because these opponents already had or quickly acquired equivalent technology. The exceptions—for instance, when Europeans had superior weapons in some parts of the Americas and in the open oceans—were largely inconsequential. This is either because other factors dominated (disease and demography) or because these limited areas of technological superiority failed to bring decisive advantage (e.g., against Asian empires, most African polities, or in a different way vis-à-vis American groups like the Mapuche). Thus the general conclusion was that the importance of a purported European technological superiority in battlefield weapons has been very overstated in many previous accounts of European expansion to 1800.

But what about after 1800? Here it might seem that battlefield technology was the decisive factor. The most apparent of these were advances in weapons, especially the repeating magazine rifle from the 1880s, and slightly later the machine gun. My claim here is that the Industrial Revolution certainly marked a divide in the power of European polities relative to their African, Asian, and other counterparts, but that non-military technology, politics, and logistics were more important than more advanced weapons. Turning to Qing China as the most powerful of the surviving Eastern empires, which was nevertheless subordinated by the Europeans, it would seem that the regime's own political and institutional decrepitude was more important in allowing small Western forces to dominate than the difference in military technology.

Even those scholars keen on a technological explanation emphasize the parallel importance of non-military technology.[26] One of these was medical advances that lowered the horrifically high death toll of Europeans falling victim to tropical diseases in Africa.[27] Another was the invention of the steamship, in particular because of its ability to deploy and support forces far inland through river networks.[28] The railway later supplemented and extended this logistical advantage, while the telegraph allowed for much closer coordination of strategy between the metropole and colonial outposts.

Beyond technology, scholars of Southeast Asia, Africa, and elsewhere emphasize a combination of logistics, planning, discipline, and strategic mobility in explaining European conquests.[29] One continuity with the early modern period was that local troops were again crucial, generally making up a majority of imperial forces. On the other side, the failure of African polities to set aside local rivalries, and the effectiveness of divide-and-rule tactics, were also critical factors in enabling European conquest.[30]

Even in the age of the greatest European triumphs, however, it was possible to see the beginnings of trends that would lead to the downfall of colonial empires, and the declining fortunes of Western expeditionary warfare more generally. Those outside Europe who practiced irregular tactics were more likely to cause persistent problems for the European invaders. In contrast, non-Western powers who sought to emulate Western methods often actually made themselves more vulnerable to European conquest.[31] To suppress such irregular opponents, rather than tiny expeditionary forces, Europeans increasingly had to commit larger and larger forces that represented an appreciable drain on their overall militaries.

Thus France committed over 100,000 troops, a third of its entire army, to "pacify" Algeria in the 1840s.[32] The Russians had to deploy an army of 155,000 in a failed effort to suppress Chechen resistance in the Caucasus in 1838, only succeeding when 250,000 troops were committed immediately after the Crimean War.[33] Just before the First World War, the Italians were forced to send over 100,000 troops to conquer Libya.[34] Although the English India Company had built its army in South Asia to over 100,000 at the start of the 1800s, a century later the British mobilized and transported almost half a million men to suppress the Boers in South

Africa.[35] In the interwar years it took 250,000 French and Spanish troops to stamp out resistance in the Rif region of Morocco after a long series of humiliating Spanish defeats. Despite these larger commitments, the European success rate began to wane. According to MacDonald, while only 18 percent of anti-imperial insurgencies were successful before 1914, after 1918 this increased to 57 percent.[36] The fact that the Europeans had to greatly out-number their opponents to win these imperial campaigns is sharply at odds with the stereotypical renderings from Cortes to Plassey to Rorke's Drift of tiny Western forces besting vastly larger enemy hosts arrayed against them.

Turning away from Africa, what about the empires of the East? Much of the book has contended that Asian empires long overshadowed their European counterparts, and that the former rather than the latter should properly be regarded as the great conquerors of the early modern era. Yet by the end of the nineteenth century the Eastern great powers had been humbled and subordinated. By the second half of the nineteenth century European forces were winning battles against Chinese armies in the same crushing and decisive manner as in Africa. The decline of the Mughals and the Ottomans has been discussed in chapters 2 and 3, but what of the Chinese? What does the "century of humiliation" mean for the broader argument about the dynamics of European expansion?

From 1840 onwards Europeans repeatedly blasted their way through Chinese coastal and inland river defenses.[37] In 1860 the Second Opium War culminated in the capture of Beijing and the flight of the emperor after his elite Mongol cavalry were routed. Britain and France were able to conclusively defeat the Qing Emperor with a force of as little as 20,000 troops.[38] What had happened to the Qing Empire? In the previous century it had not only held the Europeans at bay, but finally succeeded in suppressing the nomad threat from the steppe through a campaign of genocidal expansion into Central Asia[39]; then, as now, "China" is "an inherently imperial term, defined politically and enforced militarily."[40] Rather like the Ottomans a century before, it is not so much a story of an Asian military trapped in time, clinging to the old ways as Europeans implemented radical advances in their armies and navies. Instead, Qing armies declined in an absolute sense, losing their traditional strengths.[41] Again as with the Ottomans, military decline was firmly rooted in underlying deep domestic political and fiscal factors.[42] A series of massive rebellions, particularly the Taiping civil war, by far the nineteenth century's bloodiest conflict with many millions of deaths, saw a delegation of military and fiscal power to the provincial level as a desperate measure to save the Qing dynasty.

Almost as notable as the military defeats themselves was the Chinese court's reaction. For the paradigm-diffusion model and functionalism more generally, organizational failure is meant to be the great spur of reform. Especially for those emphasizing deliberate reform and organizational learning, a common presumption in both military history and the social sciences, a long string of battlefield defeats like those experienced by Qing forces in the Opium Wars should have produced much more rapid and thorough-going reform than they did. This failure is indicative of why improving military effectiveness through learning is so uncertain. Upon hearing of the first decisive defeats at the hands of the British in the First Opium War, the Qing leadership had to diagnose what had gone wrong and why.[43] While one faction explained the reverses as due to systemic problems that necessitated root-and-branch reform, another argued that treachery and poor leadership were the true culprits, and resisted Westernization.[44]

No doubt these contrasting conclusions were not innocent of personal agendas and courtly intrigue, but the point raised in the previous chapter with reference to the Ottomans is again pertinent: it is one thing to know that you have lost, but it is quite another to know why you have lost, or how to retrieve the situation. To repeat, scholars with the massive benefit of hindsight still find such diagnoses very difficult and controversial. Even if the Qing rulers had been able to make an accurate diagnosis and decided on remedial measures, implementation poses acute difficulties of its own. As Ralston's book on importing the European military model makes clear, those rulers outside the West who had unequivocally decided on a path of Western reform generally found it extremely difficult to bring about such a transformation. Not only was the resulting hybrid of Westernized and local models sometimes actually less militarily effective, but in the process of reform rulers often endangered the foundations of the political system that kept them in power.[45]

Overall, how then does the story of early modern European expansion look different when surveyed from the heyday of the new imperialism? Is it a case of the military revolution thesis being right after all about European expansion, just two or three centuries late? Against this last proposition, the military revolution thesis is an argument that is set in a specific historical context and formed of specifically early modern developments, technological and institutional, from the invention of cannons, to the birth of European standing armies, and the death of feudalism. It cannot be equated with a vague sense that Westerners won out over other peoples at some point in history thanks to a material-technological superiority in military affairs. Pulling back to look at the logic that underlies the military revolution thesis, the idea that international security competition ruthlessly and efficiently winnows institutional forms to promote a convergence on the best-adapted and most military effective solutions, either through rulers' rational decision making, or through Darwinian elimination via conquest, is a poor fit with the rise of European colonial empires.

Losing in the End: Decolonization and Insurgency from 1945

Can we explain European expansion without explaining European contraction also? Outside of the settler countries of the Americas and Oceania, European dominance fell even more suddenly than it had been established. By most measures, the European empires reached their greatest territorial extent in the inter-war years. Yet in the period 1945–1975 a cumulating combination of political retrenchment and military defeat saw empires replaced by an international system of unprecedented homogeneity centered on sovereign states. Once again, the aim is not to re-tell or even summarize the hugely complicated story of the collapse of European empires, but to see whether shifting the end point shifts our perspective on earlier conclusions. First, the importance of the declining legitimacy of empires reinforces earlier conclusions referenced already about the importance of culture and ideas, as distinct from the rational pursuit of power and wealth, in the making and remaking of the modern international system.[46] Second, the fact that "backward" non-Western forces have repeatedly bested "advanced" Western foes supports earlier skepticism about the significance of weapons and military technology in isolation from broader concerns.

In considering the "why" of European contraction, decolonization seems to have been at least as much a product of delegitimation as of strictly military defeats, or economic decline.[47] Britain gave up most of its colonies without a fight. When those like the Dutch, Portuguese, and especially the French fought to hold on to some parts of their empires, the result of the military struggle was still heavily determined by the climate of political opinion, in the colonies, the metropole, and the wider international community. Increasingly, shifting international norms rebalanced the calculation of costs and benefits: at home and abroad, imperial possessions were no longer regarded worth fighting for. Remembering that the ability to gain local allies and support had been one of the key enablers of both the predominantly maritime European expansion of the early modern period, and the new imperialism of the nineteenth century, as this support drained away, empires became harder and harder to hold. Whereas most of those struggling to resist European conquest in the nineteenth century fought alone, in the third quarter of the twentieth century aid from the Communist bloc, and sanctuaries in other newly liberated states, increasingly meant those fighting imperial forces had far better prospects of success. Subsequently, in the aftermath of bloody disappointments from Vietnam to Afghanistan, but also more minor U.S. reverses like Lebanon in 1983 or Somalia in 1993, many observers argue that democratic publics are casualty averse, and that contemporary democratic political systems are inherently unsuited to long, indecisive wars to an extent that more than cancels out the commanding military-technological advantage that Western forces enjoy over irregulars in other parts of the world.[48]

The wars of decolonization, and subsequent Western counterinsurgency campaigns, decisively undermine the easy assumption that victory goes to those with the most advanced technology, the largest economies, and the most developed state apparatus.[49] Winning battles but losing wars became a recurring theme for Western forces in Asia, Africa, and the Middle East.[50] This brings into question the importance of the battlefield factors. What are often taken as the fundamental "lessons" of the nineteenth-century wars of imperial conquest, that is, the primacy of Western military technology and the modern industrial state in securing victory against less advanced non-Western foes, are directly contradicted by developments from 1945 to the present. Better weapons, complete air superiority, superior communications, more advanced medical technology, far greater strategic mobility and more developed logistics, more training, far more lavish funding, and a host of other related factors somehow consistently failed to deliver victory against non-Western opponents. In the aftermath of the unsuccessful counterinsurgencies in Iraq and Afghanistan, U.S. and Western forces are perhaps even further away from solving these problems than they were fifty years earlier.[51] The current calculation among Western governments and militaries seems to be that they must avoid overseas expeditionary campaigns that involve holding territory and controlling populations, because Western forces will generally lose such contests, even when faced with objectively much weaker foes.

Claims that these kinds of insurgencies are not "real" major power wars completely fail to deal with the fact that this kind of expeditionary warfare was how Europeans built their empires and created the international system in the first place. Similarly, to say that defeats in the wars of decolonization, and subsequent U.S. losses to Communist and Islamist insurgencies have reflected political and societal factors more than military reasons, and thus that these defeats aren't relevant to the study of war, is a contrivance. This defense is especially unconvincing considering the military revolution thesis and subsequent historical treatments have been at pains to emphasize the political and societal determinants of military success, and the need to analyze how each factor influences the other. The military revolution thesis is also an institutional account of how militaries converge in the way they fight and how they are formed. According to the conventional view, modern, advanced armies associated with modern, advanced states came into conflict with inferior institutional forms, which either adapted to fit the new template, or fell by the wayside, at first in Europe, and then worldwide. Competitive success was associated with similarity. But considering the lessons of the post-1945 period, differentiation, not mimicry, has brought success for those combating Western forces, according to the idea of asymmetric warfare.

The Paradigm-Diffusion Model and an Alternative

The critique of the military revolution, and my argument about the importance of private actors, tactical adaptations, deference to non-Western great powers, and the modus vivendi facilitated by Europeans' maritime orientation, have drawn heavily and directly on historians' work to better inform social science. But if most of the arbitrage has been from history to the social sciences, is there anything that can be exchanged in return? If historians have noted the lack of contact with International Relations and other social sciences,[52] opinion is at best divided on whether this represents any loss (as discussed in the Introduction). Nevertheless, I argue below that in fact historians can learn something from social science. Perhaps ironically, historians have sometimes been unwittingly too social scientific in the basic form of their arguments. Just as social scientists' implicit historical assumptions regarding European expansion crucially shape their scholarship, so too historians are often strongly influenced by implicit social scientific models of rational learning and efficient organizational learning and change. Both groups need to bring these assumptions out into the light for much closer scrutiny.

As such, the final matter is to draw together the analysis of the common assumptions often held by historians (usually tacitly) and social scientists (somewhat more openly) concerning organizational learning, adaptation, and interaction with their environments. These are premised on the basic idea that competition promotes convergence on efficient organizational models via learning and environmental pressures. The particular example explored in this book concerns military organizations and states in war, but the same logic extends far more widely into many other domains.

As discussed in the Introduction, what is called the paradigm-diffusion model in history is often equated with functionalism in social science, but by whatever label, the idea may seem to be little more than common sense. The military revolution thesis is fundamentally dependent on this logic:

> Guns up-ended the balance because larger, wealthier, and better-organized political structures were better able to afford gunpowder warfare. Therefore, the weak, the poor, the badly organized structures died away. A feedback cycle ensued: the more control a state managed to achieve, the more revenue it could raise, the more guns it could buy, the more fortresses it could build. Thus, gunpowder warfare selected for effective, centralized states. It's a widely held notion, nearly ubiquitous.[53]

The mechanisms at work here, learning and elimination, have an evolutionary flavor to them, the first more Lamarckian,[54] the second classically Darwinian.[55] Speaking in the most general terms about the propensity to learn, McNeill reasons that "Any human skill that achieves admirable results will tend to spread from its place of origin by taking root among other peoples who encounter the novelty and find it better than whatever they had previously known or done."[56] The view of learning via military competition is based on the assumption that "after wars were over ... it became clear what had failed and what had worked."[57] The related "survival of the fittest" elimination dynamic both provides the motivation for learning and also constitutes a separate path to promoting efficiency via selecting out organizations that failed to adapt.[58]

Just as the significance of the military revolution thesis goes far beyond the battlefield in seeking to explain changes in political institutions and the international system, so too these mechanisms are held to shape states as well as armies. Thus as a recent social science treatment argues: "Because the ability to finance war was key for survival, armed conflict forced monarchs to create effective fiscal infrastructures."[59] More generally, "Like maladapted firms, maladapted states and alliances—whose organization consistently yields less than optimal policies—must reform or perish."[60] Historians often take the same line: "Early and efficient fiscal-military states gained increased power and territory, while less efficient states diminished in importance or disappeared altogether."[61] This dynamic applies with special force in warfare: "Since war provides a fundamental threat to the security of the state there should logically be every incentive for states to adopt as quickly as possible the structures, values and practices of successful militaries irrespective of issues of political, social and cultural compatibility."[62] This hard necessity of military efficiency in an arena of life-or-death struggle is said to trump the force of ideas and culture: war "does not permit culturally driven but militarily ineffective ideas and practices to prosper."[63]

What is wrong with this functionalist logic that we can equate survival over time with efficiency, and what's the alternative? The bulletproofing example discussed in the Introduction is a stark contradiction of the paradigm-diffusion model and functionalist logic more generally, but it is only one example. The elements of an alternative view have been built up throughout the book, but here I consolidate them.

The first point is that the seemingly simple idea of improving organizational performance via learning and reform actually rests on very demanding assumptions that are unlikely to be met. The earlier discussion has noted that accurately identifying the causes of military effectiveness and ineffectiveness is very difficult.[64] A huge number of factors are in play. Even long after the fact, scholars and analysts often can't agree why victories and defeats happened as they did. It is not just that discerning what causes what in the social world is difficult, but that such judgments are *deceptively* difficult. In the past and at present, people commonly think they know a lot more about cause and effect than they really do. One example might be the belief, very common among the historical actors in this book, but also in the contemporary example of bulletproofing, that battlefield results are determined by God or the intervention of supernatural entities. Adding to these huge difficulties was the fact that the military enterprise was constantly changing, in line with changes in the enemy (who of course tries to prevent any learning) and changes in contextual factors. Even if accurate knowledge could be accumulated, it would quickly become obsolete.[65]

Rather than efficient, functional learning and adaptation, the alternative perspective favored here is that the lessons actors draw about organizational performance are largely shaped by cultural considerations. Bulletproofing is an arresting example, but it is by no means unusual. Speaking of the bloody Sino-Japanese clashes in the 1590s, Lorge notes that for each side "the results of the battlefield reinforced preconceived notions of warfare. People learned the lessons they were inclined to learn, and even those were strongly affected by their political implications."[66] Considering sociologists' equivalent findings in the contemporary era, there is no reason to assume that modern Western military establishments are somehow immune to similar tendencies.[67]

Speaking of what he terms "the suicidal army," Theo Farrell describes how the Irish defense strategy of the 1920s moved away from a fairly successful and realistic approach based on guerilla war to deter a British invasion, to a prohibitively expensive and militarily infeasible posture of creating a conventional "British military in miniature."[68] Working from within a culture that privileged such conventional military templates, the Irish general staff "learned" lessons that made their army much less effective. Afterwards, Irish soldiers had three hours training on how to salute, but none on guerilla tactics.[69] It seems hard to dispute that at least in some cases contemporary militaries favor "gold-plated" high-prestige items (e.g., advanced aircraft and large warships) for symbolic reasons over priorities that would actually improve performance (e.g., more training and better maintenance of existing equipment).[70]

But assuming that rulers and generals could somehow suspend the cultural categories that inform and create their perceptions and mental categories, and learn to unravel the labyrinthine complexity of the causal relationships at work, what then? Harking back to a point made several times earlier, diagnosing a problem is in no way equivalent to solving it. The broad thrust of recent work on "war and society" in history, and military effectiveness in the social sciences, emphasizes that military performance is in large part a product of underlying institutional, societal, and cultural factors that are usually impervious to deliberate reform.[71]

What then of the view that a process of Darwinian elimination ensures efficiency and effectiveness?[72] The advantage of this account is to dispense with the implausible and unrealistic assumptions about learning as a route to effectiveness and rational reform via deliberate policy interventions. As Chase puts it of "stupid" ideas about the conduct of war: "Such notions did not survive long because the people who held them did not survive long."[73] If maladapted, ineffective militaries and polities are weeded out by the impersonal workings of military competition in the same way as failing firms in a competitive market, the presumption of efficiency and effectiveness can be reinstated.

In practice, however, the expectation of efficiency-through-elimination is frustrated. First, like the suicidal Irish army, most militaries are not tested in war most of the time, and even those at war are seldom tested to destruction. For the elimination mechanism to consistently promote convergence on an effective model, the rate of organizational "death" must be much higher than obtained during almost any historical era.[74] Systematic studies of the rate of elimination of polities from the international system via conquest not only show that such an eventuality is very rare, but that it is unrelated to factors like size, military capacity, or the presence of allies.[75] As one scholar puts it: "the survival of inefficient institutions remains a central puzzle in economic and international history."[76] Speaking of a theoretical stance closely related to the military revolution thesis, another concurs: "The classical realist position, according to which domestic institutions quickly and automatically evolve towards a single 'best adapted' form, finds little support in the research to date."[77] Similarly, rather than one dominant style of Western warfare and conquest, we are faced with the need to appreciate a diversity of forms.

Emphasizing the difficulty of understanding the complexity and diversity of historical and political processes, the depths of our ignorance, and the dangers of false certainty may be a sobering or self-defeating note on which to end a book. If we probably can't know anything, why write books at all? Rather than suggesting that such endeavors are futile, my hope is that this book will help to make us a little more reflective in thinking about our assumptions and preconceptions, a little more broad-minded in asking questions and selecting evidence, and perhaps even a little more willing to take history on its own terms.

Beyond the benefits of a better understanding of the past on its own terms, moving away from the conventional story of Western hegemony puts our current circumstances in a new light.[78] A more cosmopolitan, less ethnocentric perspective, giving due weight to regions beyond Europe, shows Western dominance of the international system as relatively fleeting, and thus makes it much less surprising if this dominance is now being challenged with the rise of powers beyond the West. A multipolar global international order becomes the historical norm rather than the exception. Although predictions are hard, especially about the future, and particularly for social scientists, if China and India were to become the mightiest of the great powers in the twenty-first century, this would in many ways be a return the situation that obtained around 1700. The questions that we ask, and fail to ask, about history change our views not only of where we have come from, but also where we are, and where we are going.

NOTES

Introduction. The Military Revolution and the First International System

1. Andrade 2016: 119; see also Roy and Lorge 2015: 1.
2. Diamond 1997.
3. Marshall 2005: 4; see also Bull and Watson 1984; Dunne and Reus-Smit 2017.
4. Black 1998; Agoston 2005; Andrade 2016: 2–3; Rodger 2011: 119.
5. Roberts 1955 [1995]: 18.
6. Thompson and Rasler 1999.
7. Tilly 1985: 78.
8. McNeil 1982: 117, 143; Rogers 1995a: 7; Glete 2002: 7; Gat 2006: 447; Andrade 2016: 115–116; de la Garza 2016: 7–9.
9. Peers 2011: 83.
10. Brewer 1989.
11. Parker 1996: 4.
12. Glete 2000; Rose 2001; Guilmartin 1974, 2002, 2011; Rommelse 2011.
13. Parker 1990: 163.
14. For the derivation of this figure, see Hoffman 2015: 3 footnote 5.
15. Among many others, see the discussion Black 1991; Rogers 1995a; Glete 2002; Gat 2006; Parrott 2012.
16. E.g., Bryant 2006; Gat 2006; Hoffman 2015; Karaman and Pamuk 2010; Gennaioli and Voth 2015; for critiques that make this point about the continuing dominance of the military revolution, see MacDonald 2014; Roy and Lorge 2015; Lee 2015; Andrade 2016.
17. Kennedy 1988; North and Thomas 1973; North 1990a.
18. Mann 1986; Hanson 1989; 2002; Keegan 1993; Diamond 1997; Jones 2003; Ferguson 2011.
19. Chase 2003; Hoffman 2015.
20. For example, Buzan and Little 2000: 246–250.
21. Thompson 1999.
22. MacDonald 2014: 18.
23. North 1990b: 24.
24. Anievas and Nişancioglu 2017: 48.
25. I thank one of the anonymous reviewers for pointing this out.
26. Frank 1998; Keene 2002; Hobson 2004, 2012.
27. Andrade 2011: 7.
28. For critiques, see Lemke 2003; Hobson 2004, 2012; Kang 2003, 2014; Hui 2005; Johnston 2012; Suzuki 2009; Zarakol 2010; Barkawi 2005, 2017; Dunne and Reus-Smit 2017; Go and Lawson 2017.

29. Black 2004b; Subrahmanyam 2006; Thornton 1999; Suzuki et al. 2014.

30. Lorge 2008: 7; see also Black 2004b: 153.

31. Frank 1998.

32. Pomeranz 2001; Bayly 2004; Glete 2002; Gat 2006; Darwin 2007; Headrick 2010; Buzan and Lawson 2013, 2015; Hoffman 2015.

33. Pomeranz 2001; Marks 2002; Rosenthal and Wong 2011.

34. Gray 2007: 85.

35. Elman and Elman 1999, 2008.

36. Thompson 1999; Spruyt 2005; MacDonald 2014.

37. Black 2004b: x; for exceptions, see Thompson 1999; Hobson 2004; Barkawi 2005; MacDonald 2014; Anievas and Nişancioglu 2015.

38. March and Olsen 1989, 1998; Powell and DiMaggio 1991b.

39. Black 2004b: 3.

40. Lee 2015: 2.

41. Elster 1989:: viii.

42. Elster 2000: 693.

43. von Clausewitz 2008: 101, 193.

44. Hoffman 2015: 45 and 39.

45. Rosen 1994.

46. Brooks 2007: 1; see also Rosen 1996.

47. Andrade 2016: 271.

48. March and Olsen 1998: 954; see also Pierson 2003: 190–191.

49. Lee 2015: 2; see also Gat 2006: 448.

50. Posen 1993: 20.

51. Waltz 1979: 77.

52. Resende-Santos 2007: 6.

53. Elster 2007: 274.

54. Alchian 1950; Friedman 1953; Nelson and Winter 1982.

55. Elster 1995: 404.

56. Elster 2000: 693.

57. Fazal 2007.

58. Sharman 2015, 2017

59. Apart from those already cited, see also Keegan 1976; Hanson 1989.

60. Meyer et al, 2006; Drori et al. 2006: 27-28; see also Meyer 2010.

61. Black 2004b: 169.

62. Black 2004b: 233.

63. Lynn 2008: xx.

64. Black 2004b: 124; Lynn 2008: xxviii.

65. Lee 2015: 6.

66. Though Powell and DiMaggio 1991a coined the term.

67. See also Hassner 2016.

68. Meyer and Rowan 1977

69. Meyer and Rowan 1977: 354.

70. Powell and DiMaggio 1991b: 3.

71. Parrott 2012: 259.

72. Parrott 2012: 306.
73. Parrott 2012: 309–310, see also Thomson 1994; Lynn 2008: 139.
74. Lynn 2008: 115.
75. Eyre and Suchman 1996; Farrell 2005.
76. Hassner 2016.
77. Charney 2004: 14–15; Kemper 2014: 26.
78. Reid 1982: 2.
79. Behrend 1999: 57–59.
80. Knight 1994.
81. Weigert 1996.
82. Vandervort 1998; Clayton 1999.
83. Wlodarczyk 2009.
84. Vandervort 1998.
85. Turner 1971.
86. Behrend 1999; Wlodarczyk 2009.
87. Weigert 1996.
88. Clayton 1999.
89. Wlodarczyk 2009.
90. Weigert 1996.
91. Behrend 1999; Weigert 1996.
92. Lan 1985.
93. Ellis 1999.
94. Gberie 2005; Wlodarczyk 2009.
95. Weigert 1996: 2.
96. Wlodarczyk 2009: 6, 35, 40; Ellis 1999: 261.
97. Ellis 1999: 264.
98. Wlodarczyk 2009: 14; see also Behrend 1999: 60.
99. George and Bennett 2004: 122.
100. Behrend 1999: 8.
101. Thornton 1999.
102. Wlodarczyck 2009: 1.
103. Behrend 1999: 61; Weigert 1996: 59, 90, 102.
104. Vandervort 1998: 139.
105. Weigert 1996: 94.
106. Gberie 2005: 83.
107. Powell and DiMaggio 1991b: 13.
108. Meyer and Rowan 1977.
109. Meyer 2010.
110. Busse et al. 2010; Jenkinson et al. 2016; Chang et al. 2016; Pace et al. 2016.

Chapter 1. Iberian Conquistadors and Supplicants

1. Marshall 2005: 4.
2. Vandervort 1998: 1; Darwin 2007: 52.
3. Cook 1998.

4. Tucker 2012.

5. Lee 2015: 259–260; Gat 2006: 483.

6. Parker 1996: 23.

7. Roberts [1955] 1995: 14.

8. Parker 1996: 18

9. Fuller 1954: 64.

10. Parker 1996: 24.

11. Parker 1996: 24, 45.

12. Tilly 1992; Glete 2002; Gat 2006; Lynn 2008; Parrott 2012; Hoffman 2015.

13. Thompson and Rasler 1999: 13.

14. van Creveld 1977; Hale 1986; Anderson 1988; Lynn 1994.

15. Clulow 2014: 4.

16. Cipolla 1965: 85.

17. Kamen 2002: 13; see also Tyce 2015.

18. Kamen 2002: 95–96

19. Hassig 2006; Kamen 2002; Restall 2003.

20. Restall 2003: 33–34.

21. Hoffman 2015: 9–12.

22. Headrick 2010; Hoffman 2015.

23. Roland 2016: 5–6.

24. Hoffman 2015: 8.

25. Guilmartin 1995: 312.

26. Lee 2011b: 4.

27. Thompson 1999: 163; Chase 2003: 80; Steele 1994: 8.

28. Headrick 2010: 97 and 114; see also Guilmartin 1995: 311.

29. Restall 2003: 143.

30. Lee 2011b: 4.

31. Guilmartin 1995: 311–312.

32. Restall 2003: 32.

33. Hassig 2006: 53; Lee 2015: 256.

34. Matthew and Oudijk 2007; Asselbergs 2008.

35. Lee 2011b: 11.

36. Hassig 2006: 5.

37. Lockhart 1999: 99.

38. Hoffman 2015: 12; see also Hassig 2006: 87; Glete 2000: 88.

39. Black 1998: 33–34; Headrick 2010: 95, 117.

40. Gat 2006: 483.

41. Disney 2009.

42. de Armond 1954: 126

43. Headrick 2010: 115–120; Lee 2011b: 7.

44. de Armond 1954: 126; Padden 1957: 111

45. de Armond 1954: 126.

46. de Armond 1954: 130.

47. Padden 1957: 111.

48. quoted in Padden 1957: 121.
49. Restall 2003: 70–72; Steele 1994: 6–37.
50. Secoy 1953; Spicer 1967; Schilz and Worcester 1987.
51. Lee 2011a: 52; Charney 2004: 18–20.
52. Malone 1991.
53. Steele 1994.
54. Lee 2011a: 69; Chase 2003: 81.
55. Watt 2002.
56. Steele 1994.
57. Carlos and Lewis 2010.
58. Black 1998; Headrick 2010
59. Hassig 2006: 3.
60. Thornton 1999, 2011; Quirk and Richardson 2014; Pearson 1998; Cook 1994; Hess 1978
61. Quirk and Richardson 2014
62. Thornton 2011: 167
63. Parker 1996: 136.
64. Thornton 2007: 148; see also Vandervort 1998: 26; Lee 2015: 259
65. Disney 2009: 28–30.
66. Disney 2009: 138.
67. Thornton 2011: 186.
68. Thornton 1999: 103–104.
69. Pearson 1998; Prestholdt 2001
70. Thornton 2007: 145
71. Pearson 1998: 131.
72. Casale 2010.
73. Disney 2009: 302; Casale 2010: 69; Headrick 2010: 144.
74. Casale 2010: 59–60; Black 1998: 35.
75. Thornton 2007: 153; Disney 2009: 166.
76. Pearson 1998: 144.
77. Isaacman 1972.
78. Subrahmanyam 2012: 205.
79. Thornton 2011: 187.
80. Vandervort 1998: 26; see also Cipolla 1965: 141.
81. Parker 1996: 136.
82. Scammel 1989: 35–38; Thornton 2007: 148.
83. Bethencourt and Curto 2007; Disney 2009; Subrahmanyam 2012.
84. Guilmartin 1995: 313.
85. Thornton 1999: 23 and 29.
86. Disney 2009: 32.
87. Disney 2009: 302.
88. Prestholdt 2001: 398.
89. Headrick 2010: 143.
90. Thornton 1999.

91. Casale 2010: 72–74.

92. Andrade 2011: 7; see also Clulow 2014: 4.

93. Subrahmanyam and Thomas 1990: 301.

94. Disney 2009: 130.

95. Tracy 1990: 5–6.

96. Subrahmanyam 1995: 756.

97. Disney 2009: 132.

98. Glete 2000: 80; Matthews 2015: 174–176.

99. Glete 2000: 79; Matthews 2015: 177.

100. Cipolla 1965.

101. Guilmartin 1995: 315.

102. Casale 2010: 69.

103. Marshall 1980: 18; Glete 2000: 81; Headrick 2010: 64 and 71.

104. E.g., Hoffman 2015.

105. Casale 2010: 70.

106. Boxer 1969; Marshall 1980: 19; Chaudhuri 1985: 66; Disney 2009: 151; Subrahmanyam 1995: 786.

107. Winius 1971: 92.

108. Pearson 1990: 77.

109. Subrahmanyam 2012: 201–202; see also Marshall 1980: 22; Black 2004a: 216.

110. Andrade 2015; 2016.

111. Andrade 2016: 127–128.

112. Andrade 2016: 129–130.

113. Andrade 2016: 130.

114. Cipolla 1965; Clulow 2009.

115. Glete 2000: 77, 87; Richards 1993: 4, 68, 75; Alam and Subrahmanyam 1998: 13–16; Tagliacozzo 2002: 85; Washbrook 2004: 512.

116. Clulow 2014: 139.

117. Biedermann 2009: 276.

118. Headrick 2010: 76.

119. Chaudhuri 1985: 78; Gommans 2002: 77; Darwin 2007: 54.

120. Quoted in Cipolla 1965: 138.

121. Clulow 2014: 2.

122. Swope 2009: 67.

123. Chaudhuri 1985: 78–79.

124. Phillips and Sharman 2015.

125. Biedermann 2009; there were other abortive efforts in Burma and Cambodia, Subrahmanyam and Thomas 1990: 305; Subrahmanyam 2007: 1372.

126. Subrahmanyam 2012: 178.

127. Winius 1971: 76.

128. Winius 1971: 22.

129. Wickremesekera 2015.

130. Winius 1971: 33.

131. Wellen 2015: 460; Wickremesekera 2015: 289.

132. Guilmartin 1995: 316; Black 1998: 33.

133. Parker 1996: 131.

134. Parker 1996: 130.

135. Parker 1996: 131.

136. Parker 1996:14.

137. Parker 2002: 203.

138. Disney 2009: 302–305, 319–320; Subrahmanyam 2012: 202–206.

139. Subrahmanyam 1990

Chapter 2. Company Sovereigns and the Empires of the East

1. Tilly 1985, 1992.

2. Tilly 1975, 1985, 1992; Downing 1992; Ertman 1997; Glete 2002.

3. Steensgaard 1973; Phillips and Sharman 2015.

4. E.g., North 1990a.

5. Erikson and Assenova 2015; Erikson 2014; Ward 2008; Weststeijn 2014; Stern 2009, 2011.

6. Stern 2006; Cavanagh 2011.

7. Galbraith 1970; Slinn 1971; Vail 1976; Neil-Tomlinson 1977.

8. Klein 1981.

9. Steensgaard 1973; Blussé and Gaastra 1981; Stern 2009; Erikson and Assenova 2015

10. Ward 2008: 15.

11. Weststeijn 2014: 28.

12. Stern 2011: viii.

13. Wilson 2015: 258.

14. Boxer 1965: 24.

15. Clulow 2014: 14; Adams 1996: 19.

16. Steensgaard 1973: 131; Pearson 1990: 85; Adams 2005.

17. Gaastra 1981; 2003.

18. Boxer 1965: 23–24.

19. See The Charter Of The Dutch East India Company. http://rupertgerritsen.tripod.com/pdf/published/VOC_Charter_1602.pdf.

20. Tracy 1990: 2; see also North 1990b: 24.

21. Quoted in Clulow 2014: 63.

22. Boxer 1965: 69; Mostert 2007: 19.

23. Tracy 1990: 7; Ward 2008: 31.

24. Weststeijn 2014: 15.

25. Chaudhuri 1985, 1990; Pearson 2003; Bose 2009.

26. Chaudhuri 1985: 84–85.

27. Biedermann 2009: 272–274.

28. Boxer 1965: 104; Kian 2008: 293; Locher-Scholten 1994: 94.

29. Milton 1999.

30. Boxer 1965: 94; Ward 2008: 15–18; Tagliacozzo 2002: 77; Weststeijn 2014: 15.

31. Ward 2008: 31.

32. Kian 2008: 297–301.

33. Koshy 1989: 4; Odegard 2014: 9.

34. Tagliacozzo 2002: 79, however elsewhere he is much more equivocal, e.g., 2002: 81, 87.

35. Lieberman 2003.

36. Mostert 2007: 6.

37. Kemper 2014: 30.

38. Lorge 2008: 20.

39. Sun 2003: 495.

40. Sun 2003: 501–506.

41. Eaton and Wagoner 2014: 10–15.

42. Ricklefs 1993: 13.

43. Chase 2003; Casale 2010.

44. E.g., Cipolla 1965; Parker 1996; Hoffman 2015.

45. Marshall 1980: 20.

46. Ricklefs 1993; Charney 2004.

47. Reid 1982; Lorge 2008; Andrade 2016.

48. Ricklefs 1993: 5; Kemper 2014: 14.

49. Nagtegaal 1996; Moertono 2009.

50. Ricklefs 1993: 37–38.

51. Charney 2004: 56.

52. Reid 1982; Kemper 2014.

53. Mostert 2007: 22.

54. Parker 2002.

55. Mostert 2007: 28–29.

56. Charney 2004: 278–279.

57. Lorge 2008: 110.

58. Lorge 2008: 98, 110; see also Boxer 1965: 100; Pearson 1998: 139.

59. Locher-Scholten 1994.

60. Charney 2004: 243.

61. Charney 2004: 263–264.

62. Black 1998: 64.

63. Andrade 2011: 36–37.

64. Andrade 2011: 47.

65. Andrade 2011: 13–15; 2016: 5.

66. Clulow 2014: 16.

67. Clulow 2009: 85.

68. Quoted in Clulow 2014: 135.

69. Koshy 1989.

70. Odegard 2014: 14.

71. Wickremesekera 2015

72. Marshall 1980: 22.

73. Tagliacozzo 2002: 87.

74. Mostert 2007: 11.

75. Quoted in Weststeijn 2014: 18.

76. Quoted in Weststeijn 2014: 22.

77. Quoted in Boxer 1965: 95.

78. Adams 1996.

79. Stern 2009.

80. Stern 2009.

81. Washbrook 2004: 513–514.

82. Watson 1980: 77.

83. Watson 1980: 77.

84. Parker 2002: 200.

85. Pearson 1990: 91.

86. Chaudhuri 1965: 64.

87. Erikson 2014.

88. Chaudhuri 1965; Clulow 2009.

89. Hasan 1991: 357.

90. Hasan 1991: 356.

91. Subrahmanyam 1992; Richards 1993; Alam and Subrahmanyam 1998; Gommans 2002; Roy and Lorge 2015; de la Garza 2016.

92. Hasan 2004.

93. Vigneswaran 2014.

94. Watson 1980: 73.

95. Richards 1993: 239–240.

96. Hasan 1991: 360; Chaudhuri 1985: 87; Kumar 2015: 188.

97. Kumar 2015.

98. Richards 1993: 241.

99. Roy 2013: 1127; Hoffman 2015: 15.

100. Prakash 2002.

101. Gommans 2002.

102. Alam and Subrahmanyam 1998.

103. Gommans 1995, 2001.

104. Koshy 1989.

105. Koshy 1989.

106. Black 2004a: 220–221.

107. Parker 1996: 133.

108. Watson 1980: 80.

109. Parker 1996: 133.

110. Tagliacozzo 2002: 87; Marshall 2005: 135, 156; Lynn 2008: 159.

111. Blussé and Gaastra 1981: 8; Pearson 1990: 95–96; Chaudhuri 1985: 86.

112. Howard 1976: 52.

113. Parker 1996: 133.

114. Marshall 2005; Roy 2011b.

115. Stern 2009.

116. Bayly 1998: 33; Marshall 2005: 230; Peers 2007: 246.

117. Roy 2011b.

118. Cooper 2003.

119. Washbrook 2004: 481–482; Peers 2015: 303.

120. Cooper 2003: 538.

121. Marshall 2005: 207.

122. Parker 1996: 133; Headrick 2010: 149–151; Hoffman 2015: 86–87.

123. Roy 2013: 1130; see also Roy 2011a: 199, 217.

124. Chase 2003: 97–98.

125. Gommans and Kolff 2001: 40; Roy 2011a: 217; Peers 2011: 81; Washbrook 2004: 293.

126. Black 2004b; Peers 2011: 82; Cooper 2003: 540–41.

127. Eaton and Wagoner 2014: 16–17; see also Gommans and Kolff 2001: 34–35.

128. Roy 2011a: 199–201; see also Gommans 2002: 152; Peers 2011: 82.

129. Chase 2003: 136.

130. Cooper 2003; Roy 2011b.

131. Rogers 1995a: 6.

132. Roy 2013: 1143.

133. Marshall 2005: 126.

134. Kolff 2001.

135. Brewer 1989; Tilly 1985, 1992.

136. Streusand 1989, 2001; Gommans 2002; de la Garza 2016.

137. Richards 1993: 24–25.

138. Richards 1993: 19–25; Gommans 2002: 80–91; Streusand 2001: 353.

139. Gommans and Kolff 2001: 23.

140. Streusand 2011: 206.

141. Streusand 2011: 208.

142. Richards 1993: 75, 185.

143. Gommans 2002; Lorge 2008, de la Garza 2016.

144. Gommans 2002: 69; Hasan 2004: 126; de la Garza 2016: 190.

145. Washbrook 2004: 501–502; Roy 2011a: 213–214.

146. Roy 2011a; Roy 2013.

147. Gommans 2001: 365–369.

148. Roy 2013: 1152.

149. Roy: 2011a: 215.

150. Peers 2011: 83.

151. Black 2004a: 219.

152. Marshall 2005: 124; Roy 2011a: 212.

153. Cooper 2003: 452; Peers 2011: 101.

154. Peers 2011: 99.

155. Gommans and Kolff 2001: 21

156. Roy 2013: 1151.

157. Marshall 2005: 230, 251.

158. Roy 2013: 1139.

159. Roy 2013: 1138–1139.

160. Lynn 2008: 157.

161. Contra Bryant 2013.

162. Washbrook 2004: 512.

163. Parker 1996: 4.

164. Taken from Eaton and Wagoner 2014: 19–21.

Chapter 3. The Asian Invasion of Europe in Context

1. Scammel 1989: 2.

2. Davies 2007.

3. Black 2004b: 76.

4. Agoston 2012: 113.

5. Casale 2010; Chase 2003; Black 1998: 31.

6. Tuck 2008: 497.

7. Wheatcroft 2008.

8. Parker 1996: 136.

9. Hodgson 1974; McNeill 1982.

10. Black 2004b: 2; see also MacDonald 2014: 27.

11. Black 1995: 99; Guilmartin 1995: 302–304; Agoston 1998: 129; Agoston 2005: 6; Agoston 2012: 110; Borekci 2006: 408.

12. Parker 1996: 35–37.

13. E.g. Downing 1992; Ertman 1997; Glete 2002; for a critique of this view, see Frost 2000; Davies 2007; Stevens 2007.

14. Parker 1996: 37.

15. Parker 1995b: 337.

16. Parker 1996: 173; see the discussion of Parker's view of the Habsburgs and the military revolution in Agoston 1998: 128 footnote 9.

17. Parker 1990: 173.

18. Agoston 1998, 2012.

19. Agoston 2012: 125.

20. Black 1995: 99.

21. Boxer 1965: 13.

22. For an exception, see Rudolph and Rudolph 2010.

23. Guilmartin 1995: 318.

24. Parker 1995b: 341.

25. Rogers 1995b: 56, 60–61.

26. Black 1995: 104; see also Guilmartin 1995: 302–304.

27. Guilmartin 1974, 1995; Glete 2000.

28. Hess 1978: 15.

29. Murphey 1993.

30. Murphey 1999: 37–39; Aksan 2011: 149; Agoston 2012: 115.

31. Murphey 1999: 45; Aksan 2011: 149–150.

32. Murphey 1999: 19, 32; Glete 2002: 39; Parrott 2012: 30; Agoston 2014: 93.

33. Agoston 2005: 23.

34. Borekci 2006; Agoston 2014: 96–98.

35. Aksan 2011.

36. Davies 2007.

37. Murphey 1999: 20.

38. Agoston 2014: 123.

39. Murphey 1999: 15; Chase 2003; Agoston 1998: 138–140; 2005.

40. Hodgson 1974; McNeill 1982.

41. Agoston 2005.

42. Chase 2003: 97.

43. Murphey 1999: 106.

44. Murphey 1999: 30–32.

45. Murphey 1999: 49; Dale 2010: 107; Aksan 2011: 143.

46. Glete 2002: 142–143.

47. Agoston 1998: 128.

48. Aksan 2007b: 268.

49. Agoston 2005.

50. Glete 2000: 96.

51. Murphey 1993; Colas 2016.

52. Murphey 1999: 32.

53. Agoston 2012: 117; Borekci 2006: 430.

54. Guilmartin 1995: 303.

55. Murphey 1999: 15.

56. Agoston 2012: 118.

57. Borekci 2006: 424–425; Agoston 2012: 111–112.

58. Murphey 1999: 21.

59. Murphey 1999: 10; Borekci 2006: 409; Agoston 2014: 124.

60. Black 1998: 108; Chase 2003: 203.

61. Aksan 2007a: 1.

62. Murphey 1999: 1.

63. Agoston 2005: 201.

64. Aksan 2007a: 55; Aksan 2011: 149; Dale 2010: 133.

65. Murphey 1999: 16.

66. Agoston 2012: 129.

67. Aksan 2007a: 38; Aksan 2011: 152, 156–158; Agoston 2012: 112; Agoston 2014: 123; Barkey 2008: 228–229.

68. Agoston 2012: 1300.

69. Aksan 2007b: 262.

70. Aksan 2002: 256.

71. Aksan 2007a: 56–57; Agoston 2012: 127.

72. Guilmartin 1995: 321; Murphey 1999: 49.

73. Aksan 2011: 159; Agoston 2005: 204; Agoston 2012: 133–134.

74. Grant 1999; Aksan 2002; Agoston 2014; Kadercan 2013/2014.

75. Murphey 1999: 14; Grant 1999: 182, 200; Chase 2003: 93–95.

76. Agoston 2012: 125.

77. Aksan 2007a: 53.

78. Tuck 2008: 498.

79. Ralston 1990; Stevens 2007.

80. Frost 2000: 13.

81. Hoffman 2015: 90; Aksan 1993: 222. In fact the Russian tsars paid tribute to the khan of the Tartars until as late as 1683 (Black 1998: 15).

82. Aksan 1993: 224.

83. Frost 2000: 320.

84. Hess 1978; Cook 1994; Black 2004b: 79.

85. Cook 1994: 83.

86. Cook 1994: 85; Disney 2009: 2.

87. Disney 2009: 11; Cook 1994: 84.

88. Hess 1978: 12.

89. Hess 1978: 32.

90. Pedreira 2007: 56, 59.

91. Hess 1978: 42.

92. Cook 1994: 124.

93. Cook 1994: 247–254.

94. Cook 1994.

95. Disney 2009: 19.

96. Hess 1978: 95.

97. Hess 1978: 121.

98. Cook 1994: 181.

99. Disney 2009: 2, 13.

100. Disney 2009: 13.

101. Cook 1994: 144; see also Glete 2000: 78.

102. Murphey 1993; Colas 2016.

103. Hess 1978: 193.

104. Rogers 1995b; Guilmartin 1995.

105. Black 1995: 100.

106. Parker 1995b: 355–356.

107. Parker 1995b: 356.

108. Black 2004b: ix.

109. Murphey 1999: 13.

110. Hoffman 2015: 147–148, 169–170.

111. Gennaioli and Voth 2015: 1409–1413.

112. Gennaioli and Voth 2015: 1437; see also Karaman and Pamuk 2010.

113. E.g., Blaydes and Chaney 2013; Hoffman 2015: 148.

114. Brewer 1989; North and Weingast 1989.

115. Andrade 2011:11; see also Glete 2000: 11.

116. Black 2004a: 212.

117. Parker 1995b: 338.

118. Mortimer 2004b.

119. Rogers 1995c.

120. Levy 1983: 10.

121. Downing 1992; Ertman 1997.

122. Ralston 1990; see Mahoney's 1999 critique of Ertman 1997.

123. Roberts [1955] 1995: 20.

124. Roberts [1955] 1995: 29.

125. E.g., Parker 1996: 3; Bayly 1998: 30; Rogers 1995b: 61–62, 74–75; Black 2004a: 218; Lorge 2008: 5–6.

126. Gat 2006.

127. Lorge 2008: 1.

128. See also Lorge 2005; Sun 2003; Swope 2005, 2009; Andrade 2011, 2016; Andrade, Kang, and Cooper 2014.

129. Sun 2003; Lorge 2008; Andrade 2016.

130. Lorge 2008: 5–6, 20–21, 177–178; see also Gommans 2002: 134–135, 159; Charney 2004: 72, 278–279; Lee 2015: 269–287.

131. Gommans 2002; Streusand 2011.

132. Gommans and Kolff 2001; Gommans 2002.

133. Eaton and Wagoner 2014.

134. Hodgson 1974; McNeill 1982: 95–96.

135. 2002; Streusand 2011; Lorge 2008; Swope 2009; Eaton and Wagoner 2014; Andrade 2011, 2016; de la Garza 2016; Gommans and Kolff 2001.

136. Johnston 2012; Kang 2010, 2014; Suzuki et al. 2014; Hobson 2004; Hui 2005; Ringmar 2012.

137. Fazal 2007; Kang 2014; Butcher and Griffiths 2017.

138. Hui 2005.

139. Hui 2005: 1.

140. Hui 2005: 36.

141. See also Lorge 2005: 2.

142. Lorge 2008: 6–7, 178; see also Black 2004b: 153.

143. Lorge 2008: 99–100.

144. Black 2004a: 215, 223–224; 2004b: 67–72.

145. Thornton 1999: 8; see also Hobson 2012; Kadercan 2013/2014; Suzuki et al. 2014.

146. Agoston 2005; Subrahmanyam 2006; Aksan 2007; Lorge 2008; Gommans 2002.

Conclusion. How the Europeans Won in the End (Before They Later Lost)

1. Philpott 2001; Crawford 2002; Keene 2002; Spruyt 2005; Reus-Smit 2013.

2. MacDonald 2014: 10.

3. Doyle 1986; Mann 1993; Gat 2006; Darwin 2007.

4. Vandervort 1998: 1.

5. MacDonald 2014: 17.

6. For differing views of the significance of the conference itself, see Craven 2015.

7. Vandervort 1998: 30.

8. See among many others Chamberlain 1974; Snyder 1991; Cain and Hopkins 1993; Mommsen 1980; Hobsbawm 2010; Hyam 2010; Darwin 2014.

9. The "capacity aggregation" idea, see Morrow 1991; Liberman 1996; Hager and Lake 2000; Spruyt 2005.

10. Spruyt 2005: 39.

11. Reus-Smit 2011.

12. Bosworth 1979; Suzuki 2009; Barnhart 2016.

13. Bosworth 1996: 99.

14. Bosworth 1996: 101.

15. Vandervort, 1998: 32–33.

16. Bosworth 1996: 94.

17. Suzuki 2005: 154.

18. Brunschwig 1966; Cooke 1973; Barnhart 2016.

19. Locher-Scholten 1994.

20. Lorge 2008: 98.

21. Lorge 2008: 110; see also Black 2004b: 154.

22. Giordani 1916; Galbraith 1970; Slinn 1971; Vail 1976; Neil-Tomlinson 1977.

23. Hoffman 2015: 208; see also Davis and Huttenback 1986.

24. Spruyt 2005: 55–77; MacDonald 2009: 61–62.

25. Barkawi 2005; 2017.

26. Headrick 1981.

27. Headrick 2010: 146–147. In comparison, in the nineteenth century the resistance by the North American Indians was consistently sapped by successive deadly epidemics, see Headrick 2010: 123–127.

28. Charney 2004: 72; Black 2004b: 159.

29. Vandervort 1998; Charney 2004; Darwin 2007; MacDonald 2014.

30. Vandervort 1998; Thompson 1999; Newbury 2003; Spruyt 2005; Darwin 2007; MacDonald 2014.

31. Ralston 1990; Charney 2004: 243, 263; Black 2004b: 219; Roy 2013: 1152; Gommans and Kolff 2001: 40; Headrick 2010: 139; Wickremesekera 2015.

32. Vandervort 1998.

33. Headrick 2010: 168.

34. Vandervort 1998: 185.

35. Judd and Surridge 2002.

36. MacDonald 2014: 231–232; see also MacDonald 2013.

37. Fay 1998; Wong 2000; Lovell 2011; Bickers 2012.

38. Hanes and Sanello 2002; Bickers 2012.

39. Perdue 2005.

40. Lorge 2005: 1.

41. Andrade 2016: 243; Mao 2016: 30.

42. Lorge 2008: 168.

43. Polachek 1991.

44. Mao 2016.

45. Ralston 1990.

46. Finnemore 1996; Wendt 1999; Finnemore 2003; Phillips 2011; Reus-Smit 2013.

47. Jackson 1993; Philpott 2001; Crawford 2002; Reus-Smit 2013.

48. Merom 2003; Arreguin-Toft 2005; Lyall and Wilson 2009; Caverley 2014.

49. Biddle 2004.

50. Mack 1975; Merom 2003; Record 2007.

51. Bacevich 2016.

52. Black 2004b: x.

53. Andrade 2016: 115–116.

54. Nelson and Winter 1982.

55. Alchian 1950.

56. McNeill 1982: 147.

57. Hoffman 2015: 53.

58. March and Olsen 1989, 1998; Pierson 2004; Sharman 2015.

59. Gennaoili and Voth 2015: 1409.

60. Rogowski 1999: 115.

61. Glete 2002: 2–3; see also p. 28.

62. Tuck 2008: 470; see also Waltz 1979: 77; Resende-Santos 2007: 6; Reid 1982: 1; Posen 1993: 120; Walt 2002: 203.

63. Gray 2007: 84, see also Chase 2003: xv.

64. Biddle 2004; Brooks 2007.

65. March and Olsen 1989: 55; 1998: 954.

66. Lorge 2008: 86.

67. Meyer and Rowan 1977; March and Olsen 1989; Powell and DiMaggio 1991.

68. Farrell 2005, 2007.

69. Farrell 2007: 147.

70. Eyre and Suchman 1996.

71. See the journal *War and Society* and book series of this name.

72. For general work on this evolutionary perspective, see Modelski and Poznanski 1996; Kahler 1999; Thompson 2001; Rapkin 2001; Spruyt 2001.

73. Chase 2003: xv.

74. Sharman 2015.

75. Strang 1991; Lake and O'Mahony 2004; Fazal 2007.

76. Kahler 1999: 164.

77. Rogowski 1999: 137.

78. Buzan and Little 2000; Hobden and Hobson 2002.

Adams, Julia. 1996. "Principals and Agents, Colonials and Company Men: The Decay of Colonial Control in the Dutch East Indies." *American Sociological Review* 61 (1): 12–28.

Adams, Julia. 2005. *The Familial State: Ruling Families and Merchant Capitalism in Early Modern Europe.* Ithaca, NY: Cornell University Press.

Agoston, Gabor. 1998. "Habsburgs and Ottomans: Defense, Military Change and Shifts in Power." *Turkish Studies Association Bulletin* 22 (1):126–141.

Agoston, Gabor. 2005. *Guns for the Sultan: Military Power and the Weapons Industry in the Ottoman Empire.* Cambridge: Cambridge University Press.

Agoston, Gabor. 2012. "Empires and Warfare in East-Central Europe, 1550–1750: The Ottoman-Habsburg Rivalry and Military Transformation." In *European Warfare 1350–1750*, edited by Frank Tallet and D.J.B. Trim, 110–135. Cambridge: Cambridge University Press.

Agoston, Gabor. 2014. "Firearms and Military Adaptation: The Ottomans and the European Military Revolution, 1450–1800." *Journal of World History* 15 (1): 85–124.

Aksan, Virginia. 1993. "The One-Eyed Fighting the Blind: Mobilization, Supply, and Command in the Russo-Turkish War of 1768–1774." *International History Review* 15 (2): 221–238.

Aksan, Virginia. 2002. "Breaking the Spell of Baron de Tott: Reframing the Question of Military Reform in the Ottoman Empire 1760–1830." *International History Review* 24 (2): 253–277.

Aksan, Virginia H. 2007a. *Ottoman Wars 1700–1870: An Empire Besieged.* Harlow: Pearson Longman.

Aksan, Virginia H. 2007b. "The Ottoman Military and State Transformation in a Globalizing World." *Comparative Studies of South Asia, Africa and the Middle East* 27 (2): 259–272.

Aksan, Virginia H. 2011. "Ottoman Military Ethnographies of Warfare, 1500–1800." In *Empires and Indigenes: Intercultural Alliances, Imperial Expansion, and Warfare in the Early Modern World*, edited by Wayne E. Lee, 141–163. New York: New York University Press.

Alam, Muzaffar, and Sanjay Subrahmanyam (eds). 1998. *The Mughal State 1526–1750.* Delhi: Oxford University Press.

Alchian, Armen A. 1950. "Uncertainty, Evolution and Economic Theory." *Journal of Political Economy* 58 (3): 211–221.

Anderson, M. S. 1988. *War and Society in Europe of the Old Regime, 1618–1789.* Montreal: McGill-Queen's University Press.

Andrade, Tonio. 2004. "The Company's Chinese Pirates: How the Dutch East India Company Tried to Lead a Coalition of Pirates to War against China, 1621–1662." *Journal of World History* 15 (4): 415–444.

Andrade, Tonio. 2011. *Lost Colony: The Untold Story of China's First Victory over the West*. Princeton: Princeton University Press.

Andrade, Tonio. 2015. "Cannibals with Cannons: The Sino-Portuguese Clashes of 1521–22 and the Early Chinese Adoption of Western Guns." *Journal of Early Modern History* 19 (4): 311–335.

Andrade, Tonio. 2016. *The Gunpowder Age: China Military Innovation and the Rise of the West in World History*. Princeton: Princeton University Press.

Andrade, Tonio, Hybok Hweon Kang, and Kirsten Cooper. 2014. "A Korean Military Revolution: Parallel Military Innovations in East Asia and Europe." *Journal of World History* 25 (1): 51–84.

Anievas, Alexander, and Kerem Nişancioglu. 2015. *How the West Came to Rule: The Geopolitical Origins of Capitalism*. London: Pluto.

Anievas, Alexander, and Kerem Nişancioglu. 2017. "How Did the West Usurp the Rest? Origins of the Great Divergence over the Longue Durée." *Comparative Studies in Society and History* 59 (1): 34–67.

Arreguin-Toft, Ivan. 2005. *How the Weak Win Wars: A Theory of Asymmetric Conflict*. Cambridge: Cambridge University Press.

Asselbergs, Florine. 2008. *Conquered Conquistadors: The Lienzo de Quauquechollan, a Nahua Vision of the Conquest of Guatemala*. Boulder: University Press of Colorado.

Bacevich, Andrew J. 2016. *America's War for the Greater Middle East: A Military History*. New York: Random House.

Barkawi, Tarak. 2005. *Globalization and War*. Langham MD: Rowman and Littlefield.

Barkawi, Tarak. 2017. *Soldiers of Empire: India and British Armies in World War II*. Cambridge: Cambridge University Press.

Barkey, Karen. 2008. *Empire of Difference: The Ottomans in Comparative Perspective*. Cambridge: Cambridge University Press.

Barnhart, Joslyn. 2016. "Status Competition and Territorial Aggression: Evidence from the Scramble for Africa." *Security Studies* 25 (3): 385–419.

Bayly, C. A. 1998. "The First Age of Global Imperialism, c.1760–1830." *Journal of Imperial and Commonwealth History* 26 (2) 28–47.

Bayly, C. A. 2004. *The Birth of the Modern World 1780–1914*. Oxford: Blackwell.

Behrend, Heike. 1999. *Alice Lakwena and the Holy Spirits: War in Northern Uganda 1986–97*. Athens: Ohio University Press.

Bethencourt, Francisco, and Diogo Ramada Curto (Eds). 2007. *Portuguese Oceanic Expansion, 1400–1800*. Cambridge: Cambridge University Press.

Bickers, Robert. 2012. *The Scramble for China: Foreign Devils in the Qing Empire 1832–1914*. London: Penguin.

Biddle, Stephen. 2004. *Military Power: Explaining Victory and Defeat in Modern Battle*. Princeton: Princeton University Press.

Biedermann, Zoltan. 2009. "The Matrioshka Principle and How It Was Overcome: The Portuguese and Hapsburg Imperial Attitudes in Sri Lanka and the Responses of the Rulers of Kotte (1506–1598)" *Journal of Early Modern History* 13 (4): 265–310.

Black, Jeremy. 1991. *A Military Revolution? Military Change and European Society 1550–1800*. London: Palgrave.

Black, Jeremy. 1995. "A Military Revolution? A 1660–1792 Perspective." In *The Military Revolution Debate: Readings in the Military Transformation of Early Modern Europe*, edited by Clifford J. Rogers, 95–116. Boulder, CO: Westview.

Black, Jeremy. 1998. *War and the World: Military Power and the Fate of Continents 1450–2000*. New Haven: Yale University Press.

Black, Jeremy. 2004a. "A Wider Perspective: War Outside the West." In *Early Modern Military History, 1450–1815*, edited by Geoff Mortimer, 212–226. Houndmills, UK: Palgrave.

Black, Jeremy. 2004b. *Rethinking Military History*. Abingdon, UK: Routledge.

Blaydes, Lisa, and Eric Chaney. 2013. "The Feudal Revolution and Europe's Rise: Political Divergence of the Christian West and the Muslim World before 1500 CE." *American Political Science Review*, 107 (1): 16–34.

Blussé, Leonard, and Femme Gaastra (eds.). 1981. *Companies and Trade: Essays on Overseas Trading Companies During the Ancien Regime*. Leiden: Leiden University Press.

Blussé, Leonard, and Femme Gaastra. 1981. "Companies and Trade: Some Reflections on a Workshop and a Concept." In *Companies and Trade: Essays on Overseas Trading Companies During the Ancien Regime*, edited by Leonard Blussé and Femme Gaastra, 3–16. Leiden: Leiden University Press.

Borekci, Gunhan. 2006 "A Contribution to the Military Revolution Debate: The Janissaries Use of Volley Fire during the Long Ottoman-Habsburg War of 1593–1606 and the Problem of Origins." *Acta Orientalia Academiae Scientarium Hungaricae* 59 (4): 407–438.

Bose, Sugata. 2009. *A Hundred Horizons: The Indian Ocean in an Age of Global Empire*. Cambridge: Harvard University Press.

Bosworth, R.J.B. 1979. *Italy, Least of the Great Powers: Italian Foreign Policy before the First World War*. Cambridge: Cambridge University Press.

Bosworth, R.J.B. 1996. *Italy and the Wider World 1860–1960*. London: Routledge.

Boxer, C. R. 1965. *The Dutch Seaborne Empire 1600–1800*. New York: Alfred Knopf.

Boxer, C. R. 1969. "A Note on Portuguese Reactions to the Revival of the Red Sea Spice Trade and the Rise of Atjeh." *Journal of Southeast Asian History* 10 (December): 415–428.

Brewer, John. 1989. *The Sinews of Power: War, Money and the English State 1688–1783*. London: Unwin Hyman.

Brooks, Risa A. 2007. "Introduction: The Impact of Culture, Society, Institutions, and International Forces on Military Effectiveness." In *Creating Military Power: The Sources of Military Effectiveness*, edited by Risa A. Brooks and Elizabeth Stanley, 1–26. Palo Alto: Stanford University Press.

Brunschwig, Henri. 1966. *French Colonialism, 1871–1914: Myths and Realities*. New York: Prager.

Bryant, G. J. 2013. *The Emergence of British Power in India 1600–1784: A Grand Strategic Interpretation*. Woodbridge: Boyall.

Bryant, Joseph M. 2006. "The West and the Rest Revisited: Debating Capitalist Origins, European Colonialism, and the Advent of Modernity." *Canadian Journal of Sociology/Cahiers Canadien de Sociologie* 31 (4): 403–444.

Bull, Hedley, and Adam Watson (eds). 1984. *The Expansion of International Society*. Oxford: Oxford University Press.

Busse, Jeffrey A., Amit Goyal, and Sunil Wahal. 2010. "Performance and Persistence in Institutional Investment Management." *Journal of Finance* 65 (2): 765–790.

Butcher, Charles R. and Ryan D. Griffith. 2017. "Between Eurocentrism and Babel: A Framework for the Analysis of States, State Systems, and International Orders." *International Studies Quarterly* 61 (2): 328–336.

Buzan, Barry, and George Lawson. 2013. "The Global Transformation: The Nineteenth Century and the Making of Modern International Relations." *International Studies Quarterly* 57 (3): 620–634.

Buzan, Barry and George Lawson. 2015. *The Global Transformation: History, Modernity and the Making of International Relations*. Cambridge: Cambridge University Press.

Buzan, Barry, and Richard Little. 2000. *International Systems in World History: Remaking the Study of International Relations*. Oxford: Oxford University Press.

Cain, P. J., and A. G. Hopkins. 1993. *British Imperialism: Innovation and Expansion 1688–1914*. London: Longman.

Carlos, Ann M., and Frank D. Lewis. 2010. *Commerce by a Frozen Sea: Native Americans and the Fur Trade*. Philadelphia: University of Pennsylvania Press.

Casale, Giancarlo. 2010. *The Ottoman Age of Exploration*. Oxford: Oxford University Press.

Cavanagh, Edward. 2011. "A Company with Sovereignty and Subjects of Its Own? The Case of the Hudson's Bay Company, 1670–1763." *Canadian Journal of Law and Society* 26 (1): 25–50.

Caverley, Jonathan D. 2014. *Democratic Militarism: Voting, Wealth and War*. Cambridge: Cambridge University Press.

Chamberlain, M. E. 1974. *The Scramble for Africa*. Harlow: Pearson.

Chang, Tom Y., David H. Solomon, and Mark Westerfield. 2016. "Looking for Someone to Blame: Delegation, Cognitive Dissonance, and the Disposition Effect." *Journal of Finance*. 71 (1): 267–302.

Charney, Michael W. 2004. *Southeast Asian Warfare 1300–1900*. Leiden: Brill.

Chase, Kenneth. 2003. *Firearms: A Global History to 1700*. Cambridge: Cambridge University Press.

Chaudhuri, K. N. 1965. *The English East India Company: The Study of an Early Joint Stock Company*. London: Frank Cass.

Chaudhuri, K. N. 1985. *Trade and Civilisation in the Indian Ocean: An Economic History from the Rise of Islam to 1750*. Cambridge University Press.

Chaudhuri, K. N. 1990. "Reflections on the Organizing Principle of Pre-Modern Trade." In *The Political Economy of Merchant Empires: State Power and World Trade 1350–1750*, edited by James D. Tracy, 421–442. Cambridge: Cambridge University Press.

Cipolla, Carlo M. 1965. *Guns, Sails and Empires: Technological Innovation and the Early Phases of European Expansion*. New York: Minerva.

Clayton, Anthony. 1999. *Frontiersmen: Warfare in Africa Since 1950*. London: Routledge.

Clulow, Adam. 2009. "European Maritime Violence and Territorial States in Early Modern Asia, 1600–1650." *Itinerario*, 33 (3): 72–94.

Clulow, Adam. 2014. *The Company and the Shogun: The Dutch Encounter with Tokugawa Japan*. New York: Columbia University Press.

Colas, Alejandro. 2016. "Barbary Coast in the Expansion of International Society: Privacy, Privateering, and Corsairing as Primary Institutions." *Review of International Studies* 42 (5): 840–857.

Cook, Noble David. 1998. *Born to Die: Disease and New World Conquest 1492–1650*. Cambridge: Cambridge University Press.

Cook, Weston F. 1994. *The Hundred Years War for Morocco: Gunpowder and the Military Revolution in the Early Modern Muslim World*. Boulder, CO: Westview.

Cooke, J. J. 1973. *New French Imperialism: The Third Republic and Colonial Expansion*. London: David and Charles.

Cooper, R.G.S. 2003. *The Anglo-Maratha Campaigns and the Contest for India: The Struggle of Control of the South Asian Military History*. Cambridge: Cambridge University Press.

Craven, Matthew. 2015. "Between Law and History: The Berlin Conference of 1884–85 and the Logic of Free Trade." *London Review of International Law* 3 (1): 31–59.

Crawford, Neta C. 2002. *Argument and Change in World Politics: Ethics, Decolonisation and Humanitarian Intervention*. Cambridge: Cambridge University Press.

Dale, Stephen F. 2010. *The Muslim Empires of the Ottomans, Safavids, and Mughals*. Cambridge: Cambridge University Press.

Darwin, John. 2007. *After Tamerlane: The Rise and Fall of Global Empires 1400–2000*. London: Penguin.

Darwin, John. 2014. *Unfinished Empire: The Global Expansion of Britain*. London: Bloomsbury.

Davies, Brian. 2007. *Warfare, State and Society on the Black Sea Steppe 1500–1700*. Abingdon, UK: Routledge.

Davis, Lance Edwin, and Robert A. Huttenback. 1986. *Mammon and the Pursuit of Empire: The Political Economy of British Imperialism 1860–1912*. Cambridge: Cambridge University Press.

de Armond, Louis. 1954. "Frontier Warfare in Colonial Chile." *Pacific Historical Review* 23 (2): 125–132.

de la Garza, Andrew. 2016. *The Mughal Empire at War: Babur, Akbar and the Indian Military Revolution, 1500–1605*. Abingdon, UK: Routledge.

Diamond, Jared. 1997. *Guns, Germs and Steel: The Fates of Human Societies*. New York: W. W. Norton.

DiMaggio, Paul J., and Walter W. Powell. 1983. "The Iron Cage Revisited: Institutional Isomorphism and Collective Rationality in Organizational Fields." *American Sociological Review* 48 (2): 147–160.

Disney, A. R. 2009. *A History of Portugal and the Portuguese Empire*. Vol. 2: *The Portuguese Empire*. Cambridge: Cambridge University Press.

Downing, Brian M. 1992. *The Military Revolution and Political Change: The Origins of Democracy and Autocracy in Early Modern Europe*. Princeton: Princeton University Press.

Doyle, Michael W. 1986. *Empires*. Ithaca, NY: Cornell University Press.

Drori, Gili S., John W. Meyer, and Hokyu Hwang. 2006. "World Society and the Proliferation of Formal Organization." In *Globalization and Organization: World Society and Organizational Change*, edited by Gili S. Drori, John W. Meyer, and Hokya Hwang, 25–49. Oxford: Oxford University Press.

Dunne, Tim, and Christian Reus-Smit (eds). 2017. *The Globalization of International Society*. Oxford: Oxford University Press.

Eaton, Richard M., and Phillip B. Wagoner. 2014 "Warfare on the Deccan Plateau, 1450–1600: A Military Revolution in Early Modern India?" *Journal of World History* 25 (1): 5–50.

Elman, Colin, and Miriam Fendius Elman. 1999. "Diplomatic History and International Relations Theory: Respecting Difference and Crossing Boundaries." *International Security* 22 (1): 5–21.

Elman, Colin and Miriam Fendius Elman. 2008. "The Role of History in International Relations." *Millennium* 37 (2): 357–364.

Ellis, Stephen. 1999. *Mask of Anarchy: The Destruction of Liberia and the Religious Dimension of an African Civil War*. New York: New York University Press.

Elster, Jon. 1989. *The Cement of Society: A Survey of Social Order*. Cambridge: Cambridge University Press.

Elster, Jon. 1995. "Functional Explanation: In Social Science." In *Readings in the Philosophy of Social Science*, edited by Michael Martin and Lee C. McIntyre, 402–413. Cambridge: MIT Press.

Elster, Jon. 2000. "Rational Choice History: A Case of Excessive Ambition." *American Political Science Review* 94 (3): 685–695.

Elster, Jon. 2007. *Explaining Social Behavior: More Nuts and Bolts for the Social Sciences*. Cambridge: Cambridge University Press.

Erikson, Emily. 2014. *Between Monopoly and Free Trade: The English East India Company 1600–1757*. Princeton: Princeton University Press.

Erikson, Emily, and Valentina Assenova. 2015. "New Forms of Organization and the Coordination of Political and Commercial Actors." In *Chartering Capitalism: Organizing Markets, States, and Publics*. Special issue of *Political Power and Social Theory* 29 (1): 1–13.

Ertman, Thomas. 1997. *Birth of Leviathan: Building States and Regimes in Medieval and Early Modern Europe*. Cambridge: Cambridge University Press.

Eyre, Dana P., and Mark C. Suchman. 1996. "Status, Norms and the Proliferation of Conventional Weapons: An Institutional Theory Approach." In *The Culture of National Security: Norms and Identity in World Politics*, edited by Peter J. Katzenstein, 79–104. New York: Columbia University Press.

Farrell, Theo. 2005. "World Culture and Military Power." *Security Studies* 14 (3): 448–488.

Farrell, Theo. 2007. "Global Norms and Military Effectiveness: The Army in Early Twentieth-Century Ireland." In *Creating Military Power: The Sources of Military Effectiveness*, edited by Risa A. Brooks and Elizabeth Stanley, 136–157. Palo Alto: Stanford University Press.

Fay, Peter Ward. 1998. *Opium War, 1840–42: Barbarians in the Celestial Empire in the Early Part of the Nineteenth Century and the War by Which They Forced her Gates*. Chapel Hill: University of North Carolina Press.

Fazal, Tanisha M. 2007. *State Death: The Politics and Geography of Conquest, Occupation and Annexation*. Princeton: Princeton University Press.

Ferguson, Niall. 2011. *Civilization: The West and the Rest*. New York: Penguin.

Finnemore, Martha. 1996. *National Interests in International Society*. Ithaca, NY: Cornell University Press.

Finnemore, Martha. 2003. *The Purpose of Intervention: Changing Beliefs about the Use of Force*. Ithaca, NY: Cornell University Press.

Frank, André Gunder. 1998. *ReORIENT: Global Economy in the Asian Age*. Berkeley: University of California Press.

Friedman, Milton. 1953. *Essays in Positive Economics*. Chicago: University of Chicago Press.

Frost, Robert I. 2000. *The Northern Wars 1558–1721*, Harlow: Pearson.

Fuller, J.F.C. 1954. *A Military of the Western World*. New York: Funk and Wagnalls.

Furber, Holden. 1976. *Rival Empires of the Trade in the Orient 1600–1800*. Minneapolis: University of Minnesota Press.

Gaastra, Femme. 1981. "The Shifting Balance of Trade of the Dutch East India Company." In *Companies and Trade: Essays on Overseas Trading Companies During the Ancien Regime*, edited by Leonard Blussé and Femme Gaastra, 47–69. Leiden: Leiden University Press.

Gaastra, Femme. 2003. *The Dutch East India Company: Expansion and Decline*. Amsterdam: Walburg Pers.

Galbraith, J. S. 1970. "Italy, the British East Africa Company, and the Benadir Coast, 1888–1893." *Journal of Modern History* 42 (4): 549–563.

Gat, Azar. 2006. *War in Human Civilization*. Oxford: Oxford University Press.

Gberie, Lansana. 2005. *A Dirty War in West Africa: The RUF and the Destruction of Sierra Leone*. Bloomington: Indiana University Press.

Gennaioli, Nicola, and Hans-Joachim Voth. 2015. "State Capacity and Military Conflict." *Review of Economic Studies* 82 (4): 1409–1448.

George, Alexander L., and Andrew Bennett. 2004. *Case Studies and Theory Development in the Social Sciences*. Cambridge: MIT Press.

Giordani, Paolo. 1916. *The German Colonial Empire: Its Beginning and Ending.* London: G. Bell and Sons.

Glete, Jan. 2000. *Warfare at Sea 1500–1650: Maritime Conflicts and the Transformation of Europe.* New York: Routledge.

Glete, Jan. 2002. *War and State in Early Modern Europe: Spain, the Dutch Republic and Sweden as Fiscal-Military States, 1500–1660.* London: Routledge.

Go, Julian, and George Lawson (Eds). 2017. *Global Historical Sociology.* Cambridge: Cambridge University Press.

Gommans, Jos J. L. 1995. *The Rise of the Indo-Afghan Empire, c.1710–1780.* Leiden: Brill.

Gommans, Jos J. L., and Dirk H. A. Kolff. 2001. "Introduction: Warfare and Weaponry in South Asia 1000–1800AD." In *Warfare and Weaponry in South Asia 1000–1800,* edited by Jos J.L Gommans and Dirk H.A. Kolff, 1–42. New Delhi: Oxford University Press.

Gommans, Jos J. L. 2001. "Indian Warfare and Afghan Innovation During the Eighteenth Century." In *Warfare and Weaponry in South Asia 1000–1800,* edited by Jos J.L Gommans and Dirk H.A. Kolff, 365–386. New Delhi: Oxford University Press.

Gommans, Jos. 2002. *Mughal Warfare: Indian Frontiers and the High Road to Empire 1500–1700.* London: Routledge.

Grant, Jonathan. 1999. "Rethinking Ottoman 'Decline': Military Technology Diffusion in the Ottoman Empire, Fifteenth to Eighteenth Centuries." *Journal of World History* 10 (1): 179–201.

Gray, Colin S. 2007. *Another Bloody Century: Future War.* New York: Phoenix.

Guilmartin, John F. 1974. *Gunpowder and Galleys: Changing Technology and Mediterranean Warfare at Sea in the 16th Century.* Cambridge: Cambridge University Press.

Guilmartin, John F. 1995. "The Military Revolution: Origins and First Tests Abroad." In *The Military Revolution Debate: Readings in the Military Transformation of Early Modern Europe,* edited by Clifford J. Rogers, 299–333. Boulder, CO: Westview.

Guilmartin, John F. 2002. *Galleons and Galleys.* London: Cassel.

Guilmartin, John F. 2011. "The Revolution in Military Warfare at Sea During the Early Modern Era: Technological Origins, Operational Outcomes and Strategic Consequences." *Journal for Maritime Research* 13 (2): 129–137.

Hager, Robert P., and David A. Lake. 2000. "Balancing Empires: Competitive Decolonization in International Politics." *Security Studies* 9 (3): 108–148.

Hale, J. R. 1986. *War and Society in Renaissance Europe, 1450–1620.* Baltimore: Johns Hopkins University Press.

Hanes, W. Travis, and Frank Sanello. 2002. *Opium Wars: The Addiction of One Empire and the Corruption of the Other.* Naperville, IL.: Sourcebooks.

Hanson, Victor Davis. 1989. *The Western Way of War: Infantry Battle in Ancient Greece.* Berkeley: University of California Press.

Hanson, Victor Davis. 2002. *Carnage and Culture: Landmark Battles in the Rise of Western Power*. New York: Anchor.

Hasan, Farhat. 1991. "Conflict and Cooperation in Anglo-Mughal Trade Relations during the Reign of Aurangzeb." *Journal of the Economic and Social History of the Orient* 34 (4): 351–360.

Hasan, Farhat. 2004. *State and Locality in Mughal India: Power Relations in Western India c. 1572–1730*. Cambridge: Cambridge University Press.

Hassig, Ross. 2006. *Mexico and the Spanish Conquest*. Norman: University of Oklahoma Press.

Hassner, Ron E. 2016. *Religion on the Battlefield*. Ithaca, NY: Cornell University Press.

Headrick, Daniel R. 1981. *Tools of Empire: Technology and European Imperialism in the Nineteenth Century*. Oxford: Oxford University Press.

Headrick, Daniel R. 2010. *Power Over Peoples: Technology, Environments, and Western Imperialism, 1400 to the Present*. Princeton: Princeton University Press.

Hess, Andrew C. 1978. *The Forgotten Frontier: A History of the Sixteenth-Century Ibero-African Frontier*. Chicago: University of Chicago.

Hobden, Stephen and John M. Hobson (eds). 2002. *Historical Sociology of International Relations*. Cambridge: Cambridge University Press.

Hobsbawm, Eric. 2010. *Age of Empire 1875–1914*. London: Hachette.

Hobson, John M. 2004. *The Eastern Origins of Western Civilization*. Cambridge: Cambridge University Press.

Hobson, John M. 2012. *The Eurocentric Conception of World Politics: Western International Theory 1760–2010*. Cambridge: Cambridge University Press.

Hodgson, Marshall G. S. 1974. *The Venture of Islam: Conscience and History in a World Civilization*. Chicago: University of Chicago Press.

Hoffman, Philip T. 2015. *Why Did Europe Conquer the World?* Princeton: Princeton University Press.

Howard, Michael. 1976. *War in European History*. Oxford: Oxford University Press.

Hui, Victoria Tin-bor. 2005. *War and State Formation in Ancient China and Early Modern Europe*. Cambridge: Cambridge University Press.

Hyam, Ronald. 2010. *Understanding the British Empire*. Cambridge: Cambridge University Press.

Isaacman, Allen. 1972. *Mozambique: The Africanization of a European Institution: Zambezi Prazos, 1750–1902*. Madison: University of Wisconsin Press.

Jackson, Robert H. 1993. "The Weight of Ideas in Decolonization: Normative Change in International Relations." In *Ideas and Foreign Policy: Beliefs, Institutions and Political Change*, edited by Judith Goldstein and Robert O. Keohane, 111–138. Ithaca NY: Cornell University Press.

Jenkinson, Tim, Howard Jones, and Jose Vincente Martinez. 2016. "Picking Winners? Investment Consultants' Recommendation of Fund Managers." *Journal of Finance* 71 (5): 2333–2370.

Johnston, Alastair Iain. 2012. "What (If Anything) Does East Asia Tell us About International Relations Theory?" *Annual Review of Political Science* 15: 53–78.

Jones, Eric. 2003. *The European Economic Miracle: Environments, Economies and Geopolitics in the History of Europe and Asia.* Cambridge: Cambridge University Press.

Judd, Dennis, and Keith Surridge. 2002. *The Boer War: A History.* London: I. B. Taurus.

Kadercan, Burak. 2013/2014. "Strong Armies, Slow Adaption: Civil-Military Relations and the Diffusion of Military Power." *International Security* 38 (3): 117–152.

Kahler, Miles. 1999. "Evolution, Choice, and International Change." In *Strategic Choice and International Relations*, edited by David A. Lake and Robert Powell, 164–96. Princeton: Princeton University Press.

Kamen, Henry. 2002. *Empire: How Spain Became a World Power 1492–1763.* London: Penguin.

Kang, David C. 2003. "Getting Asia Wrong: The Need for New Analytical Frameworks." *International Security* 27 (4): 57–85.

Kang, David C. 2010. *East Asia Before the West: Five Centuries of Trade and Tribute.* New York: Columbia University Press.

Kang, David C. 2014. "Why Was There No Religious War in Pre-Modern East Asia?" *European Journal of International Relations* 20 (4): 965–986.

Karaman, K. Kivanç, and Şevket Pamuk. 2010. "Ottoman State Finances in European Perspective, 1500–1914." *Journal of Economic History* 70 (3): 593–629.

Keegan, John. 1976. *The Face of Battle.* London: Jonathan Cape.

Keegan, John. 1993. *A History of Warfare.* London: Hutchinson.

Keene, Edward. 2002. *Beyond the Anarchical Society: Grotius, Colonialism and Order in World Politics.* Cambridge: Cambridge University Press.

Kemper, Simon. 2014. "War-Bands on Java: Military Labour Markets in VOC Sources," Masters Thesis, Leiden University.

Kennedy, Paul. 1988. *The Rise and Fall of the Great Powers.* New York: Vintage.

Kian, Kwee Hui. 2008. "How Strangers Became Kings: Javanese-Dutch Relations in Java 1600–1800." *Indonesia and the Malay World.* 36 (105): 293–307.

Klein, P. W. 1981. "The Origins of Trading Companies." In *Companies and Trade: Essays on Overseas Trading Companies During the Ancien Regime*, edited by Leonard Blussé and Femme Gaastra, 17–28. Leiden: Leiden University Press.

Knight, Ian J. 1994. *Warrior Chiefs of Southern Africa.* New York: Firebird Books.

Kolff, Dirk H. A. 2001. "The Peasantry and the Polity." In *Warfare and Weaponry in South Asia 1000–1800*, edited by Jos J. L Gommans and Dirk H. A. Kolff, 202–231. New Delhi: Oxford University Press.

Koshy, K. O. 1989. *The Dutch Power in Kerala (1729–1758)* New Delhi: Mittal.

Kumar, Amarendra. 2015. "The Politics of Military Control in the West Coast: Marathas, Mughals and the Europeans, 1650–1730." In *Chinese and Indian Warfare: From the Classical Age to 1870*, edited by Kaushik Roy and Peter Lorge, 181–199. Abingdon, UK: Routledge.

Lake, David A., and Angela O'Mahony. 2004. "The Incredible Shrinking State: Explaining Change in the Territorial Size of Countries." *Journal of Conflict Resolution* 48 (5): 699–722.

Lan, David. 1985. *Guns and Rain: Guerillas and Spirit Mediums in Zimbabwe*. Berkeley: University of California Press.

Lane, Frederick C. 1958. "The Economic Consequences of Organized Violence." *Journal of Economic History* 18 (4): 401–417.

Lee, Wayne E. 2011a. "The Military Revolution of Native North America: Firearms, Forts and Polities." In *Empires and Indigenes: Intercultural Alliances, Imperial Expansion, and Warfare in the Early Modern World*, edited by Wayne E. Lee, 49–80. New York: New York University Press.

Lee, Wayne E. 2011b. "Projecting Power in the Early Modern World: The Spanish Model?" In *Empires and Indigenes: Intercultural Alliances, Imperial Expansion, and Warfare in the Early Modern World*, edited by Wayne E. Lee, 1–16. New York: New York University Press.

Lee, Wayne E. 2015. *Waging War: Conflict, Culture and Innovation in World History*. Oxford: Oxford University Press.

Lemke, Douglas. 2003. "African Lessons for International Relations Research." *World Politics* 56 (1): 114–138.

Levy, Jack S. 1983. *War in the Modern Great Power System 1495–1795*. Lexington: University Press of Kentucky.

Liberman, Peter. 1996. *Does Conquest Pay? The Exploitation of Occupied Industrial Societies*. Princeton: Princeton University Press.

Lieberman, Evan. 2003. *Strange Parallels: Southeast Asia in Global Context*, c.800–1830. Cambridge: Cambridge University Press.

Locher-Scholten, Elsbeth. 1994. "Dutch Expansion in the Indonesian Archipelago around 1900 and the Imperialism Debate." *Journal of Southeast Asian Studies* 25 (1): 91–111.

Lockhart, James. 1999. *Of Thing of the Indies: Essays Old and New in Early Latin American History*. Cambridge: Cambridge University Press.

Lorge, Peter. 2005. *War, Politics and Society in Early Modern China 900–1795*. London: Routledge.

Lorge, Peter A. 2008. *The Asian Military Revolution: From Gunpowder to the Bomb*. Cambridge: Cambridge University Press.

Lovell, Julia. 2011. *Opium War: Drugs, Dreams and the Making of Modern China*. London: Pan Macmillan.

Lyall, Jason, and Isaiah Wilson. 2009. "Rage Against the Machines: Explaining Outcomes in Counter-Insurgency Wars." *International Organization* 63 (1): 67–106.

Lynn, John A. (ed.) 1994. *Feeding Mars: Logistics in Western Warfare from the Middle Ages to the Present*. London: Routledge.

Lynn, John A. 2008. *Battle: A History of Combat and Culture from Ancient Greece to Modern America*. New York: Basic Books.

MacDonald, Paul K. 2009. "Those who Forget Historiography Are Doomed to Repeat It: Empire, Imperialism and Contemporary Debates about American Power." *Review of International Studies* 31 (1): 45–67.

MacDonald, Paul K. 2013. "'Retribution must Succeed Rebellion': The Colonial Origins of Counterinsurgency Failure." *International Organization* 67 (2): 253–286.

MacDonald, Paul K. 2014. *Networks of Domination: The Social Foundations of Peripheral Conquest*. Oxford: Oxford University Press.

Mack, Andrew. 1975. "Why Big Nations Lose Small Wars: The Politics of Asymmetric Conflict." *World Politics* 27 (2): 175–200.

Mahoney, James. 1999. "Nominative, Ordinal and Narrative Appraisal in Macrocausal Analysis." *American Journal of Sociology* 104 (4): 1154–1196.

Malone, Patrick. 1991. *Skulking Way of War: Technology and Tactics Among the New England Indians*. Lanham MD: Madison.

Mann, Michael. 1986. *The Sources of Social Power*. Vol. 1, *A History from the Beginning to 1760 AD*. Cambridge: Cambridge University Press.

Mann, Michael. 1993. *The Sources of Social Power*. Vol. 2, *A The Rise of Classes and Nation-States, 1760–1914*. Cambridge: Cambridge University Press.

Mao, Haijian. 2016. *The Qing Empire and the Opium War: The Collapse of the Heavenly Dynasty*. Cambridge: Cambridge University Press.

March, James G., and Johan P. Olsen. 1989. *Rediscovering Institutions: The Organizational Basis of Politics*. New York: Free Press.

March, James G., and Johan P. Olsen. 1998. "The Institutional Dynamics of International Political Orders." *International Organization* 52 (4): 943–969.

Marks, Robert B. 2002. *The Origins of the Modern World: A Global and Environmental Narrative from the Fifteenth to the Twenty-First Century*. Lanham, MD: Rowman and Littlefield.

Marshall, P. J. 1980. "Western Arms in Maritime Asia in the Early Phases of Expansion." *Modern Asian Studies* 14 (1): 13–28.

Marshall, P. J. 2005. *The Making and Unmaking of Empires: Britain, India, and America c.1750–1783*. Oxford: Oxford University Press.

Matthew, Laura E., and Michel R. Oudijk (eds). 2007. *Indian Conquistadors: Indigenous Allies in the Conquest of Mesoamerica*. Norman: University of Oklahoma Press.

Matthews, K. S. 2015. "Indo-Portuguese Naval Battles in the Indian Ocean during the Early Sixteenth Century." In *Chinese and Indian Warfare: From the Classical Age to 1870*, edited by Kaushik Roy and Peter Lorge, 166–180. Abingdon, UK: Routledge.

McNeill, William H. 1982. *The Pursuit of Power: Technology, Armed Force and Society since AD 1000*. Oxford: Basil Blackwell.

Merom, Gil. 2003. *How Democracies Lose Small Wars: State, Society, and the Failures of France in Algeria, Israel in Lebanon, and the United States in Vietnam*. Cambridge: Cambridge University Press.

Meyer, John W. and Brian Rowan. 1977. "Institutionalized Organizations: Formal Structure as Myth and Ceremony." *American Journal of Sociology* 83 (2): 340–363.

Meyer, John W., John Boli, George M. Thomas, and Francisco O. Ramirez. 1997. "World Society and the Nation-State." *American Journal of Sociology.* 103 (1): 144–181.

Meyer, John W. 2010. "World Society, Institutional Theories, and the Actor." *Annual Review of Sociology* 36 (1): 1–20.

Milton, Giles. 1999. *Nathaniel's Nutmeg: Or, The Incredible True Adventures of the Spice Trader who Changed the Course of History.* London: Hodder and Stoughton.

Modelski, George, and Kazimierz Poznanski. 1996. "Evolutionary Paradigms in the Social Sciences." *International Studies Quarterly* 40 (3): 315–319.

Moertono, Soemersaid. 2009. *State and Statecraft in Old Java: A Study of the Later Mataram Period, 16th to 19th Century.* Sheffield: Equinox.

Mommsen, Wolfgang J. 1980. *Theories of Imperialism.* Chicago: University of Chicago Press.

Morrow, James D. 1991. "Alliance and Asymmetry: An Alternative to the Capacity Aggregation Model of Alliances." *American Journal of Political Science* 35 (4): 904–933.

Mortimer, Geoff. 2004a. "Introduction: Was There a 'Military Revolution' in the Early Modern Period?" In *Early Modern Military History, 1450–1815* edited by Geoff Mortimer, 1–5. Houndmills, UK: Palgrave.

Mortimer, Geoff (ed.). 2004b. *Early Modern Military History, 1450–1815.* Houndmills, UK: Palgrave.

Mostert, Tristan. 2007. "Chain of Command: The Military System of the Dutch East India Company 1655–1663." Masters Thesis, Department of History, University of Leiden.

Murphey, Rhoads. 1993. "The Ottoman Resurgence in the Seventeenth Century Mediterranean: The Gamble and its Results." *Mediterranean Historical Review* 8 (2): 186–200.

Murphey, Rhoads. 1999. *Ottoman Warfare 1500–1700.* London: New Brunswick NJ: Rutgers University Press.

Nagtegaal, Lucas. 1996. *Riding the Dutch Tiger: The Dutch East India Company and the Northeast Coast of Java, 1680–1743.* Leiden: KITLV.

Nelson, Richard R., and Sidney G. Winter. 1982. *An Evolutionary Theory of Economic Change.* Cambridge: Harvard University Press.

Neil-Tomlinson, Barry. 1977. "The Nyassa Chartered Company 1891–1929." *Journal of African History* 18 (1): 109–128.

Newbury, Colin. 2003. *Patrons, Clients, and Empire: Chieftaincy and Over-Rule in Asia, Africa, and the Pacific.* Oxford: Oxford University Press.

North, Douglass C. 1990a. *Institutions, Institutional Change and Economic Performance.* Cambridge: Cambridge University Press.

North, Douglass C. 1990b. "Institutions, Transaction Costs, and the Rise of Merchant Empires." In *The Political Economy of Merchant Empires: State Power and World Trade 1350–1750,* edited by James D. Tracy, 22–40. Cambridge: Cambridge University Press.

North, Douglass C., and Robert Paul Thomas. 1973. *The Rise of the Western World: A New Economic History.* Cambridge: Cambridge University Press.

North, Douglass C., and Barry R. Weingast. 1989. "Constitutions and Commitment: The Evolution of Institutions Governing Public Choice in Seventeenth-Century England." *Journal of Economic History* 49 (4): 803–832.

Odegard, Erik. 2014. "Fortifications and the Imagination of Colonial Control: The Dutch East India Company in Malabar 1663–1795." Paper presented at the Urban History Conference, September 3–7, 2014, Lisbon.

Oman, C.M.C. 1885 [1953]. *The Art of War in the Middle Ages, AD 378–1515.* Ithaca, NY: Cornell University Press.

Pace, Desmond, Jana Hili, and Simon Grima. 2016. "Active versus Passive Investing: An Empirical Study on the US and European Mutual Funds and ETFs." In *Contemporary Issues in Bank Financial Market*, edited by Simon Grima and Frank Bezzina, 1–35. Bingley, UK: Emerald Group.

Padden, Robert Charles. 1957. "Cultural Change and Military Resistance in Araucanian Chile, 1550–1730." *Southwestern Journal of Anthropology* 13 (1): 103–121.

Parker, Geoffrey. 1976 [1995]. "The 'Military Revolution, 1560–1660'–A Myth?" In *The Military Revolution Debate: Readings in the Military Transformation of Early Modern Europe*, edited by Clifford J. Rogers, 37–54. Boulder, CO: Westview.

Parker, Geoffrey. 1988 [1996]. *The Military Revolution: Military Innovation and the Rise of the West, 1500–1800.* Cambridge: Cambridge University Press.

Parker, Geoffrey. 1990. "Europe and the Wider World, 1500–1750: The Military Balance." In *The Political Economy of Merchant Empires: State Power and World Trade 1350–1750*, edited by James D. Tracy, 161–195. Cambridge: Cambridge University Press.

Parker, Geoffrey. 2002. "The Artillery Fortress as an Engine of European Overseas Expansion 1480–1750." In *Empire, War and Faith in Early Modern Europe*, edited by Geoffrey Parker, 192–218. London: Penguin.

Parrott, David. 2012. *The Business of War: Military Enterprise and the Military Revolution in Early Modern Europe.* Cambridge: Cambridge University Press.

Pearson, M. N. 1990. "Merchants and States." In *The Political Economy of Merchant Empires: State Power and World Trade 1350–1750*, edited by James D. Tracy, 41–116. Cambridge: Cambridge University Press.

Pearson, Michael N. 1998. *Port Cities and Intruders: The Swahili Coast, India and Portugal in the Early Modern Era.* Baltimore: Johns Hopkins University Press.

Pearson, Michael N. 2003. *The Indian Ocean.* London: Routledge.

Pedreira, Jorge M. 2007. "Costs and Financial Trends in the Portuguese Empire, 1415–1822." In *Portuguese Oceanic Expansion, 1400–1800*, edited by Francisco Bethencourt and Diogo Ramada Curto, 49–87. Cambridge: Cambridge University Press.

Peers, Douglas M. 2007. "Gunpowder Empires and the Garrison State: Modernity, Hybridity, and the Political Economy of Colonial India, circa 1750–1850." *Comparative Studies of South Asia, Africa and the Middle East* 27 (2): 245–258.

Peers, Douglas M. 2011. "Revolution, Evolution, or Devolution: The Military Making of Colonial India." In *Empires and Indigenes: Intercultural Alliances, Imperial Expansion, and Warfare in the Early Modern World*, edited by Wayne E. Lee, 81–106. New York: New York University Press.

Peers, Douglas M. 2015. "Military Revolution and State Formation Reconsidered: Mir Qasim, Haider Ali and Transition to Colonial Rule in the 1760s." In *Chinese and Indian Warfare: From the Classical Age to 1870*, edited by Roy Kaushik and Peter Lorge, 302–323. Abingdon, UK: Routledge.

Perdue, Peter C. 2005. *China Marches West. The Qing Conquest of Central Eurasia.* Cambridge: Harvard University Press.

Phillips, Andrew. 2011. *War, Religion and Empire: The Transformation of International Orders.* Cambridge: Cambridge University Press.

Phillips, Andrew, and J. C. Sharman. 2015. *International Order in Diversity: War, Trade and Rule in the Indian Ocean.* Cambridge: Cambridge University Press.

Philpott, Daniel. 2001. *Revolutions in Sovereignty: How Ideas Shaped Modern International Relations.* Princeton: Princeton University Press.

Pierson, Paul. 2003. "Big, Slow-Moving ... and Invisible: Macrosocial Processes in the Study of Comparative Politics." In *Comparative Historical Analysis in the Social Sciences*, edited by James Mahoney and Dietrich Rueschemeyer, 177–207. Cambridge: Cambridge University Press.

Pierson, Paul. 2004. *Politics in Time: History, Institutions, and Social Analysis.* Princeton: Princeton University Press.

Prestholdt, Jeremy 2001. "Portuguese Conceptual Categories and the 'Other' Encounter on the Swahili Coast." *Journal of Asian and African Studies* 36 (4): 383–403.

Polachek, James M. 1991. *The Inner Opium War.* Cambridge: Harvard University Press.

Pomeranz, Kenneth. 2001. *The Great Divergence: China, Europe and the Making of the Modern World Economy.* Princeton: Princeton University Press.

Posen, Barry R. 1993. "Nationalism, the Mass Army and Military Power." *International Security* 18 (2): 80–124.

Powell, Walter W., and Paul J. DiMaggio (eds.). 1991a. *The New Institutionalism in Organizational Analysis.* Chicago: University of Chicago Press.

Powell, Walter W., and Paul DiMaggio. 1991b. "Introduction." In *The New Institutionalism in Organizational Analysis*, edited by Walter W. Powell and Paul DiMaggio, 1–40. Chicago: University of Chicago Press.

Prakash, Om (ed.). 2002. *Downfall of Mughal Empire.* [*sic*] Delhi: Anmol.

Quirk, Joel, and David Richardson. 2014. "Europeans, Africans and the Atlantic World, 1450–1850." In *International Orders in the Early Modern World: Before the Rise of the West*, edited by Shogo Suzuki, Yongjin Zhang, and Joel Quirk, 138–158. Routledge: Abingdon.

Ralston, David B. 1990. *Importing the European Army: The Introduction of European Military Techniques and Institutions into the Extra-European World 1600–1914.* Chicago: University of Chicago Press.

Rapkin, David. 2001 "Obstacles to an Evolutionary Global Politics Research Program." In *Evolutionary Interpretations of World Politics*, edited by William R. Thompson, 52–60. New York: Routledge.

Record, Jeffery. 2007. *Beating Goliath: Why Insurgencies Win.* Washington, DC: Potomac.

Reid, Anthony. 1982. *Europe and Southeast Asia: The Military Balance.* Centre for Southeast Asia Studies, James Cook University, Occasional Paper 16.

Resende-Santos, João. 2007. *Neorealism, States, and the Modern Mass Army.* Cambridge: Cambridge University Press.

Restall, Matthew. 2003. *Seven Myths of the Spanish Conquest.* Oxford: Oxford University Press.

Reus-Smit, Christian. 2011. "Struggles for Individual Rights and the Expansion of the International System." *International Organization* 65 (2): 207–242.

Reus-Smit, Christian. 2013. *Individual Rights and the Making of the International System.* Cambridge: Cambridge University Press.

Richards, John F. 1993. *The Mughal Empire.* Cambridge: Cambridge University Press.

Ricklefs, M. C. 1993. *War, Culture and the Economy in Java, 1677–1726.* Sydney: Allen and Unwin.

Ringmar, Erik. 2012. "Performing International Systems: Two East-Asian Alternatives to the Westphalian Order." *International Organization* 66 (1): 1–25.

Roberts, Michael. 1955 [1995]. "The Military Revolution, 1560–1660." In *The Military Revolution Debate: Readings in the Military Transformation of Early Modern Europe*, edited by Clifford J. Rogers, 13–35. Boulder, CO: Westview.

Rodger, N.A.M. 2011. "From the 'Military Revolution' to the 'Fiscal-Naval State.'" *Journal for Maritime Studies* 13 (2): 119–128.

Rogers, Clifford J. 1995a. "The Military Revolution Debate in History and Historiography." In *The Military Revolution Debate: Readings in the Military Transformation of Early Modern Europe*, edited by Clifford J. Rogers, 1–12. Boulder, CO: Westview.

Rogers, Clifford J. 1995b. "The Military Revolutions of the Hundred Years War." In *The Military Revolution Debate: Readings in the Military Transformation of Early Modern Europe*, edited by Clifford J. Rogers, 55–93. Boulder, CO: Westview.

Rogers, Clifford J. (ed.). 1995c. *The Military Revolution Debate: Readings in the Military Transformation of Early Modern Europe.* Boulder, CO: Westview.

Rogowski, Ronald. 1999. "Institutions as Constraints on Strategic Choice." In *Strategic Choice and International Relations*, edited by David A. Lake and Robert Powell, 115–136. Princeton: Princeton University Press.

Roland, Alex. 2016. *War and Technology: A Very Short Introduction.* Oxford: Oxford University Press.

Rommelse, Gijs. 2011. "An Early Modern Naval Revolution? The Relationship between 'Economic Reason of State' and Maritime Warfare." *Journal for Maritime Research* 13 (2): 138–150.

Rose, Susan. 2001. *Medieval Naval Warfare.* Abingdon, UK: Routledge.

Rosen, Stephen Peter. 1994. *Winning the Next War: Innovation and the Modern Military.* Ithaca, NY: Cornell University Press.

Rosen, Stephen Peter. 1996. *Societies and Military Power: India and its Armies.* Ithaca, NY: Cornell University Press.

Rosenthal, Jean-Laurent, and R. Bin Wong. 2011. *Before and Beyond the Great Divergence: The Politics of Economic Change in China and Europe*. Cambridge: Cambridge University Press.

Roy, Kaushik. 2011a. "The Hybrid Military Establishment of the East India Company in South Asia: 1750–1849." *Journal of Global History* 6 (2): 195–218.

Roy, Kaushik. 2011b. *War, Culture and Society in Early Modern South Asia*. London: Taylor and Francis.

Roy, Kaushik, and Peter Lorge. 2015. "Introduction." In *Chinese and Indian Warfare: From the Classical Age to 1870*, edited by Kaushik Roy and Peter Lorge, 1–14. Abingdon, UK: Routledge.

Roy, Tirthankar. 2013. "Rethinking the Origins of British India: State Formation and Military-Fiscal Undertakings in an Eighteenth Century World Region." *Modern Asian Studies* 47 (4): 1125–1156.

Rudolph, Lloyd I., and Susanne Hoeber Rudolph. 2010. "Federalism as State Formation in India: A Theory of Shared Sovereignty." *International Political Science Review* 31 (5): 553–572.

Scammell, G. V. 1989. *The First Imperial Age: European Overseas Expansion c.1400–1715*. London: Unwin Hyman.

Schilz, Thomas Frank, and Donald E. Worcester. 1987. "The Spread of Firearms among the Indian Tribes on the Northern Frontier of New Spain." *American Indian Quarterly* 11 (1): 1–10.

Secoy, Frank Raymond (ed.) 1953. *Changing Military Patterns on the Great Plains*. Lincoln: University of Nebraska Press.

Sharman, J. C. 2017. "Sovereignty at the Extremes: Micro-States in World Politics." *Political Studies* 65 (4): 559–575.

Sharman, J. C. 2015. "War, Selection, and Micro-States: Economic and Sociological Perspectives on the International System." *European Journal of International Relations* 21 (1): 194–214.

Slinn, Peter. 1971. "Commercial Concessions and Politics During the Colonial Period: The Role of the British South Africa Company in Northern Rhodesia, 1890–1964." *Royal African Society* 70 (281): 365–384.

Snyder, Jack. 1991. *Myths of Empire: Domestic Politics and International Ambition*. Ithaca, NY: Cornell University Press.

Spicer, Edward H. 1967. *Cycles of Conquest: The Impact of Spain, Mexico and the United States on the Indians of the Southwest*. Tucson: University of Arizona Press.

Spruyt, Hendrik. 1994. *The Sovereign State and Its Competitors: An Analysis of Systems Change*. Princeton: Princeton University Press.

Spruyt, Hendrik 2001. "Diversity or Uniformity in the Modern World? Answers from Evolutionary Theory, Learning, and Social Adaptation." In *Evolutionary Interpretations of World Politics*, edited by William R. Thompson, 110–132. New York: Routledge.

Spruyt, Hendrik. 2005. *Ending Empire: Contested Sovereignty and Territorial Partition*. Ithaca, NY: Cornell University Press.

Steele, Ian K. 1994. *Warpaths: Invasions of North America*. Oxford: Oxford University Press.

Steensgaard, Niels. 1973. *The Asian Trade Revolution of the Seventeenth Century: The East India Companies and the Decline of the Caravan Trade*. Chicago: University of Chicago Press.

Stern, Philip J. 2006. "British Asia and British Atlantic: Connections and Comparisons." *William and Mary Quarterly* 63 (4): 693–712.

Stern, Philip J. 2009. "History and Historiography of the English East India Company: Past, Present and Future!" *History Compass* 7 (4): 1146–1180.

Stern, Philip J. 2011. *The CompanyState: Corporate Sovereignty and the Early Modern Foundations of the British Empire in India*. Oxford: Oxford University Press.

Stevens, Carol B. 2007. *Russia's Wars of Emergence 1460–1730*. Harlow: Pearson.

Strang, David. 1991. "Anomaly and Commonplace in European Political Expansion: Realist and Institutionalist Accounts." *International Organization* 45 (2): 143–162.

Streusand, Douglas E. 1989. *The Formation of the Mughal Empire*. Oxford: Oxford University Press.

Streusand, Douglas. 2001. "The Process of Expansion." In *Warfare and Weaponry in South Asia 1000–1800*, edited by Jos J. L Gommans and Dirk H. A. Kolff, 337–364. New Delhi: Oxford University Press.

Streusand, Douglas E. 2011. *Islamic Gunpowder Empires: Ottomans, Safavids, and Mughals*. Boulder, CO: Westview.

Subrahmanyam, Sanjay, and Luis Filipe F. R. Thomas. 1990. "Evolution of Empire: The Portuguese in the Indian Ocean during the Sixteenth Century." In *The Political Economy of Merchant Empires: State Power and World Trade 1350–1750*, edited by James D. Tracy, 298–331. Cambridge: Cambridge University Press.

Subrahmanyam, Sanjay. 1990. *The Political Economy of Commerce: Southern India, 1500–1650*. Cambridge: Cambridge University Press.

Subrahmanyam, Sanjay. 1992. "The Mughal State—Structure or Process? Reflections on Recent Western Historiography." *Indian Economic and Social History Review* 29 (3): 291–321.

Subrahmanyam, Sanjay. 1995. "Of *Imârat* and *Tijârat*: Asian Merchants and State Power in the Western Indian Ocean, 1400–1750." *Comparative Studies in Society and History* 37 (4): 750–780.

Subrahmanyam, Sanjay. 2006. "A Tale of Three Empires: Mughals, Ottomans and Habsburgs in a Comparative Context." *Common Knowledge* 12 (1): 66–92.

Subrahmanyam, Sanjay. 2007. "Holding the World in Balance: The Connected Histories of the Iberian Overseas Empires 1500–1640." *American Historical Review* 112 (5): 1359–1385.

Subrahmanyam, Sanjay. 2012. *The Portuguese Empire in Asia, 1500–1700: A Political and Economic History*. Hoboken, NJ: Wiley.

Sun, Laichen. 2003. "Military Technology Transfer from Ming China and the Emergence of Northern Mainland Southeast Asia (c. 1390–1527)" *Journal of Southeast Asian Studies* 34 (3): 495–517.

Suzuki, Shogo. 2005. "Japan's Socialization into Janus-Faced European International Society." *European Journal of International Relations* 11 (1): 137–164.

Suzuki, Shogo. 2009. *Civilization and Empire: China and Japan's Encounter with International Society*. Abingdon, UK: Routledge.

Suzuki, Shogo, Yongjin Zhang, and Joel Quirk. 2014. "Introduction: The Rest and the Rise of the West." In *International Orders in the Early Modern World: Before the Rise of the West*, edited by Shogo Suzuki, Yongjin Zhang, and Joel Quirk, 1–11. Abingdon, UK: Routledge.

Swope, Kenneth. 2005. "Crouching Tiger, Secret Weapons: Military Technology Employed During the Sino-Japanese-Korean War, 1592–1598." *Journal of Military History* 69 (1): 11–41.

Swope, Kenneth M. 2009. *A Dragon's Head and a Serpent's Tail: Ming China and the First Great East Asian War*. Norman: University of Oklahoma Press.

Tagliacozzo, Eric. 2002. "Trade, Production and Incorporation: The Indian Ocean in Flux, 1600–1900." *Itinerario* 26 (1): 75–106.

Thompson, William R. 1999. "The Military Superiority Thesis and the Ascendancy of Western Eurasia in the World System." *Journal of World History* 10 (1): 143–178.

Thompson, William R., and Karen Rasler. 1999. "War, the Military Revolution(s) Controversy, and Army Expansion." *Comparative Political Studies* 32 (1): 3–31.

Thompson, William R. (ed.) 2001. *Evolutionary Interpretations of World Politics*, New York: Routledge.

Thomson, Janice E. 1994. *Mercenaries, Pirates and Sovereign: State-Building and Extra-Territorial Violence in Early-Modern Europe*. Princeton: Princeton University Press.

Thornton, John K. 1999. *Warfare in Atlantic Africa 1500–1800*. London: Routledge.

Thornton, John K. 2007. "The Portuguese in Africa." In *Portuguese Oceanic Expansion, 1400–1800*, edited by Francisco Bethencourt and Diogo Ramada Curto, 138–160. Cambridge: Cambridge University Press.

Thornton, John K. 2011. "Firearms, Diplomacy, and Conquest in Angola." In *Empires and Indigenes: Intercultural Alliances, Imperial Expansion, and Warfare in the Early Modern World*, edited by Wayne E. Lee, 167–192. New York: New York University Press.

Tilly, Charles (ed.) 1975. *The Formation of National States in Western Europe*. Princeton: Princeton University Press.

Tilly, Charles. 1985. "War Making and State Making as Organized Crime." In *Bringing the State Back In*, edited by Peter B. Evans, Dietrich Rueschemeyer, and Theda Skocpol, 169–191. Cambridge: Cambridge University Press.

Tilly, Charles. 1992. *Capital, Coercion and European States, A.D. 990–1992*. Oxford: Blackwell.

Tracy, James D. 1990. "Introduction." In *The Political Economy of Merchant Empires: State Power and World Trade 1350–1750*, edited by James D. Tracy, 1–21. Cambridge: Cambridge University Press.

Tuck, Christopher. 2008. "'All Innovation Leads to Hellfire': Military Reform and the Ottoman Empire in the Eighteenth Century." *Journal of Strategic Studies* 31 (3): 467–502.

Tucker, Molly. 2012. *Bloodwork: A Tale of Medicine and Murder in the Scientific Revolution.* New York: W. W. Norton.

Turner, Victor (Ed). 1971. *Colonialism in Africa,* Vol.3. Cambridge: Cambridge University Press.

Tyce, Spencer R. 2015. "German Conquistadors and Venture Capitalists: The Welser Company's Commercial Experiment in Sixteenth Century Venezuela and the Caribbean World." Ph.D. Dissertation, Ohio State University.

Vail, Leroy. 1976. "Mozambique's Chartered Companies: The Rule of the Feeble." *Journal of African History* 17 (3): 389–416.

van Creveld, Martin. 1977. *Supplying War: Logistics from Wallenstein to Patton.* Cambridge: Cambridge University Press.

Vandervort, Bruce. 1998. *Wars of Imperial Conquest in Africa 1830–1914.* Bloomington: Indiana University Press.

Vigneswaran, Darshan. 2014. "A Corrupt International Society: How Britain was Duped into Its First Indian Conquest." In *International Orders in the Early Modern World: Before the Rise of the West,* edited by Shogo Suzuki, Yongjin Zhang, and Joel Quirk, 94–117. (Abingdon, UK: Routledge).

von Clausewitz, Carl. 2008. *On War.* Princeton: Princeton University Press.

Walt, Stephen M. 2002. "The Enduring Relevance of the Realist Tradition." In *Political Science: State of the Discipline,* edited by Ira Katznelson and Helen V. Milner, 197–230. New York: W. W. Norton.

Waltz, Kenneth N. 1979. *Theory of International Politics.* Reading MA: Addison-Wesley.

Ward, Kerry. 2008. *Networks of Empire: Forced Migration in the Dutch East India Company.* Cambridge: Cambridge University Press.

Washbrook, David. 2004. "South India 1770–1840: The Colonial Transition." *Modern Asian Studies* 38 (3): 479–516.

Watson, I. Bruce 1980. "Fortifications and the 'Idea' of Force in Early English East India Company Relations with India." *Past and Present* No. 88: 70–87.

Watt, Robert N. 2002. "Raiders of a Lost Art? Apache War and Society." *Small Wars and Insurgencies* 13 (3): 1–28.

Weigert, Stephen L. 1996. *Traditional Religion and Guerilla Warfare in Modern Africa,* Houndmills, UK: Macmillan.

Wellen, Kathryn. 2015. "The Danish East India Company's War against the Mughal Empire, 1642–1698." *Journal of Early Modern History* 19 (5): 439–461.

Wendt, Alexander. 1999. *Social Theory of International Politics.* Cambridge: Cambridge University Press.

Weststeijn, Arthur. 2014. "The VOC as a Company-State: Debating Seventeenth-Century Dutch Colonial Expansion." *Itinerario* 38 (1): 13–34.

Wheatcroft, Andrew. 2008. *The Enemy at the Gate: Habsburgs, Ottomans and the Battle for Europe.* London: Bodley Head.

Wickremesekera, Channa. 2015. "European Military Experience in South Asia: The Dutch and British Armies in Sri Lanka in the Eighteenth Century." In *Chinese and Indian Warfare: From the Classical Age to 1870,* edited by Kaushik Roy and Peter Lorge, 289–301. Abingdon, UK: Routledge.

Wills, John E. 1993. "Maritime Asia, 1500–1800: The Interactive Emergence of European Domination." *American Historical Review* 98 (1): 83–105.

Wilson, Nicholas Hoover. 2015. "'A State in Disguise of a Merchant?' The English East India Company as a Strategic Action Field, ca. 1763–1834." In *Chartering Capitalism: Organizing Markets, States, and Publics.* Special issue of *Political Power and Social Theory* 29 (1): 257–285.

Winius, George Davidson. 1971. *The Fatal History of Portuguese Ceylon: Transition to Dutch Rule,* Cambridge: Harvard University Press.

Wlodarczyk, Nathalie. 2009. *Magic and Warfare: Appearance and Reality in Contemporary African Conflict and Beyond,* New York: Palgrave.

Wong, J. Y. 2000. "The Limits of Naval Power: British Gunboat Diplomacy in China from the Nemesis to the Amethyst, 1839–1949." *War and Society* 18 (2): 93–120.

Zarakol, Ayşe. 2010. *After Defeat: How the East Learned to Live with the West.* Cambridge: Cambridge University Press.

INDEX

Aceh, 58, 60, 76
Afghanistan, 86, 144, 145
Agoston, Gabor, 104, 105
Aksan, Virginia H., 112
Albuquerque, Afonso de, 57, 60, 118
Alcazarquivir, Battle of (1578), 49, 116
Algeria, 117, 118, 137, 140
Algiers, 115, 117, 118, 120
Alvaro, Kongo king, 50
Ambon, 72
anachronism, 33, 119, 123, 129–30
Andorra, 22
Andrade, Tonio, 59, 78, 124
Angola, 29, 49–51, 67
Araucanians, 44–46, 139
asymmetric warfare, 7, 44, 77, 146
Auma, Alice, 28
Aurangzeb, Mughal emperor, 84–85
Austrian Succession, War of (1740–48), 88
Aztec empire, 40–46, 103, 117, 135, 141

Baghdad, 101
Balkans, 100–106, 108, 110
Banda Islands, 72
Barbarossa brothers, 117
Barbary privateers, 106, 108, 118
Belgian Congo, 135
Belgrade, 108
Bengal, 82, 86–88, 111
Berlin Conference (1884–85), 135
Bijapur, 97
Black, Jeremy, 18, 119–20, 129; on
    Eurocentrism, 124; on military
    effectiveness, 23–24; on paradigm-
    diffusion model, 19, 37, 76
Boer War (1899–1902), 140–41
Bombay, 85
Bosworth, R. J. B., 137
Boxer, C. R., 70
Brazil, 44, 46, 50–51, 67
Breitenfeld, Battle of (1631), 37–38, 47

Burke, Edmund, 7
Burma, 56, 74

Cambodia, 76
Canary Islands, 40
cavalry tactics, 11, 90–93, 104; guns and,
    127; Ottoman, 106–7
Ceuta, 114–16, 118
Ceylon, 60–63, 72, 124; Dutch conflict
    over, 61–62, 79–81
Chaldiran, Battle of (1514), 101
Charles V, Holy Roman emperor, 34, 108,
    117
chartered companies, 2, 47, 53, 65, 122;
    of "new imperialism," 67. See also
    company sovereigns
Chase, Kenneth, 90, 107, 149
Chaudhuri, K. N., 60–61
Chechnya, 140
Child, Josiah, 84–85
China, 2–5, 22, 77–79, 122, 126–31; Dutch
    East India Company and, 68, 77–79;
    gunpowder weapons of, 59, 74, 78,
    126–27; infantries of, 78; Japanese
    conflicts with, 148–49; as modern
    rising power, 4, 151; Mughal empire
    and, 96; naval technology of, 14, 59,
    78; Opium Wars and, 20, 141, 142;
    Ottoman military and, 141–42;
    Russian conflicts with, 36; Taiping
    Rebellion in, 142. See also Ming
    dynasty
"civilizing mission," 137
Clausewitz, Carl von, 19–20
Clive, Robert, 88
Cochin, 72
Cold War, 6–7, 145
Columbus, Christopher, 1, 40
Compagnie Française des Indes Orien-
    tales. See French East India Company
company sovereigns, 5, 35, 53, 65–98;
    functions of, 69–70; hybrid

company sovereigns (*continued*)
   organization of, 68, 82; local allies of,
   68, 73–75, 80; monopolies of, 69, 82.
   See also chartered companies
competition, 150; innovation from, 19,
   100–101, 104; military, 7, 9–10, 12, 148;
   Parker on, 102; Waltz on, 21
Congo, 29, 50, 55, 135
conquistadors, 39–47, 66, 103, 117, 135,
   141; allies of, 122; limitations of, 43–47;
   local allies of, 42–43; Portuguese
   expansionism and, 47–48, 53–54
Cook, Weston F., 118
Correlates of War and Great Power Wars
   database, 127
Cortes, Hernan, 40–43, 103, 117, 135, 141
counterinsurgency wars, 7–8, 133, 144–45
Coxinga (Zheng Chenggong), 77–78
Crimea, Tatars of, 101, 104, 107, 112
crossbows, 11–12, 42, 55, 78
cultural approach to military history,
   23–27

da Gama, Vasco, 1, 51, 58, 103
Darwinian selection, 9, 20–23, 94, 134,
   137, 143, 147–50
de la Garza, Andrew, 92
decolonization, 7–8, 15–16, 143–46; state-
   making after, 66, 132; wars of, 133
Diamond, Jared, 35
disease, 72; as factor in European
   expansion, 35–36, 43–46, 122, 140;
   manpower shortage in Americas from,
   43–44; as natural selection, 46
Dutch East India Company (VOC), 36, 56,
   67–81; bankruptcy of, 86; in Ceylon,
   61–62, 79–81; charter of, 71; decline
   of, 79–81; in East Asia, 68, 77–79;
   English conflicts with, 83; founding
   of, 70–71; local allies of, 68, 73–75,
   80; maritime protection racket of,
   72; Portuguese conflicts with, 46,
   50–51, 61–62, 67–72, 77–81; resources
   of, 72; in Southeast Asia, 61–62, 68,
   71–77
Dutch West India Company, 46, 67; slave
   trade of, 50–51

Egypt, 57–58, 101, 107, 116, 117
EIC. *See* English East India Company
Elizabeth I, English queen, 81
Ellis, Stephen, 29
Elster, Jon, 18, 19, 21–22
encomienda system, 40, 66
English East India Company (EIC), 36,
   56, 67–68, 81–87, 131; charter of, 81;
   Court of Directors of, 70; Dutch
   conflicts with, 83; military-fiscalism
   of, 91–95; Ottomans and, 111; troops
   of, 90–91, 93, 112, 140
English Royal Africa Company, 67
Eritrea, 137
Ethiopia, 55, 101, 137
Eurocentrism, 2, 13–16, 100, 123–29
Executive Outcomes (mercenary outfit),
   29

Farrell, Theo, 149
Ferdinand of Austria, 109
firearms. *See* gunpowder weapons
"fiscal-military" state thesis, 9, 74, 121–22,
   147; India and, 69, 80, 92
"fog of war," 19–20
fortifications, 9, 11, 39, 71; in Africa, 54,
   117; in Americas, 47; in Asia, 75, 77–78,
   84; in India, 62, 63; Ottomans and,
   109, 111; in Persian Gulf, 57, 83
France, 46–47, 95; African colonies of,
   135–37, 140, 141, 144; China and,
   141; India and, 64, 68–69, 88, 90;
   Napoleonic Wars of, 86, 111, 120, 131;
   population of, 108; Prussian war with,
   137
Frederick II , Prussian king, 114
French East India Company, 67–69,
   87–88, 90, 93
Frost, Robert I., 114
functionalism, 22, 23, 147–48. *See also*
   rational-functionalist logic
fur trade, 47, 67

Gama, Vasco da, 1, 51, 58, 103
Gennaioli, Nicola, 121
Germany, African colonies of, 135–36
Gibbon, Edward, 7

Goa, 53–54, 57, 63, 87, 118
Gomman, Jos J. L., 92
Great Northern War (1700–21), 113
Guilmartin, John F., 42, 109, 119
Guinea, 49
Guinea Bissau, 29
Gujarat, 56, 101
gunpowder empire thesis, 102, 107, 127
gunpowder weapons, 9, 11, 55–56, 126,
    147; in Africa, 54, 55; in Americas,
    41–42; in China, 59, 74, 78, 126–27;
    invention of, 6; MacDonald on, 11;
    magical beliefs about, 27–33; Otto-
    man, 102, 106, 107; rockets as, 90; in
    Southeast Asia, 74; volley fire by, 4, 8,
    38–39, 78, 88, 107
Gustavus Adolphus, Swedish king, 8,
    37–38

Habsburg dynasty, 101–2, 104–5; army of,
    107–12; North Africa and, 114, 115, 117,
    118
Hasan, Farhat, 84, 92
Hassig, Ross, 42–43, 47–48
Headrick, Daniel R., 55
Hegel, G. W. F., 129
Hess, Andrew C., 106
Hobson, John M., 127
Hodgson, Marshall G. S., 102
Hoffman, Philip, 20, 63, 121
Holy League, 110, 113
Holy Spirit Movement (Uganda), 28–30
Hormuz, 118; English capture of, 83;
    Portuguese capture of, 57
Hudson's Bay Company, 46, 67
Hui, Victoria Tin-bor, 127–28
Hungary, 101, 104–5, 108–9

Inca empire, 40–46, 103, 135
India, 74; English conquest of, 67, 82;
    English East India Company in, 82–
    87; French in, 64, 68–69, 88; Maratha
    Confederacy of, 63, 84–86, 89, 94; as
    modern rising power, 4, 151;
    Portuguese in, 53–64, 72. See also
    Mughal empire
Indian "Mutiny" (1857), 89

Industrial Revolution, 15, 90, 120, 133–34,
    139
institutional isomorphism, 24–26, 134–35
insurgency wars, 7–8, 133, 144–45
International Relations, 17, 136; Euro-
    centrism of, 124, 127–28; historians'
    views of, 16–18, 37, 121, 146; on
    military competition, 21
international system, 2–3, 125, 151;
    anarchical nature of, 21; contem-
    porary, 132; imperialism and, 133–35,
    134–35, 143–44
investment managers, 33
Iraq, 144, 145
Ireland, 149, 150
Islamist insurgencies, 7–8, 145
Italy, 46, 104, 137, 140

James I, English king, 83
Janissaries, 107, 109, 112, 113
Japan, 3, 5, 60, 127; Chinese conflicts
    with, 148–49; Dutch East India
    Company and, 68, 79; imperialism
    of, 137; Korea and, 60
Java, 68, 71, 73–76, 80, 86
João I, Kongo king, 50
Johnston, Alastair Iain, 127
joint-stock companies, 70

Kamen, Henry, 40
Kang, David C., 127
Karlowitz, Treaty of, 110
Kenya, 29, 51–52, 54
Kharg Island, 80
Kongo kingdom, 50, 55
Korea, 56, 60

Laichen, Sun, 74
Lamarck, Jean-Baptiste de, 147
Lebanon, 144
Lee, Wayne E., 18
Lepanto, Battle (1571), 117, 118
Levy, Jack S., 124–25
Liberia, 29, 30
Libya, 118, 140
Liechtenstein, 22
Lockhart, James, 43

Lorge, Peter A., 75–76, 126, 128–29, 138, 149
Lynn, John, 24, 27

Macau, 77
MacDonald, Paul K., 11, 141
Madras, 84, 85, 88
magical beliefs: about bulletproofing, 27–33, 148; about healing diseases, 36, 72
Malabar Coast, 79–80, 87
Malacca, 57, 62, 72–74, 81, 118
Maldives, 58
Mamluks, 57–58, 101, 107, 117
Manchu dynasty. *See* Qing dynasty
Mapuche, 44–46, 139
Maratha Confederacy, 63, 84–86, 89, 94
McNeill, William H., 63, 102, 124, 147
Melilla, 115
Mexico, Spanish conquest of, 40–46, 66, 103, 117, 135, 141
Meyer, John, 18, 23–26
military entrepreneurs, 26–27, 122. *See also* pirates
military revolution thesis, 94–95, 100–102, 121–30, 145–47; company sovereigns and, 35, 67–69, 73–74; conquistadors and, 40–43; elements of, 7–8, 11, 37–39; Eurocentrism of, 13–16, 123–29; Ottoman empire and, 102–6, 119–21; Portuguese and, 52–55, 63; rise of the West and, 9–13, 17, 127–29; social scientists and, 16–18; sovereign companies and, 67–68
military superiority thesis, 11, 41, 68
Mill, John Stuart, 7
Ming dynasty, 2, 3, 121, 129–30; Dutch East India Company and, 68, 77–79; Portuguese warfare with, 59; world exploration by, 14, 60. *See also* China
Mohács, Battle of (1526), 108–9
Moluccas, 57, 76, 82, 83
monopolies, 69, 82
Montesquieu, 7
Morocco, 49, 105–6, 114–16, 118, 141
Mozambique, 29–31, 51
Mughal empire, 3, 5; China and, 96; decline of, 68, 85–86, 129–30; Dutch

East India Company and, 68; English East Indies Company and, 68, 84; Portuguese and, 54, 56, 60, 63; rise of, 6, 93, 122, 127. *See also* India
Murphey, Rhoads, 107–8, 120
Muscat, 57, 59
Muscovy Company, 67
Museveni, Yoweri Kaguta, 28–29
Mysore, 80, 88–89, 97

Nadir Shah, Persian emperor, 86
Napoleonic Wars, 86, 111, 120, 131
natural selection. *See* Darwinian selection
naval warfare: Chinese, 14, 59, 77; development of, 10, 42; Dutch, 76; financing of, 66, 108; Omani, 54; Ottoman, 51–52, 58, 106, 108; Portuguese, 58, 72
Ndongo kingdom, 50
Netherlands, 65–66, 71, 138; decline of, 119, 129; English East India Company and, 83, 86; independence of, 46, 70, 104, 105; population of, 74
"new imperialism," 6, 12, 132, 135–43; chartered companies of, 67; means of, 139–43; motives of, 136–39
Nigeria, 29
North, Douglass, 11–12
North Africa, 48–49, 101–2, 105–6, 114–20
nutmeg, 72

Oceania, 131, 143
Oman, 52, 54, 57, 59
Opium Wars, 20, 141, 142
organizational theory, 18–19, 21, 148; dysfunctional beliefs and, 33, 149–50; institutional isomorphism and, 24–26, 134–35
Ottoman empire, 22, 99–122; Chinese military and, 141–42; decline of, 111–14, 119, 129–30; European campaigns of, 108–11; Indian Ocean and, 51–52, 97; Janissaries of, 107, 109, 112, 113; military revolution thesis and, 102–8, 119–22; naval warfare of, 51–52, 58, 106, 108; North Africa and, 5; Persia and, 101, 107–9, 117; Portuguese and, 51–52, 64; religious

toleration in, 107–8; rise of, 6, 122; Russian conflicts with, 36, 100, 102, 110–13; Venice and, 102, 110, 111, 120

paradigm-diffusion model, 19, 37, 76, 97, 146–48; alternative to, 148–51; Amerindian resistance and, 44; rationalizations of, 78, 122

Parker, Geoffrey, 9–10, 15, 36, 119–20; on African imperialism, 53; on Battle of Breitenfeld, 37–38; Eurocentrism and, 124; on Indian Ocean settlements, 56, 62; on military competition, 102; on Polish-Lithuanian Commonwealth, 104; on siege warfare, 111; on statemaking, 66, 91, 94

Pearson, M. N., 52

Persia, 5, 86, 120; English East India Company and, 83–84; Ottomans and, 101, 107–9, 117. *See also* Safavid empire

Persian Gulf, 57, 80, 83, 101

Peru, Spanish conquest of, 40–46, 66, 103, 135

Pescadores Islands, 77

Peter I, Russian tsar, 110–11, 113–14

pirates, 71, 117, 122; Barbary, 106, 108, 118; Chinese, 77

Pizarro, Francisco, 40–43, 135

Plassey, Battle of (1757), 82, 88, 102, 141

Polish-Lithuanian Commonwealth, 22, 102, 105, 110

Pondicherry, 88

Portugal, 52–55; African explorations by, 47–55, 105, 114–18; China and, 59, 77; conquistadors and, 47–48, 53–54; decline of, 119, 129; Dutch conflicts with, 46, 50–51, 61–62, 67–72, 77–81; English conflicts with, 83; in India, 53–64, 72; Mughal empire and, 54–56, 60, 63; naval warfare of, 58, 72; Ottoman empire and, 51–52, 64; slave trade of, 51; Spain and, 47–49, 53–54, 116, 129

Prester John legend, 49

Qing dynasty, 2–3, 77–79, 129–31; decline of, 22, 133, 141–42; rise of, 122; Taiping Rebellion and, 142. *See also* China

racial theories, 13, 86

Ralston, David B., 142

rational-functionalist logic, 13, 22–25, 134, 143, 147–48

Ricklefs, M. C., 75

Ringmar, Erik, 127

Roberts, Michael, 7–9, 104, 119; on statemaking, 66, 91, 126; on Swedish armies, 38

Roe, Thomas, 82

Rogers, Clifford J., 119

Romanov dynasty, 101, 113

Rourke's Drift, Battle of (1879), 141

Roy, Kaushik, 90

Russia, 67, 101; Chechnya and, 140; Chinese conflicts with, 78; Ottoman conflicts with, 36, 100, 102, 110–13; Swedish conflict with, 113

Safavid empire, 56, 83, 120; Ottomans and, 101, 107, 108, 117. *See also* Persia

San Marino, 22

Santa Catarina (Portuguese ship), 71

Schumpeter, Joseph A., 7

Sebastian, Portuguese king, 49, 116

Selim I, Ottoman sultan, 101

Seven Years' War (1756–63), 88

siege warfare, 109, 111, 127

Sierra Leone, 29, 31

slave trade, 49; Dutch, 50–51; English, 67; Portuguese, 51

Smith, Adam, 7

social Darwinism, 23–24, 137, 143, 147. *See also* Darwinian selection

Somalia, 144

South Africa, 29, 140–41

Spain, 141; Armada of, 60, 117; Columbus and, 1, 40; decline of, 119; Dutch conflicts with, 46, 70, 104, 105; North Africa and, 114–18; Portugal and, 47–49, 53–54, 116, 129; Reconquista of, 114, 115. See also conquistadors

Spice Islands. *See* Moluccas

spice trade, 56–59, 64; Dutch and, 72, 76, 83; English and, 82, 83

Sri Lanka. *See* Ceylon

state-making: after decolonization, 66;
    war-making and, 8, 66, 91, 126, 128,
    147–48
steel weapons/armor, 41–42, 55
Stern, Philip J., 70
sub-Saharan Africa, 48
Suleiman the Magnificent, 108
Sumatra, 58, 60, 76, 101
Suzuki, Shogo, 127
Swahili Coast, 51–52, 54, 60
Sweden, 8, 37–38, 113, 129
Syria, 101
Szapolyai, John, 109

Tagliacozzo, Eric, 73
Taiping Rebellion (1850–64), 142
Taiwan, 77–78
Tangiers, 115
Tanzania, 29, 51
Tatars, 101, 104, 107, 112
telegraph, invention of, 140
teleological bias, 129–30
Tenochtitlan, Battle of (1521), 40, 42
Thirty Years War (1618–48), 8, 34, 102,
    104; military entrepreneurs of, 26–27;
    military model of, 37–38; Ottomans
    and, 110
Thompson, William R., 11
Thornton, John K., 129
Tilly, Charles, 8, 66, 88
timariot system, 107, 111–12
trace italienne forts. *See* fortifications
Transylvania, 109

Travancore kingdom, 79–80
Tripoli, 117
Tunis, 117, 118

Uganda, 28–30
Uzbekistan, 101

Valdivia, Pedro de, 44–45
Vandervort, Bruce, 136
Venice, 57, 58, 108; Ottomans and, 102,
    110, 111, 120
Vienna, 109, 110, 120
Vietnam, 74, 144
Vijayanagara empire, 97
VOC (Vereenigde Oostindische
    Compagnie). *See* Dutch East India
    Company
Voth, Hans-Joachim, 121

Waltz, Kenneth, 21
Ward, Kerry, 70
Weigert, Stephen L., 29
Westphalia, Treaty of (1648), 8, 105
Wilson, Nicolas Hoover, 70
Winius, George Davidson, 61
Wlodarczyk, Nathalie, 29–30
world order. *See* international system

Yemen, 101

Zanzibar, 54
Zheng Chenggong (Coxinga), 77–78
Zimbabwe, 29, 52

A NOTE ON THE TYPE

THIS BOOK has been composed in Miller, a Scotch Roman typeface designed by Matthew Carter and first released by Font Bureau in 1997. It resembles Monticello, the typeface developed for The Papers of Thomas Jefferson in the 1940s by C. H. Griffith and P. J. Conkwright and reinterpreted in digital form by Carter in 2003.

Pleasant Jefferson ("P. J.") Conkwright (1905–1986) was Typographer at Princeton University Press from 1939 to 1970. He was an acclaimed book designer and AIGA Medalist.

The ornament used throughout this book was designed by Pierre Simon Fournier (1712–1768) and was a favorite of Conkwright's, used in his design of the *Princeton University Library Chronicle*.

CPSIA information can be obtained
at www.ICGtesting.com
Printed in the USA
JSHW050851201020
8893JS00002B/2